First Edition 2006.

The Clay Sanskrit Library is co-published by
New York University Press
and the JJC Foundation.

Further information about this volume
and the rest of the Clay Sanskrit Library
is available on the following Websites:
www.claysanskritlibrary.com
www.nyupress.org.

ISBN 0-8147-8815-7

Artwork by Robert Beer.
Printed in Great Britain by St Edmundsbury Press Ltd,
Bury St Edmunds, Suffolk, on acid-free paper.
Bound by Hunter & Foulis Ltd, Edinburgh, Scotland.

THE CLAY SANSKRIT LIBRARY

FOUNDED BY JOHN & JENNIFER CLAY

WWW.CLAYSANSKRITLIBRARY.COM

WWW.NYUPRESS.ORG

THE RECOGNITION OF SHAKÚNTALA

BY KĀLIDĀSA

EDITED AND TRANSLATED BY
SOMADEVA VASUDEVA

NEW YORK UNIVERSITY PRESS
JJC FOUNDATION
2006

Library of Congress Cataloging-in-Publication Data
Kālidāsa
[Śakuntalā. English & Sanskrit]
The recognition of Shakuntala / by Kalidasa ;
edited and translated by Somadeva Vasudeva.
p. cm. – (The Clay Sanskrit library)
Play.
In English and Sanskrit; includes translation from Sanskrit.
Includes bibliographical references and index.
ISBN 0-8147-8815-7 (cloth : alk. paper)
I. Vasudeva, Somadeva. II. Title. III. Series.
PK3796.S4V37 2006
891'.22 2 22 2004029513

CONTENTS

CSL CONVENTIONS

SANSKRIT ALPHABETICAL ORDER

Vowels:	*a ā i ī u ū ṛ ṝ ḷ ḹ e ai o au ṃ ḥ (f)*
Gutturals:	*k kh g gh ṅ*
Palatals:	*c ch j jh ñ*
Retroflex:	*ṭ ṭh ḍ ḍh ṇ*
Dentals:	*t th d dh n*
Labials:	*p ph b bh m*
Semivowels:	*y r l v*
Spirants:	*ś ṣ s h*

GUIDE TO SANSKRIT PRONUNCIATION

a	b*u*t
ā, â	r*a*ther
i	s*i*t
ī, î	f*ee*
u	p*u*t
ū, û	b*oo*
ṛ	vocalic *r*, American p*ur*dy or English p*re*tty
ṝ	lengthened *ṛ*
ḷ	vocalic *l*, ab*le*
e, ê, ē	m*a*de, esp. in Welsh pronunciation
ai	b*i*te
o, ô, ō	r*o*pe, esp. Welsh pronunciation; Italian s*o*lo
au	so*u*nd
ṃ	*anusvāra* nasalizes the preceding vowel
ḥ, f	*visarga*, a voiceless aspiration (resembling English *h*), or like Scottish lo*ch*, or an aspiration with a faint echoing of the preceding vowel so that *taiḥ* is pronounced *taih*ⁱ. In Kashmirian practice, when *visarga* is followed by *p* or *ph* it is replaced by *upadhmānīya*, here written as *f*, and pronounced as an unvoiced, short blow of air.
k	lu*ck*
kh	blo*ckh*ead
g	*g*o
gh	bi*gh*ead
ṅ	a*n*ger
c	*ch*ill
ch	mat*chh*ead
j	*j*og
jh	aspirated *j*, he*dgeh*og
ñ	ca*ny*on
ṭ	retroflex *t*, *t*ry (with the tip of tongue turned up to touch the hard palate)
ṭh	same as the preceding but aspirated
ḍ	retroflex *d* (with the tip

	of tongue turned up to touch the hard palate)
ḍh	same as the preceding but aspirated
ṇ	retroflex *n* (with the tip of tongue turned up to touch the hard palate)
t	French *t*out
th	ten*t h*ook
d	*d*inner
dh	guil*dh*all
n	*n*ow
p	*p*ill
ph	u*ph*eaval
b	*b*efore
bh	a*bh*orrent
m	*m*ind
y	*y*es
r	trilled, resembling the Italian pronunciation of *r*
l	*l*inger
v	*w*ord
ś	*sh*ore
ṣ	retroflex *sh* (with the tip of the tongue turned up to touch the hard palate)
s	hi*ss*
h	*h*ood

CSL PUNCTUATION OF ENGLISH

The acute accent on Sanskrit words when they occur outside of the Sanskrit text itself, marks stress, e.g. Ramáyana. It is not part of traditional Sanskrit orthography, transliteration or transcription, but we supply it here to guide readers in the pronunciation of these unfamiliar words. Since no Sanskrit word is accented on the last syllable it is not necessary to accent disyllables, e.g. Rama.

The second CSL innovation designed to assist the reader in the pronunciation of lengthy unfamiliar words is to insert an unobtrusive middle dot between semantic word breaks in compound names (provided the word break does not fall on a vowel resulting from the fusion of two vowels), e.g. Maha·bhárata, but Ramáyana (not Rama·áyana). Our dot echoes the punctuating middle dot (·) found in the oldest surviving samples of written Indic, the Ashokan inscriptions of the third century BCE.

The deep layering of Sanskrit narrative has also dictated that we use quotation marks only to announce the beginning and end of every direct speech, and not at the beginning of every paragraph.

CSL PUNCTUATION OF SANSKRIT

The Sanskrit text is also punctuated, in accordance with the punctuation of the English translation. In mid-verse, the punctuation will not alter the *sandhi* or the scansion. Proper names are capitalized, as are the initial words of verses (or paragraphs in prose texts). Most Sanskrit metres have four "feet" *(pāda):* where possible we print the common *śloka* metre on two lines. The capitalization of verse beginnings makes it easy for the reader to recognize longer metres where it is necessary to print the four metrical feet over four or eight lines. In the Sanskrit text, we use French *Guillemets* (e.g. *«kva saṃcicīrṣuḥ?»*) instead of English quotation marks (e.g. "Where are you off to?") to avoid confusion with the apostrophes used for vowel elision in *sandhi*.

Sanskrit presents the learner with a challenge: *sandhi* ("euphonic combination"). *Sandhi* means that when two words are joined in connected speech or writing (which in Sanskrit reflects speech), the last letter (or even letters) of the first word often changes; compare the way we pronounce "the" in "the beginning" and "the end."

In Sanskrit the first letter of the second word may also change; and if both the last letter of the first word and the first letter of the second are vowels, they may fuse. This has a parallel in English: a nasal consonant is inserted between two vowels that would otherwise coalesce: "a pear" and "an apple." Sanskrit vowel fusion may produce ambiguity. The chart at the back of each book gives the full *sandhi* system.

Fortunately it is not necessary to know these changes in order to start reading Sanskrit. For that, what is important is to know the form of the second word without *sandhi* (pre-*sandhi*), so that it can be recognized or looked up in a dictionary. Therefore we are printing Sanskrit with a system of punctuation that will indicate, unambiguously, the original form of the second word, i.e., the form without *sandhi*. Such *sandhi* mostly concerns the fusion of two vowels.

In Sanskrit, vowels may be short or long and are written differently accordingly. We follow the general convention that a vowel with no mark above it is short. Other books mark a long vowel either with a bar called a macron (*ā*) or with a circumflex (*â*). Our system uses the macron, except that for initial vowels in *sandhi* we use a circumflex to indicate that originally the vowel was short, or the shorter of two possibilities (*e* rather than *ai*, *o* rather than *au*).

When we print initial *â*,	before *sandhi* that vowel was *a*
î or *ê*,	*i*
û or *ô*,	*u*
âi,	*e*
âu,	*o*
ā,	*ā* (i.e., the same)
ī,	*ī* (i.e., the same)
ū,	*ū* (i.e., the same)
ē,	*ī*
ō,	*ū*
āi,	*ai*
āu,	*au*
’, before *sandhi* there was a vowel *a*	

FURTHER HELP WITH VOWEL SANDHI

When a final short vowel (*a*, *i* or *u*) has merged into a following vowel, we print ’ at the end of the word, and when a final long vowel (*ā*, *ī* or *ū*) has merged into a following vowel we print ” at the end of the word. The vast majority of these cases will concern a final *a* or *ā*.

Examples:

What before *sandhi* was *atra asti*	is represented as *atr’ âsti*
atra āste	*atr’ āste*
kanyā asti	*kany” âsti*
kanyā āste	*kany” āste*
atra iti	*atr’ êti*
kanyā iti	*kany” êti*
kanyā īpsitā	*kany” ēpsitā*

Finally, three other points concerning the initial letter of the second word:

(1) A word that before *sandhi* begins with *ṛ* (vowel), after *sandhi* begins with *r* followed by a consonant: *yatha” rtu* represents pre-*sandhi* *yathā ṛtu*.

(2) When before *sandhi* the previous word ends in *t* and the following word begins with *ś*, after *sandhi* the last letter of the previous word is *c* and the following word begins with *ch*: *syāc chāstravit* represents pre-*sandhi syāt śāstravit*.

(3) Where a word begins with *h* and the previous word ends with a double consonant, this is our simplified spelling to show the pre-*sandhi* form: *tad hasati* is commonly written as *tad dhasati*, but we write *tadd hasati* so that the original initial letter is obvious.

COMPOUNDS

We also punctuate the division of compounds (*samāsa*), simply by inserting a thin vertical line between words. There are words where the decision whether to regard them as compounds is arbitrary. Our principle has been to try to guide readers to the correct dictionary entries.

EXAMPLE

Where the Deva·nágari script reads:

कुम्भस्थली रक्षतु वो विकीर्णसिन्दूररेणुर्द्विरदाननस्य ।
प्रशान्तये विघ्नतमश्छटानां निष्ठ्यूतबालातपपल्लवेव ॥

Others would print:

kumbhasthalī rakṣatu vo vikīrṇasindūrareṇur dviradānanasya /
praśāntaye vighnatamaśchaṭānāṃ niṣṭhyūtabālātapapallaveva //

We print:

kumbha|sthalī rakṣatu vo vikīrṇa|sindūra|reṇur dvirad'|ānanasya
praśāntaye vighna|tamaś|chaṭānāṃ niṣṭhyūta|bāl'|ātapa|pallav" êva.

And in English:

"May Ganésha's domed forehead protect you! Streaked with vermilion dust, it seems to be emitting the spreading rays of the rising sun to pacify the teeming darkness of obstructions."

"Nava·sáhasanka and the Serpent Princess" I.3 by Padma·gupta

DRAMA

Classical Sanskrit literature is in fact itself bilingual, notably in drama. There women and characters of low rank speak one of several Prakrit dialects, an "unrefined" *(prākṛta)* vernacular as opposed to the "refined" *(saṃskṛta)* language. Editors commonly provide such speeches with a Sanskrit paraphrase, their "shadow" *(chāyā)*. We mark Prakrit speeches with ⌜opening and closing⌟ corner brackets, and supply the Sanskrit *chāyā* in endnotes. Some stage directions are original to the author but we follow the custom that sometimes editors supplement these; we print them in italics (and within brackets, in mid-text).

WORDPLAY

Classical Sanskrit literature can abound in puns *(śleṣa)*. Such paronomasia, or wordplay, is raised to a high art; rarely is it a *cliché*. Multiple meanings merge *(śliṣyanti)* into a single word or phrase. Most common are pairs of meanings, but as many as ten separate meanings are attested. To mark the parallel senses in the English, as well as the punning original in the Sanskrit, we use a *slanted* font (different from *italic*) and a triple colon *(⁝)* to separate the alternatives. E.g.

> yuktaṃ Kādambarīṃ śrutvā kavayo maunam āśritāḥ
> *Bāṇa|dhvanāv* an|adhyāyo bhavat' îti smṛtir yataḥ.
>
> It is right that poets should fall silent upon hearing the Kádambari, for the sacred law rules that recitation must be suspended when *the sound of an arrow ⁝ the poetry of Bana* is heard.

Soméshvara·deva's "Moonlight of Glory" I.15

INTRODUCTION

The eloquence of great poets, streaming with such suggestive essence, reveals a coruscating extra-ordinary genius, whereby in this world, crowded with a succession of diverse poets, only two, three, or perhaps five or six, headed by Kali·dasa, can be reckoned "great poets."[1]

Dhvany/āloka 1.6

KALI·DASA's "The Recognition of Shakúntala" *(Abhijñāna/śākuntala)* was one of the first examples of Indian literature to be seen in Europe, first translated into English, and then into German. It attracted considerable attention (from Goethe, among others) and, indeed, pained surprise that such a sophisticated art form could have developed without the rest of the world noticing.

It tells the story of the hermit girl Shakúntala, the daughter of the celestial nymph Ménaka and the sage Vishva·mitra. The poet Kali·dasa intends Shakúntala to be the focus of attention. This is not the story of King Dushyánta, or their son Bhárata, who, according to the "Maha·bhárata" is the emperor whose rule gives India its Sanskrit name: Bhárata.

The Poet

The poet Kali·dasa is traditionally linked to a ruler called Vikramáditya. This is most probably a Gupta emperor.

The Gupta dynasty rose to prominence in the late third century CE, winning control of Mágadha. "Year one" of the Gupta era is 319/320 CE, but it is not clear if this marks the accession of Chandra·gupta I or rather the year he proclaimed himself an independent and sovereign ruler. In the following decades military conquest and marital alliances expanded the Gupta empire until, when Samúdra·gupta died in 380 CE, it included the entire Indus valley in the west, reached into what is now Myanmar in the east, incorporated Nepal in the north, and reached the river Nármada in the south, with Ujjain becoming the new capital city.

The courtly culture sponsored by the imperial Guptas has been called a conservative, conscious effort to restore the customs of the Vedic past: Samúdra·gupta revived the royal horse sacrifice, and all titles and inscriptions issued were in elegant classical Sanskrit, abandoning the spoken tongues hitherto favored. INGALLS (1976) notes that this perception is also contradicted by remarkable innovations. Many scholars have called the ensuing blossoming of the fine arts and philosophy an Indian Golden Age. The Chinese pilgrim Fa Hsien, arriving in India in 404 CE (and writing for a Buddhist audience in China) describes a well-governed and prosperous land with beautiful cities, hospitals and universities. He notes that the people are free to move at will, not subject to corporal punishment, and that official salaries are fixed. He particularly draws attention to the amenities available to travellers. Kali·dasa similarly describes a happy land, and the meager evidence at our disposal makes it plausible that Gupta rule was benign not just for monks and courtier poets but for the common people too, at least in days of peace and prosperity.

Kali·dasa may have lived during the reign of one or all of the following three Gupta emperors: Chandra·gupta II "Vikramáditya" (*reg.* 375–413 CE), Kumára·gupta "Mahéndráditya" (*reg.* 413–455 CE), or Skanda·gupta "Vikramáditya" (*reg.* 455–467 CE).

Bakker (2006:165–187) has put forward the theory that Kali·dasa's drama "Málavika and Agni·mitra" *(Mālavik"/âg-nimitra)* uses an ancient love story to describe a contemporary Gupta succession struggle. In its wake a geo-political triangle with Vídisha and Vídarbha which had ensured Gupta power and prosperity disintegrated, sealing the doom of the "Golden Age."

Other playwrights wrote similarly political plays (though more explicitly so),[2] and Vishákha·datta even wrote a work about the Shaka-Gupta wars, the now lost *Devī/candragupta* (much of its plot has been reconstructed from citations and allusions by Raghavan[3]). Kali·dasa's political subtext is however less obvious and still awaits fuller unveiling and discussion (in the prologue to "Málavika and Agni·mitra" he himself draws attention to his originality in this matter[4]).

If Kali·dasa's "Málavika and Agni·mitra" alludes to actual events, is it possible that his other works do too?[5] It would be interesting to study whether the character of Kali·dasa's Shakúntala might have anything to do with either Dhruva·devi, wife of Chandra·gupta II and mother of Kumára·gupta, or with his wife Anánta·devi.[6]

Similarly the "Birth of Kumára" *(Kumāra/sambhava)* tells of events leading up to the birth of Skanda Karttikéya, the God of war and saviour of the Gods *(deva)* in a cosmic struggle against the Titans *(asura)*. In an interesting parallel, Kumára·gupta was at war with an expanding confederacy of Hunnic tribes based in Tokharistan and called the Kidarites (sometimes just "Red Huns") after their leader Kidara. In 455 CE, during the confusion of the last year of Kumára·gupta's reign, the Gupta armies, led by his son Skanda·gupta, inflicted a defeat on another Hunnic group that had invaded the shortlived Kidarite state, the Hephthalites (Xionites or "White Huns"). Kali·dasa may have personally seen these Hunnic tribes (he refers to either of them indiscriminately as *Hūṇa*s although in other Sanskrit sources the more descriptive *Śveta/hūṇa,* "White Hun," is also found), for he gives details about them not known to other Sanskrit writers. In his "Lineage of Raghu" *(Raghu/vaṃśa)* he notes that they live on the river *Vaṅkṣu* (Oxus) and that the wives of a fallen chieftain gouge their cheeks in mourning.[7] A number of such apparently observed details in Kali·dasa's work has led many to conclude that he was a widely travelled man. This is not beyond dispute. In the "Lineage of Raghu" as transmitted by the earliest commentator Vállabha·deva, Kali·dasa erroneously seems to think that Raghu finds himself in Kerala as soon as he crosses the River Káveri. Isaacson & Goodall (2003) discuss this to demonstrate how subsequent commentators "corrected" Kali·dasa's text to remove such perceived inconsistencies. Kali·dasa's apparently accurate geographical knowledge may not be a feature of the earliest witnesses of his work.

Around 480 CE the Hephthalites, led by Toramána, renewed their onslaught and the financial strain of fighting this prolonged war of annihilation proved too much for the Gupta empire; by 510 CE Ujjain was destroyed and the Western provinces devastated. In the aftermath of the catastrophic Hephthalite invasion the shrinking empire entered into a long phase of decline as local feudatories asserted their independence.

BAKKER places Kali·dasa's literary activity between 415 and 445 CE, a time of political stability between the Gupta empire, Vídisha and Vídarbha. WARDER had tentatively placed Kali·dasa's literary activity between 430 and 470 CE, INGALLS between 400 and 450 CE. These approximate dates gain support from chronological lists of poets found in eulogies incorporated into many dateable works.[8]

THE PLOT

ACT 1: In the course of a hunting expedition King Dushyánta chances upon the hermitage of the sage Kanva. He is welcomed by the absent sage's daughter Shakúntala, with whom he falls in love. Dushyánta learns that Shakúntala is the daughter of the nymph Ménaka and the seer Vishvámitra, abandonded in the wild and fostered by the sage Kanva.

ACT 2: The king, aided by the buffoon, seeks a pretext to enter the hermitage to see Shakúntala again when he is suddenly summoned by the ascetics to protect their rites from malevolent demons.

ACT 3: Shakúntala and Dushyánta meet in secret and contract a *gandharva* marriage of mutual consent. Upon the succesful completion of the seers' rites Dushyánta returns to his capital city, leaving a signet ring with Shakúntala as a token of his affection. Absentminded with love, Shakúntala unknowingly slights the irascible seer Durvásas and is cursed by him: whoever she was thinking of will not remember her. Her companions manage to win a reprieve from the angered sage: a token of recognition can break the curse.

ACT 4: The patriarch Kanva returns and is delighted with events so far. When no word from Dushyánta arrives, the now heavily pregnant Shakúntala is despatched to his court and in a famous and moving scene bids farewell to her hermitage home.

ACT 5: At court the amnesic king disavows her; she tries to show him his signet ring to prove her story but cannot find it. Humiliated, Shakúntala is suddenly borne away into the sky by her mother.

ACT 6: A fisherman finds the ring in the guts of a fish. A zealous police chief recognizes the royal signet ring and shows it to the king who at once regains his memory. Dushyánta then torments himself with remorse until he is summoned by Indra, king of the Gods, to fight against the demons.

ACT 7: Six years later Dushyánta is returning in an airborne chariot when he alights in a celestial hermitage. He sees a young boy called Sarva·dámana playing with a lion cub. It dawns on him that this is his son, the prophesied world emperor later called Bhárata. Shakúntala herself appears and forgives Dushyánta. Blessed by the sages and the Gods, the reunited family returns to the world of mortals and Dushyánta's capital.[9]

SHAKÚNTALA BEFORE KALI·DASA

The plot of "The Recognition of Shakúntala" is a carefully conceived expansion of an episode found in the "Maha·bhárata." By adding the device of a curse to account for Dushyánta's loss of memory, Kali·dasa casts him in a more favorable light; in the "Maha·bhárata" he seems to have simply forgotten about Shakúntala once he returned to the pleasures of his palace. The "Maha·bhárata" also explains the origin of Shakúntala's name. Abandonded in the wilderness, the infant was shielded from predators by birds *(śakunta)* when the sage Kanva chanced upon her; and as the daughter of an *apsaras* nymph she possesses the power of flight, which Kali·dasa's drama deprives her of.

Related versions of the tale, presumed to be derivative, exist in Puranic texts as well.

A very similar story is also found in a Játaka tale of one of the Buddha's previous lives.[10] King Brahma·datta encounters a woman gathering firewood in a grove and at once falls in love with her. They make love there and then and the Bodhi·sattva is conceived. The king gives her a signet ring and instructs her to bring the child to him if it is a boy. A few years later the king, embarrassed before his court, denies both the child and the ring. The mother then throws the child up and he remains floating cross-legged in midair. The king then acknowledges the son as his heir and makes the firewood collector his chief queen. Of all these retellings of the story, Kali·dasa's is the most intricate.

Kali·dasa's Dramatisation

One of the most immediate joys of reading and rereading Kali·dasa's play lies in the discovery of the relevance of the many subtle strategic pairings of acts and parallelisms that Kali·dasa has worked into the plot.

Gerow (1979–80) has shown how Kali·dasa uses complex mirroring and inversion of events to structure and punctuate his narrative.

Among the more striking is the symmetry between the beginning and the end of the play. In the first act the eager Dushyánta and his human charioteer are in pursuit of the pleasure of hunting. He is borne up a slope to the mountain hermitage, a place of religious duty, where he enters a kind of higher plane of natural spontaneity inhabited by the semi-divine Shakúntala, and is bidden to combat the local demons. In the last act the listless Dushyánta is descending with the divine charioteer Mátali in an aerial chariot from heaven where he has taken part in a war against universal demons at the bidding of Indra. They alight in a celestial hermitage again halfway between heaven and earth, where a very different meeting with Shakúntala takes place.

Similarly, act 2 is mirrored in act 6, and act 3 in 5. The celebrated fourth act is the central pivot around which all of this symmetry turns. In this act Kali·dasa shows Shakúntala—already suffering from the separation of her beloved Dushyánta—undergoing a painful farewell from her foster father, her dear friends, and the natural world of the hermitage of which she had considered herself an integral part. For the spectator or reader, aware of the curse, her naïve hopes for a happy future are all the more poignant. In this act, Kali·dasa effectively seems on the verge of killing off Shakúntala the shy, innocent forest girl for the reader—it is a character that cannot possibly cope with the world she will encounter at court. But what happens next is unexpected. Of all of the characters Shakúntala alone does not develop into a "more evolved" character, assuming a new persona as she enters the "real world" beyond the hermitage. Dushyánta does not appear at all in this central act, and when she meets him again it is as a stranger. Dushyánta is not merely changed by the curse, he has assumed an entirely new "public" identity far removed from Shakúntala's expectations. Kali·dasa shows her as a simple girl humiliated and awkwardly out of place as she tries to defend herself at the royal court, but he will not let her compromise her character. Since her presence at court is so incongruent, he whisks her away in a supernatural flash of light. The effect on the reader is shocking. It is as if Kali·dasa has let us watch her walk slowly towards a precipice, and finally over it.

What does he intend with this?

There is no simple answer, for Kali·dasa has not written a simple work by following a single set of rules. A series of partial explanations of what he has done can be given according to various models of interpretation.

It would be a mistake to assume from the above synopsis that "The Recognition of Shakúntala" concludes with a banal happy ending. While the play does not end on the same note of optimistic innocence with which it begins, it is clearly not intended as a tragedy either.

This is not because Sanskrit drama is completely unaware of tragedies as is frequently claimed in secondary literature, but because the play ends in what is called *abhyudaya,* a positive result. A tragic genre of Sanskrit drama called *utsṛṣṭik'/âṅka,* interpreted as "marked by death," (though probably originally "one-act-play about death") in which are depicted death and lamenting[II] may or may not end in such *abhyudaya.*

Scholiastic Theories

The earliest surviving Sanskrit dramaturgical treatise, the *Nāṭya/śāstra* ("Science of drama") of Bhárata (redacted into its present composite form[12] by c. 200 CE), mentions "instruction" *(hit'/ôpadeśa)* and "entertainment" *(krīḍā, sukha, viśrānti)* as the purposes of drama, but all of the "four goals" *(puruṣ'/ârtha)* of brahminical culture are prominent in its initial justificatory chapter: pleasure, wealth, justice, and spiritual liberation. Drama should depict all kinds of emotions and all kinds of states, it should imitate events in the world.[13]

> *In part about religion, in part about entertainment, in part about money, in part about tranquility, in part about comedy, in part about war, in part about love, in part about killing.*[14]

Dramaturgical theory from Bhárata onwards discusses a peculiar idealised plot structure that progresses through five "transitions" or "junctions" *(sandhi)*.[15]

The [1.] "origin" *(mukha)* states the "seed" *(bīja)* of the plot in outline; the [2.] "incident" *(pratimukha)* develops the "seed" by alternating episodes showing a balance of both "gain" *(prāpti)* and "loss" *(aprāpti)* of the "aim" *(phala)*; in the [3.] "germ" *(garbha)* the likelihood of "gain" outweighs the possibility of "loss," the attainment of the "aim" seems likely; in the [4.] "crisis" *(vimarśa)* the likelihood of "loss" outweighs "gain," all hope of securing the aim seems lost; in the [5.] "completion" *(nirvahaṇa)* all narrative currents converge towards the final consummation.

Erudite commentators will alert the inattentive reader to the occurrence of these as the play progresses.

Stepping back from such learned discussions about which transition happens exactly where and why, and reconsidering the logic of Kali·dasa's plot on the basis of this inherent structure one might reduce as follows: We start with what might be called an *idyll (A).* This is reversed to *not-idyll* ($\neg A$). *Not-idyll* is countermanded, but the end-result is not a reversal back to *idyll* (either the original *A* or a new *idyll B)*, but a strange, ambivalent situation *quasi-idyll (A′).* It is striking that in the final act Kali·dasa uses essentially the same setting, and the same characters as he does in his opening act. Nor can the differing action, dialogue or diction alone account for the disparate effect on the spectator or reader. This means that the new situation *quasi-idyll (A′)* differs from *idyll (A)* for the spectator or reader because he has witnessed the characters be subjected to a series of symmetries and reversals.

In other words, Kali·dasa has brought his audience to a point where they respond differently and even perceive as different a very similar situation because of what they know about it. Events (and the spectator's deepening involvement in them) have made a return to the original, unqualified innocence impossible.

This brings us to an influential Indian theory of aesthetic appreciation.[16]

Aesthetic Sentiment

The key terms to understanding the theory of "aesthetic sentiment" *(rasa)* are: "determinant emotional states" *(vi-*

bhāva), "consequent emotional states" *(anubhāva),* "transient emotional states" *(vyabhicāri/bhāva),* and "permanent emotional states" *(sthāyi/bhāva).* In the *Nāṭya/śāstra* and its derivatives these are used primarily prescriptively to teach an elaborate grammar of emotional response. Later aestheticians expanded on this by minutely analysing the mechanisms of aesthetic appreciation in the spectator (as taught in the sixth book of the *Nāṭya/śāstra*). Here *rasa* must be understood as a technical term. Nothing but obfuscation is gained by importing the vague allusions or associations that a literal translation of the term evoke. Tieken (2000:118) rightly deplores the use of the term as a "magic word" to justify all manner of absurd speculation on the purpose of Indian drama, broadening it "to such a point that it becomes an utterly meaningless concept with which one can indeed explain virtually everything."[17] Before going further, therefore, I fear I cannot spare the reader from a brief explanation of what it is that the mature theory attempts to explain. It is not, in essence, a complicated doctrine, admitting of simplification and paraphrase. Hopefully, many of us have had a similar experience to the following.

An Example

Imagine that you find yourself going to see a performance of "Romeo and Juliet." You are in the right mood for the play, no mundane worries preoccupy your mind, you have agreeable company, and the theatre, the stage, the director and the actors are all excellent—capable of doing justice to a great play. Your seat in the theatre is comfortable and gives an unobstructed view.

The play begins and you find yourself drawn into the world Shakespeare is sketching. The involvement deepens to an immersion where the ordinary, everyday world dims and fades from the center of attention, you begin to understand and even share the feelings of the characters on stage—under ideal conditions you *might* reach a stage where you begin to participate in some strange way in the love being evoked.

Now, if at that moment you were to ask yourself: "Whose love is this?" a paradox arises.

It cannot be Romeo's love for Juliet, nor Juliet's love for Romeo, for they are fictional characters. It cannot be the actors', for in reality they may despise one another. It cannot be your own love, for you cannot love a fictional character and know nothing about the actors' real personalities (they are veiled by the role they assume), and, for the same reasons, it cannot be the actors' love for either you or the fictional characters. So it is a peculiar, almost abstract love without immediate referent or context.

A Sanskrit aesthete would explain to you that you are at that moment "relishing" *(āsvādana)* your own "fundamental emotional state" *(sthāyi/bhāva)* called "passion" *(rati)* which has been "decontextualised" *(sādhāraṇīkṛta)* by the operation of "sympathetic resonance" *(hṛdaya/saṃvāda)* and heightened to become transformed into an "aesthetic sentiment" *(rasa)* called the "erotic sentiment" *(śṛṅgāra)*.

This "aesthetic sentiment" is a paradoxical and ephemeral thing that can be evoked by the play but is not exactly caused by it, for many spectators may have felt nothing at all during the same performance. You yourself, seeing it again next week, under the same circumstances, might experience nothing. It is, moreover, something that cannot be adequately explained through analytic terms, the only proof for its existence is its direct, personal experience.[18]

The fourteenth century Orissan literary critic Vishva·natha has summarised his predecessors' deliberations on the strange ontological status of this "aesthetic sentiment" as a series of paradoxes:[19]

> *It cannot be made known for its existence cannot be separated from its experience. Since it depends in essence upon the aggregation of determinants etc. it cannot be an effect; nor is it eternal since it is not perceived before [the determinants etc.], when not perceived it does not even exist. Nor is it something that will exist [eternally or independently in the future] since it is self-manifest immediate bliss. Nor does it exist presently, since it is different from an effect or a knowable thing. Nor is its perception indeterminate knowledge since it becomes objective by the experience of the determinants etc., and since sensitive readers experience it directly as supreme delight. Nor is it perceived as determinate knowledge since it does not admit contact with analytical terms. It is not imperceptible since it can arise from words, yet its manifestation is not perceptible. Therefore connoisseurs should truly regard it as non-ordinary. Since this [aesthetic sentiment] is not different from one's own experience, the learned consider it proven by pleasurable experience.*

It is, moreover, a blissful experience. The fact that sensitive readers often weep while reading poetry does not mean that they are suffering, rather the tenderness of the work has succeeded in melting the contraction of their minds or hearts.

The non-ordinary nature of such aesthetic sentiments makes it possible for the spectator or reader to derive a pleasurable experience even from what in ordinary life would be causes of grief.[20]

Technical Details

The *Rasa/sūtra* in the *Nāṭya/śāstra* of Bharata states:[21]

> *Rasa is evoked by the conjunction of determinants, consequents and transient emotional states.*

For example: In a play based on the story of the "Ramáyana," the characters Rama, Sita and the demon Rávana might be the "objective determinants." The season, garlands, and the appropriate makeup are the "excitant determinants."[22] The "bodily consequents" are the gestures and stances the characters assume on stage.[23] The "verbal consequents" are peculiar intonations which may, for instance, reveal if a statement is sarcastic. The "involuntary consequents" are spontaneous reactions such as tears and tremors.[24] The accessory consequents are such as Rama wearing armor and a helmet. The many transients support the emerging *rasa*: When Sita sees Rávana, the consequents "paralysis, trembling, and perspiration" are supported by the transients "worry, fear, and effort."[25]

But how exactly is this aesthetic sentiment evoked?

The theory is considered a "doctrine of transformation" *(pariṇāma/vāda)*.

What is it that is transformed into an aesthetic sentiment? Eight pre-existing "foundational emotions" *(sthāyi/bhāva)* are postulated. These can be transmuted into "aesthetic sentiments" by the presence of all of the other emotional processes and conditions mentioned above. Even though many of these may be at the time more prominent than a "foundational emotion," only the foundational emotions can be transmuted into aesthetic sentiments.

> *Just as a king alone—though he may be surrounded by a great retinue—deserves his title, and not some other man, however exalted, so a fundamental emotion, attended by determinant, consequent, and transient emotional states, receives the designation "aesthetic sentiment."*[26]

The aesthetic sentiment is in this way categorically different from the other sentiments. The fundamental emotions generate aesthetic sentiments as follows:

Foundational state		Aesthetic sentiment
1. passion *(rati)*	>	erotic *(śṛṅgāra)*
2. energy *(utsāha)*	>	heroic *(vīrya)*
3. revulsion *(jugupsā)*	>	disgust *(bībhatsa)*
4. anger *(krodha)*	>	wrathful *(raudra)*
5. fun *(hāsa)*	>	comic *(hāsya)*
6. wonder *(smaya)*	>	amazing *(adbhuta)*
7. fear *(bhaya)*	>	fearful *(bhayānaka)*
8. grief *(śoka)*	>	compassionate *(karuṇa)*
9. world-weariness *(śama/nirveda)*	>	quietist *(śānta)*

The much-discussed "quietist" emotional state is not universally accepted. It may be a later addition, and some argue it cannot be staged and is thus confined to poetry.

Another theory further reduces this list by dividing the first eight of these into two paired groups, the former being capable of generating the latter.[27]

Love

For many theoreticians the erotic sentiment is considered the most important since it requires the greatest sensitivity in handling:[28]

> *The erotic alone is the sweetest, most captivating aesthetic sentiment. The quality of evocativeness arises from poetry imbued with this sentiment.*

Ábhinava·gupta, on the other hand, considers the quietist sentiment as fundamental to all others. The variety of amorous relationships depicted in classical Sanskrit poetry are governed by well-defined conventions. Rhetoricians stipulate that the erotic sentiment as it ought to be depicted in poetry is twofold, happy and sad: "love-in-union" *(saṃbhoga)*, and "love-in-separation" *(vipralambha)*. Love-in-separation is further subdivided rather clinically into ten developmental stages:[29] [1.] longing *(abhilāṣa)*, [2.] pondering *(cintana)*, [3.] remembrance *(smṛti)*, [4.] praising *(guṇa/kīrtana)*, [5.] agitation *(udvega)*, [6.] babbling *(pralāpa)*, [7.] madness *(unmāda)*, [8.] fever *(saṃjvara)*, [9.] torpor *(jaḍatā)*, and finally [10.] death *(maraṇa)*.

The *Satta/saī* of Hala, a Prakrit anthology of amorous verse compiled in the early centuries CE may well have served as the model for the formulation of the conventions of love, since almost all amorous situations discussed by the scholiasts can be traced in it.

Impediments

A playwright wishing to write a work capable of evoking this relishing of an aesthetic sentiment *(rasanā, camat/kāra, ras'/āsvāda)*[30] must guard against a number of pitfalls. These are summarised as seven impediments to the experience of the aesthetic sentiment, and apply equally to the spectator.[31] They are [1.] lack of credulity, a sympathetic response must be possible; [2.] a too personal identification with the characters or narrative must be avoided by the use of not only realistic conventions *(loka/dharmin)* but also theatrical conventions *(nāṭya/dharmin)* in drama, or, in poetry, naturalistic expression *(svabhāv'/ôkti)* and artificial expression *(vakr'/ôkti);* [3.] preoccupation with personal affairs; [4.] lack of proper means of perception; [5.] lack of clarity, abstract theatrical conventions must be balanced by the presence of everyday conventions; [6.] lack of predominance of a single aesthetic sentiment; [7.] presence of doubt as to how the consequents are to be interpreted: tears may ambiguously represent joy, anger, fear etc. unless they are properly combined with other emotional states.

Recensions Or Versions?

What is presented here is the first complete translation of the Kashmirian recension of the "The Recognition of Shakúntala." "Recension" here designates the product of conscious redactional choices. This differs from what might be called a "version" of a text which simply comes into existence as scribal errors accumulate with each generation of copying. Some scribes may consult other manuscripts to correct obvious errors,[32] but as long as this is done unsystematically, the resulting conflated text remains a "version."

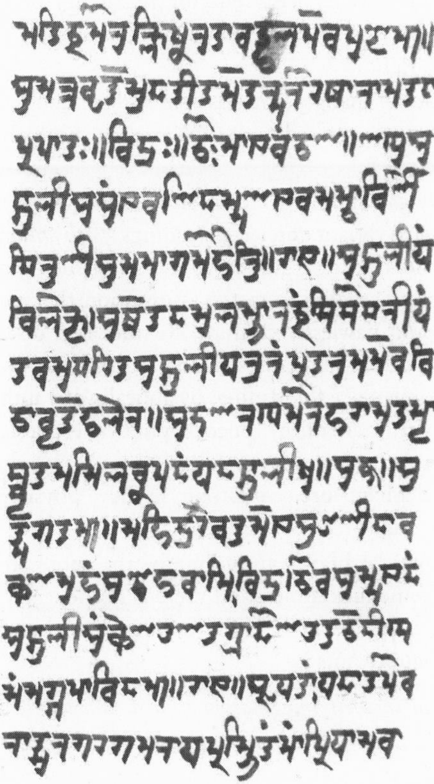

Fol. 50r of the Shrinagar manuscript showing § 6.114–120.

The boundary between recension and version is neccessarily a blurred one. Some scribes might redact parts of their text, while some redactors might be inept. Nevertheless, in principle, the activity of the redactor (redacting) differs from that of the scribe (copying) enough to be usefully studied in its own right.[33]

The kinds of changes, emendations and corrections such a redactor (or group of redactors) will make are not impossible to deduce.

In lucky cases the redactor is also a commentator, who might discuss variant or rejected readings *(pāṭh'|ântara, apapāṭha)*. The kind of argument adduced in such cases can be telling, proceeding from the assumption that a play or poem should flawlessly conform to rules laid down in a number of technical treatises. Thus commentators will justify their preference for readings by appealing to authorities on grammar, dramaturgy, poetics, politics, erotics, metallurgy/chemistry, gemology, medicine, astronomy/astrology, archery, elephant-lore, equestrian science, physiognomy, gambling, and sorcery.[34]

The more celebrated an author is, the more stringent this requirement becomes, and there is no poet writing in Sanskrit more celebrated than Kali·dasa. As the aesthete Ábhinava·gupta puts it:[35]

> *Not even in their imagination in a dream would connoisseurs impute even the most minute imperfection to his poetry.*

This might be read as tantamount to a license to emend away whatever offends a pedantic scholiast, and such commentarial projects have indeed been documented. Only recently Goodall & Isaacson have made a successful effort to evaluate such criteria to weight variant readings in their critical text and recover an older stratum of one of Kali·dasa's works, the *Raghu/vaṃśa*.

A closer reading reveals that such wilful "purification" (as Vámana puts it) of a poet's work, is not, in fact, sanctioned by all rhetoricians. Instead of advocating a rigid application of inflexible rules, a benign, contextually sensitive reading of poetry is preferred by some of the most prominent writers. Dandin allows breaches of rules as long as the learned are not offended. Mámmata, the author of the most popular text-book on aesthetics, teaches that defects can become virtues if appropriately used.[36] Ábhinava·gupta puts it most bluntly: these rules are not "royal edicts."[37]

What does such an editorial policy mean for the current volume?

Let us look at an example: the third metrical foot of verse 6.9 (§6.114 in this book) is marred by a number of unsatisfactory or banal readings in the Deva·nágari and Bengal recensions. The Kashmirian recension presents a syntactical difficulty with the predicate *(vidheya)* being predominant. The Míthila recension reads the word *sudatī* ("fine-toothed woman") as the predominant subject *(uddeśya)* in place of the Kashmirian *tad atītam* ("passed beyond"). Now this is exciting: we may surmise that there exists ample motivation for redactors to remove the word *sudatī*, for the rhetorician Vámana (active in Kashmir in the 8th cent. CE) had taught that it is grammatically suspect.[38] The messy readings thus show us various attempts to repair the damage done by wilfully replacing *sudatī* with conjectures. A further problem: in place of the Kashmirian recension's *mam' âiṣa* the Míthila recension reads *mam' âiva*. Now there exists again a compelling reason for this. Here the Kashmirian reading is probably original, the problem for the Míthila redactor is that it presents us with a metaphor *(rūpaka)* where the subject *(upameya)* and object *(upamāna)* are in different genders, the "fine-toothed woman" *(sudatī* fem.) and the "precipice" (*prapātaḥ* masc.). As a general rule, rhetoricians censure such gender incongruence, but Kali·dasa does not always adhere to such formal requirements. The Míthila redactor appears to have wilfully read precipice as a fem. *(prapātā),* and then changed the masc. pronoun *eṣaḥ* to the syntactically redundant particle *eva*.

But note how appropriate is the use of "fine-toothed" for the juxtaposition with the gaping, jagged cliff precipice if we adopt the following reading (a combination of the Míthila and Kashmirian) as original: *s" âsannivṛttyai sudatī mam' âiṣa,* "She, the fine-toothed woman, became for me this [precipice. . .] from which there is no return."

Such textual criticism explains how the Kashmirian recension translated here comes to have its peculiar reading in this place and it also indicates what Kali·dasa may have originally written. That no printed text of "The Recognition of Shakúntala" gives this reading shows just how much we stand to gain from a careful reevaluation of the recensions in the light of the Kashmirian text.

The study of the writings of Sanskrit rhetoricians and literary critics is thus indispensable for anyone wishing to edit Sanskrit literature; not because it provides insightful tools to analyze the text (which, of course, it does) but because generations of scribes, redactors and even the original poets have made decisions based on rhetorical works prominent in their place and time.

The Recensions

With the exception of the Deva·nágari recension (named after the script its manuscripts were written in), the surviving recensions of "The Recognition of Shakúntala" are usually named for the regions they are found in.

The Deva·nágari recension, often published with Rághava·bhatta's commentary, is probably the most popular. Despite this, there exists no critical text of this recension.

Of the Bengal recension there exists a pioneering critical edition by Richard Pischel published in its final form in the Harvard Oriental Series 16. Pischel's editorial decision to standardize the Prakrit to that of the grammarians has been called into question.

The Southern recension is available in print with a number of commentaries, notably the *Diṅ/mātra/darśanī* of *Abhirāma Bhaṭṭa*, the *Kumāra/giri/rājīya* of *Kāṭayavema*, the *Sāhitya/sāra* of *Śrīnivāsa Bhaṭṭa* and a learned, anonymous *Carcā* commentary published by the Trivandrum Sanskrit Series.

The Mithila recension's readings were published by the Mithilā Research Institute in Darbhanga in 1957, based on the two commentaries of *Śaṅkara* and *Narahari*.

Besides these, there are many more unpublished commentaries by well known medieval commentators such as *Ghanaśyāma, Dakṣināvartanātha,* and *Nīlakaṇṭha* (as well as a large number of modern Sanskrit commentaries). It would be of inestimable value to know what relation the texts of these early commentators bear to the published recensions.

In 1884 Karl BURKHARD published a provisional edition of the Kashmirian recension from a single manuscript brought to Poona by Georg BÜHLER after one of his tours to collect manuscripts in Kashmir. The same was reprinted in Deva·nágari by S.K. BELVALKAR in 1965 *(Sāhitya Academy)*. BURKHARD had previously (1882) published another manuscript written in the Kashmirian *Śāradā* script preserved in Bikaner which he believed to be the Kashmirian recension. This, however, is a *Śāradā* manuscript of the Deva·nágari recension with a few emendations based on the Kashmirian text. In 1980 Dilīp Kumār KANJILĀL attempted to reconstruct Kali·dasa's original text from the various recensions. His is the only work, so far, to make use of the STEIN manuscripts of the Kashmirian recension preserved in Oxford. KANJILĀL's pioneering effort is greatly hampered by the fact that the regional recensions are not yet properly critically edited.

The text published here in the Clay Sanskrit Library is the first stage of a work in progress; much more careful textual criticism is required before we can have a clearer picture of the Kashmirian recension. The surviving Kashmirian manuscripts allow us to restore the text to the form it assumed in Kashmir some time after about 700 CE but before the end of the first millenium CE, dates tentatively deduced by the detectable influence of Vámana and by Ábhinava·gupta's knowledge of (some parts of) the text as presently constituted.

Concerning the Prakrit Passages

Not all characters in a Sanskrit drama speak Sanskrit. A substantial part of both verse and dialogue is sung or spoken in various forms of Prakrit. These are not intended as regional dialects, but rather as something approaching "sociolects:" gender, status and age determine the language.

Differing approaches to editing these additional languages have been attempted, and the controversy is ongoing. I do not find it advisable, in this edition, to adopt either Pischel's "strong program" of disregarding the manuscript evidence as unreliable, and emending the text to conform to the rules of the Prakrit grammarians, nor its opposite. It is uncertain that the Kashmirian redactors used a grammar at all, and if they did, it remains unclear which grammar this might have been. Salomon (1982) believed that Pischel's (and Hillebrandt's *Mudrā/rākṣasa*) approach had become dubious at least since Lüders (1911) published the Central Asian fragments of Ashva·ghosha's plays because their Prakrit predates and diverges from what is prescribed by the grammarians. Because this might have little bearing on the post Vara·ruchi (3rd–4th cent CE) period of Kali·dasa and the other classical poets, the dispute is reevaluated in Steiner (1997:§9).

As regards the *deśī* ("provincial," "local")[39] terms encountered, the most likely surviving source for Prakrit lexicography that comes close to what the Kashmirian redactors of "The Recognition of Shakúntala" might have used (if they used anything at all) is the *Pāialacchīnāmamālā* of Dhana·pala (he styles himself *Dhanavāla* in Prakrit), composed in *Vikrama/saṃvat* 1029=972 CE in Dhara, the capital city of the Para·mara dynasty of Malava, and Hema·chandra's influential *Deśi/nāma/mālā*.

As a result the presentation of Prakrit is still somewhat uneven; sometimes the manuscript evidence favored forms which accord with the norms of the grammarians, sometimes they did not. I did not use either as evidence for a normative "Kashmirian Dramatic Prakrit" but have rather preserved much of this eclecticism, removing only what I judged to be copyists errors: more work on the regional variation of the transmission of dramatic Prakrits is needed before either of the two procedures mentioned above could be seriously entertained in the present case.

ACKNOWLEDGMENTS

I am grateful to Harunaga Isaacson and Eivind Kahrs for their many corrections.

BIBLIOGRAPHY

Hans Bakker, "A newly found statue from Nagardhan," *South Asian Archeology* 1991, ed. A.J. Gail & G.J.R. Mevissen, Stuttgart 1993, pp. 303–11.

—"A Theatre of Broken Dreams, Vidiśā in the Days of Gupta Hegemony," in *Interrogating History, Essays for Hermann Kulke,* ed. Martin Brandtner & Shishir Kumar Pande, New Delhi 2006.

Lyne Bansat-Boudon, "Le texte accompli par la scene: observations sur les versions de Śakuntalā." *Journal asiatique 282* (1994), pp. 280–333.

Carl (Karl) Burkhard, *Lectiones codicis Çâkuntali Bikânîrensis,* Achter Jahresbericht über das k.k. Franz Joseph Gymnasium, Wien 1882.

—*Die kaçmirer Çakuntalâ Handschrift,* Sitzungsberichte der kaiserlichen Akademie der Wissenschaften, Philosoph. Hist. Classe, Vol. cvii, Wien 1884.

Edwin GEROW, "Plot structure and the Development of Rasa in the Śakuntalā, Pts. I and II," *Journal of the Amercian Oriental Society,* 99:4 (1979), pp. 559–72; 100:3 (1980), pp. 267–82.

Dominic GOODALL & Harunaga ISAACSON, *The Raghupañcikā of Vallabhadeva,* Vol. 1, Groningen Oriental Studies XVII, Groningen 2003.

Daniel H.H. INGALLS "Kālidāsa and the Attitudes of the Golden Age." *Journal of the American Oriental Society,* Vol. 96, No. 1 (Jan.–Mar., 1976), pp. 15–26.

Eivind KAHRS, "What is a tadbhava word," *Indo-Iranian Journal* 35 (1992), pp. 225–249.

Dilīp Kumār KANJILĀL, *A reconstruction of the Abhijnanasakuntalam of Kalidasa,* Calcutta Sanskrit College Research Series No. 90, 1980.

Friedrich LÜDERS *Bruchstücke buddhistischer Dramen,* Hrsg. von Heinrich LÜDERS, Berlin 1911. (Kleinere Sanskrit-Texte. 1)

Nāṭyaśāstra of Bharatamuni with the Commentary Abhinavabhāratī by Abhinavaguptācārya. Ed. M. RAMAKRISHNA KAVI, revised [. . .] by K.S. RAMASVAMI SHASTRI, 2nd ed. Baroda 1956, (Gaekwad Oriental Series 36).

Claude RAPIN, *Indian Art from Afghanistan. The legend of Sakuntala and the Indian Treasure of Eucratides at Ai Khanum.* New Delhi 1996.

Richard SALOMON "The Original Language of the Karpûra-manjarî," In: ZDMG 132, pp. 119–141.

S.A. SHRINIVASAN, *On the Composition of the Nāṭyaśāstra,* Studien zur Indologie und Iranistik. Monographie I, Reinbeck 1980.

Roland STEINER "Untersuchungen zu Harsadevas Nâgânanda und zum indischen Schauspiel," Swisttal-Odendorf 1997, *(Indica et Tibetica. 31.)*

Hermann TIEKEN, "On the Use of rasa in Studies of Sanskrit Drama." *Indo-Iranian Journal 43* (2000), pp. 115–138.

—"The Structure of Kalidasa's Raghuvamsa." *Studien zur Indologie und Iranistik 15* (1989), pp. 151–158.

V. RAGHAVAN *Bhoja's Śṛṅgāraprakāśa,* Madras 1963.

A.K. WARDER *Indian Kāvya Literature,* Vol. 3, Delhi 1977.

ZEIMAL, E.V., *The Kidarite Kingdom in Central Asia.* History of Civilizations of Central Asia, vol. 3 (Paris: UNESCO, 1996).

NOTES

1 Ananda·várdhana, *Vṛtti* to *Dhvany/āloka* 1.6: *tad vastu/tattvaṃ niḥṣyandamānā mahatāṃ kavīnāṃ bhāratī a/loka/sāmānyaṃ pratibhā/viśeṣaṃ parisphurantam abhivyanakti yen' âsminn ativicitra/kavi/paramparā/vāhini saṃsāre Kālidāsa/prabhṛtayo dvi/trāḥ pañca/ṣā vā mahā/kavaya iti gaṇyante.*

2 For example the *Mudrā/rākṣasa.*

3 RAGHAVAN 1963:858–880.

4 See WARDER 1977:129ff, and TIEKEN 2001.

5 TIEKEN had speculated that the "Málavika and Agni·mitra" is unique in this respect.

6 It would go too far to suppose that this in itself implies that there was a suspicion of illegitimacy surrounding the succession. Kali·dasa's works were not crude vehicles for Gupta propaganda. But it is noteworthy how much emphasis is laid on establishing Bhárata's claim to succession in the play.

7 *Raghu/vaṃśa* 4.67 as read by the oldest commentator, Vállabha·deva. The presence of the Huns on the River Oxus also serves as a confirmation of Kali·dasa's date.

8 BAKKER 1993 has suggested that a sculpture of Kali·dasa survives.

9 For a very beautiful series of plaques made of inlaid shells depicting the story see C. RAPIN 1996.

10 *Kaṭṭhahāri/jātaka.*

11 According to the aesthetician Ábhinava·gupta this term is to be rendered as lit. "marked *(aṅkita)* by death."

12 See S.A. SHRINIVASAN 1980.

13 *Nāṭya/śāstra* 1.112: *nānā/bhāv'/ôpasaṃpannaṃ nān"/āvasth"/ ântar"/âtmakam / loka/vṛtt'/ânukaraṇaṃ nāṭyam etan mayā kṛtam.*

14 *Nāṭya/śāstra* 1.108: *kva/cid/dharmaḥ kva/cit/krīḍā kva/cid/ arthaḥ kva/cic/chamaḥ/ kva/cid/dhāsyaṃ kva/cid/yuddhaṃ kva/cit/kāmaḥ kva/cid/vadhaḥ.*

15 For a succinct treatment of these not deriving from the *Daśa/rūpaka* see *Nāṭaka/lakṣaṇa/ratna/kośa* of Ságara·nandin (ca. 1225CE) chapter 8.

16 H. TIEKEN questions the value of this in "On the Use of rasa in Studies of Sanskrit Drama," Indo-Iranian Journal 43 (2000) 115–138.

17 As examples of this abuse TIEKEN (2000:118) cites the work of Lyne BANSAT BOUDON, concluding: "We are dealing with *rasa* as a kind of comforting mantra here. This third type of use of the term *rasa* properly belongs to the realm of fiction and need not be considered any further."

18 Adapted mainly from Ábhinava·gupta's discussion of *Dhvany/āloka* 2.4, using as example the love of Rama and Sita.

19 *Sāhitya/darpaṇa* 3.20cd–26: *n' âyaṃ jñāpyaḥ, sva/sattāyāṃ pratīty/avyabhicārataḥ // yasmād eṣa vibhāv'/âdi/samūh'/ālamban'/ātmakaḥ / tasmān na kāryaḥ, no nityaḥ pūrva/saṃvedan"/ôjjhitaḥ / a/saṃvedana/kāle hi na bhāvo 'py asya vidyate // nāpi bhaviṣyan sākṣād ānanda/maya/prakāśa/rūpatvāt / kārya/jñāpya/vilakṣaṇa/bhāvān no vartamāno 'pi // vibhāvādi/parāmarśa/ viṣayatvāt sa/cetasām / parānanda/mayatvena saṃvedyatvād api sphuṭam // na nirvikalpakaṃ jñānaṃ tasya grāhakam iṣyate / tathābhilāpasaṃsargayogyatvavirahān na ca // savikalpakasaṃvedyaḥ sākṣāt kāratayā na ca / parokṣas tatprakāśo nāparokṣaḥ śabda/saṃbhavāt // [Vṛtti: tat kathaya kīdṛg asya tattvam aśru-t'/âdṛṣṭa/nirūpaṇa/prakārasyety āha] tasmād alaukikaḥ satyaṃ vedyaḥ sahṛdayair ayam / [Vṛtti: tat kiṃ punaḥ pramāṇaṃ tasya sadbhāve?] pramāṇaṃ carvaṇaivātra svābhinne viduṣāṃ matam //26//. [atra=rase, svābhinne=carvaṇāsvarūpe].*

20 *Sāhitya/darpaṇa* 3.4–8: *karuṇ"/ādāv api rase jāyate yat paraṃ sukham, sa/cetasām anubhavaḥ pramāṇaṃ tatra kevalam. kiṃ ca teṣu yadā duḥkhaṃ na ko 'pi syāt tad/unmukhaḥ, tathā Rāmāyaṇ'/ādīnāṃ bhavitā duḥkha/hetutā. hetutvaṃ śoka/harṣāder gatebhyo loka/saṃśrayāt. śoka/harṣ'/ādayo loke jāyantāṃ nāma laukikāḥ, alaukika/vibhāvatvaṃ prāptebhyaḥ kāvya/saṃśrayāt. sukhaṃ saṃjāyate tebhyaḥ sarvebhyo 'p' îti kā kṣatiḥ, aśru/pāt'/ādayas tadvad drutatvāc cetaso matāḥ.*

21 *Nāṭya/śāstra* 6: *vibhāv'/ânubhāva/vyabhicāri/saṃyogād rasa/niṣpattiḥ.*

22 Determinant emotional states can be either "objective" *(ālambana),* the objects towards which the emotional responses are directed, e.g. the dramatis personæ, or "excitant" *(uddīpana),* these include the setting, the season, etc.

23 The "consequents" are responses to the emotional states. They are of four kinds: bodily, verbal, involuntary, and accessory. (*Daśa/rūpaka* 4.3ab, *Bhāva/prakāśana* 1.141cd–145ab.)

24 Of particular importance to the theory are the eight "involuntary emotional responses" *(sāttvik'/ânubhāva).* They are: paralysis, unconsciousness, horripilation, perspiration, loss of color, trembling, tears, stammering. (*[1.] stambha, [2.] pralaya, [3.] romañca, [4.] sveda, [5.] vaivarṇya, [6.] vepathu, [7.] aśru and [8.] vaisvarya).* See *Bhāva/prakāśana* 1.151cd–163ab.

25 The "transient emotional states" *(vyabhicāribhāva)* are counted as thirty-three: *[1.] nirveda, [2.] glāni, [3.] śaṅkā, [4.] śrama, [5.] dhṛti, [6.] jaḍatā, [7.] harṣa, [8.] dainya, [9.] augrya, [10.] cintā, [11.] trāsa, [12.] īrṣyā, [13.] āmarṣa, [14.] garva, [15.] smṛti, [16.] maraṇa, [17.] mada, [18.] supta, [19.] nidrā, [20.] vibodha, [21.] vrīḍā, [22.] apasmāra, [23.] moha, [24.] mati, [25.] ālasya, [26.] āvega, [27.] tarka, [28.] avahittha, [29.] vyādhi, [30.] unmāda, [31.] viṣāda, [32.] utsuka, [33.] cāpala.*

26 *Abhinava/bhāratī* 7.8: *yathā nar'/êndro bahu/jana/parivāro 'pi sa eva nāmo labhate n' ânyaḥ sumahān api puruṣaḥ*

tathā vibhāv'|ânubhāva|vyabhicāri|parivṛtaḥ sthāyī bhāvo rasa|nāma labhate.

27 *Nāṭya|śāstra* 6.39. For a discussion of this see KÖLVER 1991.

28 *Dhvany|āloka* 2.7: *śṛṅgāra eva madhuraḥ paraḥ prahlādano rasaḥ / tanmayaṃ kāvyam āśritya mādhuryaṃ pratitiṣṭhati.*

29 See *Daśa|rūpaka* 4.51cd–52.

30 Defined at *Abhinava|bhāratī* Vol. 1, p. 279: *sa c' âtṛpti|vyatirekeṇ' â|vichinno bhog'|āveśa ity ucyate.*

31 *Abhinava|bhāratī* Vol. 1, p. 280–284; see also *Dhvany|āloka* 3.17–19 on the six obstructors *(virodhin)* of *rasa.*

32 In fact textual critics have had to evolve various strategies to deal with such "conflation."

33 BANSAT-BOUDON, following CAPELLER ("pseudo-recensions") and CHAND ("temporary fictions"), calls the recensions versions. My own view is that they are recensions, i.e. versions that have been consciously revised to remove inconsistencies accumulated by accidents of transmission.

34 A list provided by the eleventh-century Kashmirian poet and literary critic Ksheméndra.

35 Ábhinava·gupta, *Ghaṭa|karpara|vivṛti* 20: *na c' âsya kāvye tṛṇa|mātram api kalaṅka|pātram utprekṣitavanto manorathe 'pi supte 'pi sahṛdayāḥ.*

36 *Kāvya|prakāśa* 7.59.

37 *Ghaṭa|kharpara|kulaka* 20: *na h' îyaṃ rāj'|ājñā.*

38 *Kāvy'|âlaṅkāra|sūtra|vṛtti* 5.2.67: *sudaty|ādayaḥ pratividheyāḥ.*

39 *Deśi* terms are words encountered in standard Prakrit works which cannot be explained by Sanskrit dictionaries, the derivations of the Prakrit grammarians, or by *lakṣaṇā* (indicative usage). All other Prakrit words are classed as either *tat|samas* or *tad|bhavas.* To explain: *indu* ("the moon") is a *tat|sama,* it has the same form and meaning in both Sanskrit and Prakrit.

Prakrit *gaha*, ("planet," or "house"), is a *tad/bhava*, it can be derived from the Sanskrit *graha* or *gṛha* by following the rules of the Prakrit grammarians. The Prakrit word *ceṃcchaï* ("unchaste woman") is a *deśi* word of uncertain etymology and formation. Similarly, the Prakrit compound *valaya/bāhu* ("bracelet") is a *deśi* word even though both of its members are *tat/sama*s: this is because the correct Sanskrit compound should be *bāhu/valaya*. For further detail see E. Kahrs (1992).

DRAMATIS PERSONÆ

In order of appearance:

Sūtra/dhāraḥ:	STAGE DIRECTOR
Naṭī:	ACTRESS
Rājā, Duṣyantaḥ:	KING DUSHYÁNTA
Sūtaḥ:	His CHARIOTEER
Tapasvī, Tāpasaḥ:	ASCETIC
Sakhyau:	TWO FRIENDS
Śakuntalā:	SHAKÚNTALA
Priyaṃvadā:	PRIYAM·VADA
Anasūyā:	ANASÚYA
Vidūṣakaḥ, Mādhavyaḥ:	BUFFOON
Dauvārikaḥ, Revakaḥ:	DOOR-KEEPER
Senā/patiḥ:	GENERAL
Parijanaḥ:	RETINUE
Tāpasau, Ṛṣī	TWO ASCETICS, TWO SAGES
Karabhakaḥ:	KARÁBHAKA, Royal Envoy
Śiṣyaḥ:	Kanva's DISCIPLE
Tāpasī:	Two Female ASCETICS
Ṛṣi/kumārakau	TWO YOUNG SAGES
Gautamī:	GÁUTAMI
Durvāsas:	DURVÁSAS, An Irascible Sage
Kāśyapaḥ, Kaṇvaḥ:	KÁSHYAPA, KANVA
Śiṣyāḥ:	Three DISCIPLES
Śārṅgaravaḥ:	SHARNGA·RAVA
Kañcukī, Maudgalyaḥ:	CHAMBERLAIN
Pratihārī:	PORTRESS
Vaitālikaḥ:	HERALD
Śāradvataḥ:	SHARAD·VATA
Purohitaḥ, Purodhāḥ, Somarāta:	PRIEST
Ṛṣayaḥ:	SEERS
Rakṣiṇau:	TWO GUARDS
Puruṣaḥ:	Man, a FISHERMAN
Śyālaḥ:	POLICE CAPTAIN, the king's brother-in-law

Akṣamālā:	Aksha·mala
Ceṭī:	Two Female Gardeners
Lipi/kārī, Medhāvinī:	Artist, Scribe
Mātali:	Mátali
Cūtamañjarī:	Chuta·máñjari, First Dancer
Pārijātamañjarī:	Parijáta·máñjari, Second Dancer
Bālaḥ:	Boy
Tāpasī:	Two Female Ascetics
Mārīcaḥ:	Marícha
Aditiḥ:	Áditi

PROLOGUE

YĀ SRAṢṬUḤ SṚṢṬIR ĀDYĀ pivati vidhi|hutaṃ,
yā havir, yā ca hotrī,
ye dve kālaṃ vidhattaḥ, śruti|viṣaya|guṇā
yā sthitā vyāpya viśvam,
yām āhuḥ «sarva|bīja|prakṛtir» iti, yayā
prāṇinaf prāṇavantaḥ,
pratyakṣābhif prasannas tanubhir avatu nas
tābhir aṣṭābhir Īśaḥ!

nāndy|ante.

SŪTRA|DHĀRAḤ: *(nepathy'|âbhimukham avalokya)* ārye! yadi nepathya|vidhānam avasitaṃ tad itas tāvad āgamyatām.

praviśya naṭī.

1.5 NAṬĪ: ⌜ayya! ia mhi. āṇavedu ayyo ko ṇioo aṇuciṭṭhīadu tti.⌟

SŪTRA|DHĀRAḤ: *(dṛṣṭvā)* abhirūpa|prāya|bhūyiṣṭh" êyaṃ pariṣat. asyāṃ ca kila Kālidāsa|grathita|vastunā navena nāṭaken' ôpasthātavyam asmābhiḥ. tat pratipātram āsthīyatāṃ yatnaḥ.

NAṬĪ: ⌜suvihida|ppaoadāe ayyassa ṇa kiñci paḍihāissadi.⌟

SŪTRA|DHĀRAḤ: *(smitaṃ kṛtvā)* ārye. kathayāmi te bhūt'|ârtham.

ā paritoṣād viduṣāṃ
na sādhu manye prayoga|vijñānam.
balavad api śikṣitānām
ātmany apratyayaṃ cetaḥ.

May God, kindly disposed, protect us
with eight manifest bodies:
The first creation of the creator, that drinks
the ritual offering,
And the offering,
The sacrificer,
The two which regulate time,
That which pervades the universe, audible to
the ear,
That which is called "the source of all seeds,"
And that which gives living beings their vital
energy!*

At the end of the benediction.

STAGE DIRECTOR: *(looking toward the curtain)* Madam! If everyone has prepared their parts!

Enter the actress.

ACTRESS: Sir! Here I am. What are your instructions? 1.5

STAGE DIRECTOR: *(looking)* This audience is overwhelmingly made up of very sophisticated spectators, and we have to entertain them with a new play, its plot devised by Kali·dasa. Let each role be seen to with care.

ACTRESS: With your careful directing, nothing can go awry.

STAGE DIRECTOR: *(smiling)* Lady, let me tell you a truth.

I cannot be confident of my directorial proficiency until the literati are satisfied. The heart of even those who have rehearsed diligently is racked by self-doubt.

1.10 NAṬĪ: ⌜evaṇ·ṇ·edaṃ.* aṇantara|karaṇīaṃ dāṇiṃ ayyo āṇabedu.⌟

SŪTRA|DHĀRAḤ: *(dṛṣṭvā)* kim anyat, asyāś pariṣadaḥ śruti|pramoda|hetor imam eva n' âticira|pravṛttam upabhoga|kṣamaṃ grīṣma|kālam adhikṛtya gīyatāṃ tāvat.

saṃprati hi—

subhaga|salil'|âvagāhāḥ
  pāṭala|saṃsarga|surabhi|vana|vātāḥ
pracchāya|sulabha|nidrā
  divasāś pariṇāma|ramaṇīyāḥ.

NAṬĪ: ⌜taha.⌟ *(gāyati.)*

1.15 ⌜khaṇa|cumbiāī bhamarehī
  suhaa|suumāra|kesara|sihāiṃ
odaṃsaanti pamadā
  daamāṇāo sirīsa|kusumāiṃ.⌟

SŪTRA|DHĀRAḤ: suṣṭhu gītam! eṣa hi gīta|rāg'|ânubaddha|citta|vṛttir ālikhita iva sarvato raṅgaḥ. tad idānīṃ katamat prakaraṇam āśritya janam ārādhayiṣyāvaḥ?

NAṬĪ: ⌜ṇaṃ paḍhamaṃ yyeva ayyeṇ' āṇattaṃ jahā "Abhiṇṇāṇa|saüntalā" ṇāma apuruvaṃ ṇāḍaaṃ paoeṇa adhikarīadu tti.⌟

SŪTRA|DHĀRAḤ: bhavati! samyag anuprabodhito 'ham. asmin kṣaṇe khalu vismṛtaṃ mayā tat. kutaḥ?

ACTRESS: How true. Now tell me what must be done next, sir. 1.10

STAGE DIRECTOR: *(looking)* What other than sing about this season of summer, not long upon us, suited to enjoyment, to delight the ears of this gathering.

For now,

> Are the days:
> when plunging into water is a joy,
> with woodland breezes fragrant by contact
> with *pátala* blossoms,
> where sleep comes with ease in deep shade,
> delightful in their twilight.

ACTRESS: As you wish. *(Sings.)*

> Sympathetic women adorn 1.15
> themselves with *shirísha* flowers,
> their exceedingly delicate filaments
> fleetingly kissed by bees.*

STAGE DIRECTOR: Beautifully sung! For this audience all around me, engrossed in the melody of the song, seems as if it were painted. Now, then, what play shall we stage to regale these people?

ACTRESS: Surely, sir, you just said at the outset: "Stage the new play called 'The Recognition of Shakúntala'?"

STAGE DIRECTOR: Madam, I am justly reminded. Right now it had simply slipped my mind. Why?

tav' âsmi gīta|rāgeṇa hāriṇā prasabhaṃ hṛtaḥ. . .

1.20 *(nepathy'|âbhimukham avalokya.)*

. . . eṣa rāj" êva Duṣyantaḥ sāraṅgeṇ' âtiraṃhasā.

iti niṣkrāntau.

prastāvanā.

I was irresistibly carried away
by the captivating melody of your song. . .

(glancing toward the curtain.) 1.20

. . . just as this king Dushyánta was
by a swift antelope.

With this they exit.

End of the prologue.

ACT ONE: THE CHASE

tataf praviśati ratha|yātakena mṛg'|ânusārī cāpa|hasto Duṣyantaḥ Sūtaś ca.

1.25 SŪTAḤ: *(rājānaṃ mṛgaṃ c' âvalokya)* āyuṣman!

kṛṣṇa|sāre dadac cakṣus tvayi c' âdhijya|kārmuke
mṛg'|ânusāriṇaṃ sākṣāt paśyām' îva Pinākinam.

RĀJĀ: sārathe! sudūram anena kṛṣṇa|sāreṇa vayam ākṛṣṭāḥ. ayam idānīm api,

grīv'|ābhaṅg'|âbhirāmaṃ muhur anupatati
    syandane datta|dṛṣṭiḥ
  paśc'|ârdhena praviṣṭaḥ śara|patana|bhayād
    bhūyasā pūrva|kāyam
śaṣpair ardh'|âvalīḍhaiḥ śrama|vitata|mukha|
    bhraṃśibhiḥ kīrṇa|vartmā
  paśy' ôdagra|plutitvād viyati bahutaraṃ
    stokam urvyāṃ prayāti.

katham? anupātina eva me prayatna|prekṣaṇīyaḥ saṃvṛttaḥ!

1.30 SŪTAḤ: āyuṣman! udghātinī bhūmir iyaṃ mayā raśmi|saṃyamanād rathasya mandīkṛto vegaḥ. ten' âiṣa mṛgo viprakṛṣṭ'|ântaraḥ saṃvṛttaḥ. saṃprati tu sama|deśa|vartī na te durāsado bhaviṣyati.

Enter King Dushyánta in a chariot, pursuing a deer, bow in hand, accompanied by his charioteer.

CHARIOTEER: *(glancing at king and deer)* Your Majesty! 1.25

As I cast my eye upon the deer, and you
with your bow strung,
I seem to see before my very eyes
the Bow-bearer Shiva chasing the Deer.*

KING: Charioteer! We have been drawn far by this black antelope. Even now he,

Repeatedly darts a glance at the pursuing chariot,
gracefully twisting his neck,
with his haunches drawn acutely forward
into his forebody
out of fear of the arrow's strike,
scattering the path with grass half-chewed,
dropping from his mouth gaping
with exhaustion.
Look! With his lofty leaps he moves
more through the sky
and hardly touches the ground.

How? Even though I am hard on his heels he has become hard to make out!

CHARIOTEER: Your Majesty! The terrain is uneven.* By 1.30
curbing in the reins I have reduced the chariot's speed. Thereby the antelope has made good some ground. But now the ground is level, you will have no trouble getting him.

RĀJĀ: mucyantām abhīśavaḥ.

SŪTAḤ: yad ājñāpayaty āyuṣmān. *(tathā kṛtvā veg'|ântaraṃ nirūpayan)* āyuṣman! paśya paśya! ete

muktеṣu raśmiṣu nirāyata|pūrva|kāyā
  niṣkampa|cāmara|śikhā nibhṛt'|ōrdhva|karṇāḥ
ātm'|ôddhatair api rajobhir alaṅghanīyā
  dhāvanty amī mṛga|jav'|âkṣamay" êva rathyāḥ.

RĀJĀ: satyam atītya Hari|harīn api harayo vartante. tathā hi

1.35 yad āloke sūkṣmaṃ
    vrajati sahasā tad vipulatām
  yad ardhe vicchinnaṃ
    bhavati kṛta|saṃdhānam iva tat
prakṛtyā yad vakraṃ
    tad api sama|rekhaṃ nayanayoḥ
  na me dūre kiṃ cin
    na ca bhavati pārśve ratha|javāt.

SŪTAḤ: āyuṣman! asya khalu te bāṇa|patha|vartinaḥ kṛṣṇa|sārasy' ântare tapasvinaḥ.

RĀJĀ: *(sa|saṃbhramam)* tena hi nigṛhyantāṃ vājinaḥ!

SŪTAḤ: tathā karomi. *(ity uktvā rathaṃ sthāpayati.)*

tataf praviśati ātmanā|tṛtīyas tapasvī.

1.40 TAPASVĪ: *(sa|saṃbhramaṃ hastam udyamya)* rājan! rājan! āśrama|mṛgo 'yaṃ! āśrama|mṛgo 'yaṃ!

KING: Let loose the reins!

CHARIOTEER: As Your Majesty commands. *(does so; acts a change in speed)* Your Majesty! Look, look!

> The reins being loosened, these chariot horses,
> their flanks fully extended,
> their yak-tail plumed crests unshaking,
> their ears stiff,
> unreachable even by the dust they themselves throw up,
> sprint as though unable to tolerate
> the speed of the antelope.

KING: Truly the horses are outstripping the horses of Indra. For,

> What looked tiny to my eyes 1.35
> suddenly becomes immense,
> what really is divided in half appears joined,
> what is inherently crooked appears straight.
> Because of the chariot's speed,
> nothing is far from me,
> and nothing remains at my side.

CHARIOTEER: Your Majesty! Ascetics have come between you and the black antelope your arrow is aimed at!

KING: *(alarmed)* Then restrain the horses!

CHARIOTEER: I'm doing so. *(So saying, he stops the chariot.)*

Enter an ascetic with two companions.

ASCETIC: *(raising up his hand agitatedly)* King! King! This is 1.40
a hermitage antelope. This is a hermitage antelope.

tat sādhu kṛta|saṃdhānaṃ pratisaṃhara sāyakam
ārta|trāṇāya te śastraṃ na prahartum anāgasi.

RĀJĀ: eṣa pratisaṃhṛtaḥ. *(yath" ôktaṃ karoti.)*

TĀPASAḤ: *(sa|harṣam)* sādhu bhoḥ! sadṛśam etat Puru|vaṃśa|jātasya bhavataḥ. sarvathā cakra|vartinaṃ putram avāpnuhi.

RĀJĀ: *(sa|praṇāmam)* pratigṛhītaṃ tapo|dhana|vacanam.

1.45 TĀPASAḤ: samid|āharaṇāya prasthitā vayam. eṣa c' âsmad|guroḥ Kāśyapasya saṃsakta|Himavat|sānur anu|Mālinī|tīram āśramo dṛśyate. na ced anya|kāry'|âtipātas tadā tat praviśy' âtra pratigṛhyatām atithi|satkāraḥ. api ca,

dhanyās tapo|dhanānāṃ
  pratihata|vighnāḥ kriyāḥ samālokya
jñāsyasi: «kiyad bhujo me
  rakṣati maurvī|kiṇ'|âṅka iti!»

RĀJĀ: ayaṃ saṃnihito 'tra kula|patiḥ?

TĀPASAḤ: ady' âiv' ânavadyāṃ duhitaraṃ Śakuntalām atithi|satkārāya saṃdiśya pratikūlam asyā daivaṃ śamayituṃ Somatīrtha|Prabhāsaṃ gataḥ.

Therefore withdraw
your well-aimed arrow.
Your weapon is meant to protect the afflicted,
not to strike the innocent.

KING: It is withdrawn. *(He does as said.)*

ASCETIC: *(rejoicing)* Well done, sir! This becomes you, scion of the lineage of Puru. Without fail, may you have a son who will be a universal emperor.

KING: *(bowing)* The words of the ascetic are welcome.

ASCETIC: We have set out to collect firewood. Yonder, along 1.45
the banks of the River Málini, clinging to the escarpments of the Himálaya, you can see the hermitage of our master Káshyapa. If it does not interfere with other duties, then enter it and receive the welcome due a guest. Moreover,

Watching the worthy sacrifices of ascetics
rich in penance,
carried out without obstructions,
you will appreciate:
"How much my bowstring-scarred arm protects!"

KING: Is the patriarch at home?

ASCETIC: This very day he bid his faultless daughter Shakúntala provide hospitality and departed to Prabhása at the sacred Moon-ford to work a reprieve from her adverse fate.

RĀJĀ: *(ātma|gatam)* bhavatu. tām eva drakṣyāmi. sā māṃ vidita|bhaktiṃ maha"|rṣeḥ kariṣyati.

1.50 TĀPASAḤ: sādhayāmas tāvat. *(iti sa|śiṣyo niṣkrāntaḥ.)*

RĀJĀ: Sūta! coday' âśvān! puṇy'|āśrama|darśanena tāvad ātmānaṃ punīmahe.

SŪTAḤ: yad ājñāpayaty āyuṣmān. *(parikramya ratha|yātakaṃ nirūpayati.)*

RĀJĀ: *(samantād vilokya)* Sūta! akathito 'pi jñāyata eva yath" âyam ābhogas tapo|vanasy' êti.

SŪTAḤ: katham iti?

1.55 RĀJĀ: kiṃ na paśyati bhavān? iha hi,

nīvārāḥ śuka|garbha|koṭara|mukha|
  bhraṣṭās tarūṇām adhaḥ
 prasnigdhāḥ kva cid iṅgudī|phala|bhidaḥ
  sūcyanta ev' ôpalāḥ
viśvās'|ôpagamād abhinna|gatayaḥ
  śabdaṃ sahante mṛgāḥ
 toy'|ādhāra|pathāś ca valkala|śikhā|
  niḥṣyanda|lekh'|âṅkitāḥ.

SŪTAḤ: sarvam upapannam.

KING: *(aside)* So be it. It is her I shall see. She will make my devotion known to the great seer.

ASCETIC: We must go now. *(Exit with his disciples.)* 1.50

KING: Charioteer! Drive on the horses! First of all, we will purify ourselves by the sight of the sacred hermitage.

CHARIOTEER: As Your Majesty commands. *(Walks about, acts the steering of the chariot.)*

KING: *(looking around)* Charioteer! Even without being told, it is evident that these are the outskirts of a penance grove.

CHARIOTEER: How so?

KING: Can you not see? For here, 1.55

Beneath the trees are grains of wild rice
dropped from tree hollows harboring parrots,
elsewhere one sees stones,
oily from crushing *íngudi* fruits;
the fawns are so trusting
they will tolerate speech without stopping
in their tracks,
the paths to the ponds are marked by lines
of water drops from the corners
of bark-garments.

CHARIOTEER: It all fits.

RĀJĀ: *(stokam antaraṃ gatvā)* api ca,

kuly'|âmbhobhif prasṛta|capalaiḥ
śākhino dhauta|mūlā
bhinno rāgaḥ kisalaya|rucām
ājya|dhūm'|ôdgamena
ete c' ârvāg|upavana|bhuvi
cchinna|darbh'|âṅkurāyāṃ
naṣṭ'|āśaṅkā hariṇa|śiśavo
manda|mandaṃ caranti.

1.60 mā tapo|vana|nivāsināṃ uparodho bhūt! tad etāvaty eva rathaṃ sthāpaya yāvad avatarāmi.

SŪTAḤ: dhṛtāf pragrahāḥ. avataratv āyuṣmān.

RĀJĀ: *(avatīrya)* vinīta|veṣeṇa praveśyāni tapo|vanāni. tad idaṃ tāvat pragṛhyatām. *(iti sūtāy' ābharaṇaṃ dattvā dhanuś c' ôtsṛjya)* sūta! yāvad aham upāsya maha"|rṣīn upāvarte tāvad ārdra|pṛṣṭhāḥ kriyantāṃ vājinaḥ.

SŪTAḤ: yad ājñāpayaty āyuṣmān. *(iti niṣkrāntaḥ.)*

RĀJĀ: *(parikramy' âvalokya ca)* idam āśrama|dvāraṃ yāvat praviśāmi. *(praviśya, nimittaṃ sūcayan vimṛśati.)*

1.65 śāntam idam āśrama|padaṃ
sphurati ca bāhuḥ. kutaf phalam ih' âsya?
athavā bhavitavyānāṃ
dvārāṇi bhavanti sarvatra.

KING: *(proceeds a bit)* Moreover,

> Trees have their roots washed
>   by turbulent canal streams,
> the gleam of their tendrils is mixed
>   with the rising smoke
>   from clarified butter offerings,
> and here fawns lazily graze without inhibition
>   on the lawn before us where the shoots
>   of *darbha* grass have been cut.

Let no disturbance hinder the hermitage inmates! Stop the chariot on this verge for me to descend. 1.60

CHARIOTEER: The reins are secure. Descend, Your Majesty.

KING: *(descends)* Hermitages should be entered in modest dress. Therefore take this now. *(with which he gives the charioteer his ornaments and lays aside his bow)* Charioteer! Until I return from paying homage to the great seers douse the horses' backs.

CHARIOTEER: As Your Majesty commands. *(Exit.)*

KING: *(walking around and observing)* I shall enter through this gateway to the hermitage. *(He enters, displays a portentous twitch and reflects.)*

> Tranquil is the hermitage ground, 1.65
>   yet my arm throbs.
> How can this happen here? Or rather,
>   the gates to what must come to pass
>   are everywhere.

NEPATHYE: ⌜ido ido pia|sahī.⌟

RĀJĀ: *(karṇaṃ dattvā)* aye! dakṣiṇena kusuma|pādapa|vīthīm ālāpa iva. yāvad atra gacchāmi. *(parikramy' âvalokya ca)* etās tapasvi|kanyakāḥ sva|pramāṇ'|ânurūpaiḥ secana|ghaṭakair bāla|pādapān siñcantya ita ev' âbhivartante. *(nipuṇaṃ nirūpya)* aho mādhurya|kāntaṃ khalu darśanam āsām. yāvad etāṃ chāyām āśritya pratipālayāmi. *(vilokayan sthitaḥ.)*

tataf praviśati yath"|ôkta|vyāpārā saha sakhībhyāṃ Śakuntalā.

SAKHYAU: ⌜halā Saüntale! taïtto vi kkhu tāda|Kassavassa assama|rukkhaā pia tti takkemha jeṇa nomāliā|pelavā|vi tumaṃ edassa ālavāla|pūraṇe ṇiuttā.⌟

I.70 ŚAKUNTALĀ: ⌜ṇa kevalaṃ tāda|nioo tti. bahu|māṇo jāva mam' âvi. sodarī|siṇeho edesu atthi yyeva.⌟ *(vṛkṣa|sekaṃ rūpayati.)*

UBHE: ⌜halā Saüntale! udaaṃ lambhidā gimha|kāla|kusuma|dāiṇo gumaā. idāniṃ adikkanta|samae vi rukkhae siñcamha. tasuṇo aṇahisandhida|puravo dhammo bhavissadi.⌟

ŚAKUNTALĀ: ⌜ahiṇandaṇīaṃ mantedha.⌟ *(nāṭyena siñcati.)*

RĀJĀ: *(nirvarṇya sa|kautukam)* katham? iyaṃ sā Kaṇva|duhitā? aho vismayaḥ!

BEHIND THE SCENES: This way, this way, dear friends!

KING: *(listening)* Ah! There appears to be a conversation to the right of the flower-tree path.* I will go there. *(walks around and looks)* It is the daughters of the ascetics, sprinkling the young trees with watering pots proportioned to themselves, coming this way. *(appraising them expertly)* Oho! How lovely they are to behold. I will take to this shade and wait. *(Keeps looking.)*

Enter Shakúntala, engaged as described, accompanied by two friends.

FRIENDS: Shakúntala, dear! We do believe that the hermitage trees are dearer to father Káshyapa than even you are, since you, as tender as the *nava·málika* jasmine, have been appointed to fill their basins.

SHAKÚNTALA: This is not just an order from father, but my 1.70
own respect; I truly do feel a sisterly affection toward them. *(Mimes sprinkling the trees.)*

BOTH: Shakúntala, dear! The copses of summer-blossoming trees are slaked with water. Now let's water the trees no longer in season. Then we can expect some unforeseen merit.

SHAKÚNTALA: What you say is commendable. *(Mimes sprinkling.)*

KING: *(watching, surprised)* What? This is the daughter of Kanva? How amazing!

śuddh'|ânta|durlabham idaṃ
  vapur āśrama|vāsino yadi janasya
dūrīkṛtāḥ khalu guṇair
  udyāna|latā vana|latābhiḥ.

1.75 bhavatu. pādap'|ântarita eva viśvasta|bhāvām enāṃ paśyāmi. *(tathā karoti.)*

ŚAKUNTALĀ: ⌜eso vād'|ērida|pallav'|âṅgulīhiṃ tuvarāvedi via maṃ baüla|rukkhao. jāva ṇaṃ sambhāvemi.⌟ *(rājñaḥ saṃnikarṣam āgacchati.)*

RĀJĀ: *(nirvarṇya)* a|sādhu|darśī tatra|bhavān Kāśyapo ya imām āśrama|dharma|caraṇe niyuṅkte.

idaṃ kil' âvyāja|mano|haraṃ vapuḥ
  tapaḥ|kṣamaṃ sādhayituṃ ya icchati
dhruvaṃ sa nīl'|ôtpala|patra|dhārayā
  samil|latāṃ chettum ṛṣir vyavasyati.

ŚAKUNTALĀ: ⌜halā Aṇasūe! ati|piṇaddheṇa Piaṃvadāe vakkaleṇa ṇiantida' mhi. seḍhilehi tā dāva ṇaṃ. *(Anasūyā śithilayati.)*⌟

1.80 PRIYAṂVADĀ: *(sa|smitam)* ⌜ittha pao|hara|vitthāraïttaaṃ appaṇo jovvaṇaṃ uvālaha.⌟

RĀJĀ: kāmam, a|pratirūpam asya vayaso valkalaṃ na punar alaṅkāra|śriyaṃ na puṣyati. kutaḥ?

If the figure of this person,
  scarcely to be found in royal apartments,
is that of a hermitage-dweller, then indeed
  the garden vine is outclassed in virtues
  by the forest creeper.

Be that so. Concealed by this tree I will observe her freed from inhibition. *(Does so.)* 1.75

SHAKÚNTALA: This *bákula* tree seems to hasten me on with its wind-stirred tendril-fingers. I will attend to it. *(Comes close to the king.)*

KING: *(watching)* His honor Káshyapa must be blind, that he should employ her in hermitage duties.

The sage who tries to make
  this guilelessly appealing figure capable
  of enduring penance:
surely he has set about cutting hard firewood
  with the edge of a blue water-lily petal.

SHAKÚNTALA: Anasúya, dear! I am pinioned by the bark-garment tightened by Priyam·vada. Please loosen it now. *(Anasúya loosens it.)*

PRIYAM·VADA: *(smiling)* For this you had better scold your own youth, which expands your breasts. 1.80

KING: Admitted, the bark-cloth is not apposite to her youthful prime, yet it does not fail to adorn her. How?

sarasi|jam anuviddhaṃ śevalen' âpi ramyaṃ
  malinam api him'|âṃśor lakṣma lakṣmīṃ tanoti.
iyam adhika|mano|jñā valkalen' âpi tanvī:
  kim iva hi madhurāṇāṃ maṇḍanaṃ n' ākṛtīnām?

PRIYAṂVADĀ: ⌜halā Saüntale! esā tāda|Kassabeṇa tumaṃ via saṃvaḍḍhidā alindae māhavī|ladā. pekkha ṇaṃ. kiṃ visumāridā de?⌟

ŚAKUNTALĀ: ⌜att" âbi visumarissadi.⌟ *(iti tat|samīpaṃ gacchati.)*

1.85 PRIYAṂVADĀ: ⌜halā Saüntale! ciṭṭha idha yyeva muhuttaaṃ dāva baüla|rukkha|samībe.⌟

ŚAKUNTALĀ: ⌜kiṃ ti?⌟

PRIYAṂVADĀ: ⌜tae samība|ṭṭhidāe ladā|saṇādho via me baüla|rukkhao paḍibhādi.⌟

ŚAKUNTALĀ: ⌜ado kkhu Piaṃvad' âsi.⌟

RĀJĀ: priyam api tathyam āh' âiṣā. asyāḥ khalu

1.90 adharaḥ kisalaya|rāgaḥ
  komala|viṭap'|ânukāriṇau bāhū
kusumam iva lobhanīyaṃ
  yauvanam aṅgeṣu saṃnaddham.

A lotus entangled with *sháivala* weed is still
attractive,
the spot on the moon, though a blemish,
sheds beauty,
this slender maiden is most captivating even
wearing a bark-cloth:
For what could not serve as an adornment
to sweet figures?

PRIYAM·VADA: Shakúntala, dear! Here in this natural verandah* is the *mádhavi* vine raised by father Káshyapa as if it were you yourself. See to it. Or have you forgotten it?

SHAKÚNTALA: As likely as I might forget myself. *(With this she approaches it.)*

PRIYAM·VADA: Shakúntala, dear! Pause for a moment, right 1.85
by the *bákula* tree.

SHAKÚNTALA: Why?

PRIYAM·VADA: With you standing beside it, the *bákula* tree seems to me as if it were embraced by a vine.

SHAKÚNTALA: That is why you are Priyam·vada ("Sweet-talker").

KING: What she says is sweet but also true. For her

Lower lip has the hue of a sprouting tendril, 1.90
her arms imitate tender branches.
Youth, desirable like a flower, is primed
in her physique.

ANASŪYĀ: ⌜halā Saüntale! iaṃ saaṃ|vara|vahū saha|ārassa tae kida|ṇāma|heassa Vaṇa|dosiṇo ṇo|māliā.⌟

ŚAKUNTALĀ: *(upagamy' âvalokya ca)* ⌜halā! ramaṇīe kāle imassa pādaba|mihuṇassa vadiaro saṃvutto. iaṃ ṇava|kusuma|jovvaṇā. aaṃ bi baddha|phaladāe uvabhoa|kkhamo saha|āro.⌟ *(paśyantī tiṣṭhati.)*

PRIYAṂVADĀ: ⌜halā Aṇasūe! jāṇāsi kiṃ|ṇimittaṃ Saüntalā Vaṇa|dosiṇaṃ adimettaṃ pekkhadi tti.⌟

ANASŪYĀ: ⌜ṇa kkhu vibhāvemi.⌟

I.95 PRIYAṂVADĀ: ⌜jadhā Vaṇa|dosiṇā aṇusadiseṇa pādabeṇa saṅgadā ṇo|māliā, avi ṇāma evaṃ ahaṃ pi attaṇo aṇurūvaṃ varaṃ lahemi tti.⌟

ŚAKUNTALĀ: ⌜eso ṇūṇaṃ de attaṇo citta|gado maṇo|radho!⌟ *(iti kalaśam āvarjayati.)*

RĀJĀ: api nāma kula|pater iyam a|sa|varṇa|kṣetra|sambhavā syāt? atha vā

asaṃśayaṃ kṣatra|parigraha|kṣamā
  yad evam asyām abhilāṣi me manaḥ
satāṃ hi saṃdeha|padeṣu vastuṣu
  pramāṇam antaḥ|karaṇa|pravṛttayaḥ.

tath" âpi tattvata enāṃ veditum icchāmi.

I.100 ŚAKUNTALĀ: *(bhramara|saṃpātaṃ nāṭayati)* ⌜ammo! salila|sea|saṃbhanto ṇo|māliaṃ ujjhia vaaṇaṃ me mahu|aro aṇuvaṭṭadi.⌟ *(bhramara|bādhāṃ nirūpayati.)*

ANASÚYA: Shakúntala, dear! This is the *nava·málika* jasmine, the bride who chose as her husband the mango tree named by you "Pleaser of the Forest."

SHAKÚNTALA: *(approaching and looking)* My dear! The union of this pair of root-drinking plants has taken place at a happy time. She is youthful with fresh blossoms. The mango tree, bedecked with fruits, is ready to be enjoyed. *(Remains gazing.)*

PRIYAM·VADA: Anasúya, dear! Do you know why Shakúntala is staring at "Pleaser of the Forest" so ardently?

ANASÚYA: I cannot imagine.

PRIYAM·VADA: She's thinking: "Just as the *nava·málika* jas- 1.95
mine is united with 'Pleaser of the Forest,' a worthy tree, so may I too win a suitable bridegroom."

SHAKÚNTALA: Surely that's a wish in your own heart! *(empties her pot.)*

KING: Can it be that she is born in a caste different from the patriarch's?* Or, rather,

> Doubtless she is fit to be wed by a warrior,
>   since my heart desires her so.
> For the good, the inclinations
>   of their inner faculties
>   are authoritative in matters of doubt.

Nevertheless, I wish to know the truth about her.

SHAKÚNTALA: *(acting the attack of a bee)* Ah! A bee confused 1.100
by the sprinkling of water has left the jasmine and is now assailing my face. *(Mimes fending off the bee.)*

RĀJĀ: *(vilokya sa/spṛham)*

cal'|âpāṅgāṃ dṛṣṭiṃ
    spṛśasi bahuśo vepathumatīṃ
  rahasy'|ākhyāy" îva
    svanasi mṛdu karṇ'|ântika|gataḥ
karau vyādhunvatyāḥ
    pivasi rati|sarvasvam adharaṃ
  vayaṃ devair maugdhyān
    madhukara hatās tvaṃ khalu kṛtī.

ŚAKUNTALĀ: ⌜halā! parittāadha maṃ iminā kusuma|pāḍaccareṇa ahibhūamāṇaṃ!⌟

UBHE: *(vihasya)* ⌜ke vaaṃ parittāṇe? Dussantaṃ ākanda! rāa|rakkhidāiṃ khu tavo|vaṇāiṃ honti.⌟

1.105 RĀJĀ: avasaraḥ khalv ayaṃ mam' ātmānaṃ darśayitum. *(upasṛtya)* na bhetavyam! na bhetavyam! *(ity ardh'/ôkte 'pavārya)* evaṃ rāj" âham iti pratijñātaṃ bhavati. bhavatu! atithi|samucit'|ācāram avalambiṣye.

ŚAKUNTALĀ: *(sa/trāsaṃ)* ⌜ṇa eso me purado aïdhaṭṭho viramadi. tā aṇṇado gamissaṃ. *(iti paṭ'/ântareṇa sthitvā sa/dṛṣṭi/kṣepaṃ)* haddhī! kadhaṃ ido bi maṃ aṇusaradi.⌟

RĀJĀ: *(sa/tvaram upetya)*

kaḥ Paurave vasumatīṃ
  śāsati śāsitari durvinītānām
ayam ācaraty avinayaṃ
  mugdhāsu tapasvi|kanyāsu?

sarvā rājānaṃ dṛṣṭvā kiñ cid iva sambhrāntāḥ.

KING: *(gazing longingly)*

You repeatedly touch her darting eye,
so that it quivers;
approaching her ear you hum
sweetly as if confiding a secret;
and while she flails her hands you drink
from her lower lip the treasure of love.
I, perplexed, am foiled by the Gods,
while you, bee, enjoy success.

SHAKÚNTALA: My friends! Protect me, I am assailed by this flower-bandit!

BOTH: *(laughing)* Who are we to protect you? Call for Dushyánta! Penance groves are under the protection of the king.

KING: This is the opportunity to reveal myself. *(approaching)* 1.105
Fear not! Fear not! *(stops in mid-sentence, aside)* Like this I will acknowledge that I am the king. Never mind. I will enjoy the welcome due a guest.

SHAKÚNTALA: *(trembling)* This bold villain will not leave me alone. I'll go elsewhere. *(stands behind a curtain, casting glances)** Oh, no! Why must he follow me even here?

KING: *(approaching hastily)*

Who dares harass innocent hermitage daughters,
while the scion of Puru,
chastiser of the wicked, rules the earth?

Seeing the king, they are all somewhat taken aback.

I.110 ANASŪYĀ: ⌜ṇa kkhu kiṃ|ci accāhidaṃ. iaṃ uṇa ṇo pia|sahī mahu|areṇa āülīkiamāṇā kādarī|bhūdā.⌟ *(Śakuntalāṃ darśayati.)*

RĀJĀ: *(Śakuntalām upetya)* bhavati! api tapas te vardhate?

ŚAKUNTALĀ: *(sa|sādhvas" âvanata|mukhy avacanā tiṣṭhati.)*

ANASŪYĀ: *(rājānaṃ prati)* ⌜idāṇiṃ adidhi|visesa|lāheṇa.⌟

PRIYAṂVADĀ: ⌜sāadaṃ ayyassa!⌟

I.115 ANASŪYĀ: ⌜halā Saüntale! gaccha tumaṃ uḍaādo phala|missaṃ agghaṃ uvāhara, idha pād'|ôdaaṃ atthi yyeva.⌟

RĀJĀ: bhavatu! sūnṛtay" âiva kṛtam ātithyam.

PRIYAṂVADĀ: ⌜teṇa imassiṃ dāva pādava|cchāā|sīdalāe satta|vaṇṇa|vediāe ayyo uvavisia muhuttaaṃ parīsamaṃ avaṇedu.⌟

RĀJĀ: nanu yūyam apy anena dharma|karmaṇā pariśrāntāḥ. tan muhūrtam upaviśata.

PRIYAṂVADĀ: *(jan'|ântikam)* ⌜halā Saüntale! uidaṃ ṇo adidhi|payyuvāsaṇaṃ. tā idha uvavisamha.⌟ *(sarvā upaviśanti.)*

I.120 ŚAKUNTALĀ: *(ātma|gatam)* ⌜kiṃ ṇu kkhu imaṃ pekkhia tabo|vaṇa|virohiṇo viārassa gamaṇīa mhi saṃvuttā?⌟

ANASÚYA: There is no cause for alarm. This dear friend of ours, upset by a bee, became frightened. *(Presents Shakúntala.)* I.110

KING: *(approaching Shakúntala)* Madam! Does your penance thrive?

SHAKÚNTALA: *(remains speechless, looks downward timidly.)*

ANASÚYA: *(to the king)* Now it does, by winning such a distinguished guest.

PRIYAM·VADA: Welcome, lord!

ANASÚYA: Shakúntala, dear! Go and fetch a mixed fruit offering from the leaf-hut. Water to wash his feet we have here. I.115

KING: Do not trouble yourselves! Your friendly conversation has already performed the rite of hospitable welcome.

PRIYAM·VADA: Then, lord, sit on this terrace surrounding the Seven-leaf tree, cooled by its shade, and dispel your fatigue.

KING: Surely you too are wearied by this religious labor, so please be seated for a while.

PRIYAM·VADA: *(in private)* Shakúntala, dear! It is our duty to wait upon a guest. So let us sit down here. *(The women all sit down.)*

SHAKÚNTALA: *(to herself)* What is this? No sooner have I seen him than I have become susceptible to feelings out of place in this penance grove. I.120

RĀJĀ: *(sarvā vilokya)* aho! samāna|vayo|rūpa|ramaṇīyaṃ sauhārdaṃ bhavatīnām.

PRIYAṂVADĀ: *(jan'|ântikam)* ⌜Aṇasūe! ko ṇu kkhu eso caüra|gambhīr'|āidī mahuraṃ piaṃ ālavanto pahavantaṃ dakkhiṇṇaṃ via karedi?⌟

ANASŪYĀ: *(jan'|ântikam eva)* ⌜sahi! mam' âvi kodūhalaṃ atthi yyeva. tā pucchissaṃ dāva ṇaṃ.⌟ *(prakāśam)* ⌜ayyassa ṇo mahur'|ālāva|jaṇido vīsambho mantāvedi. kadamaṃ uṇa ayyo vaṇṇaṃ alaṅkaredi? kiṇ|ṇimittaṃ vā suumāreṇa ayyeṇa tabo|vaṇ'|āgamaṇa|parīsamassa attā patthī|kado?⌟

ŚAKUNTALĀ: *(ātma|gatam)* ⌜hiaa, mā uttamma! jaṃ tae cintidaṃ taṃ Aṇasūā mantedi.⌟

I.125 RĀJĀ: *(sva|gatam)* katham idānīm ātmānam āvedaye? kathaṃ v"| ātm'|âpahāraṃ karomi? bhavatu! evaṃ tāvad enāṃ vakṣye. *(prakāśam)* bhavati! Veda|vid asmi Pauraveṇa rājñā dharm'|âdhikāre niyuktaḥ. so 'ham āśramiṇām avighna|kriy"|ôpalambhāya dharm'|âraṇyam idam āyātaḥ.

ANASŪYĀ: ⌜sa|ṇādhā dhamma|āriṇo.⌟

ŚAKUNTALĀ: *(śṛṅgāra|lajjāṃ nirūpayati.)*

SAKHYAU: *(ubhayor ākāraṃ viditvā, jan'|ântikaṃ)* ⌜halā Saüntale! jadi ajja tādo idha saṇṇihido bhave. . .⌟

ŚAKUNTALĀ: *(sa|bhrū|bhedam)* ⌜tado kiṃ bhave?⌟

KING: *(looking at all of them)* Ah! Your ladyships' friendship is delightful because you are alike in age and beauty.

PRIYAM·VADA: *(in private)* Anasúya! Who is this man with elegant and dignified demeanor, who, speaking to us with affectionate gentleness, seemingly shows us extraordinary courtesy?

ANASÚYA: *(also in private)* My dear, I too am curious. Let me ask him. *(aloud)* The confidence evoked by your lordship's gentle talk prompts me to speak. Which caste does your lordship adorn? And on what account has a refined lord given himself the toil of visiting a penance grove?

SHAKÚNTALA: *(to herself)* My heart! Do not be faint. Anasúya has asked what you want to know.

KING: *(to himself)* How now should I introduce myself? 1.125
Or how should I conceal my identity? Very well! I will tell her this: *(aloud)* Lady! I am a knower of the Vedas appointed by the Páurava to the office of supervising religion.* I have come to this sacred forest to ascertain that the rites of the hermits are not obstructed.

ANASÚYA: The followers of righteousness have a champion!

SHAKÚNTALA: *(mimes infatuated coyness.)*

THE FRIENDS: *(realizing the pair's condition, to the audience)* Shakúntala, dear! If only father were here now. . .

SHAKÚNTALA: *(knitting her brows)* What would happen then?

I.130 UBHE: ⌜tado imaṃ adidhiṃ jīvida|savvasseṇ' âbi kad|atthaṃ kare.⌟

ŚAKUNTALĀ: *(sa|roṣam)* ⌜ayi! avedha! kiṃ pi hiae karea mantedha! ṇa khu suṇissaṃ.⌟ *(parāvṛtya tiṣṭhati.)*

RĀJĀ: vayam api tāvad bhavatyau sakhī|gataṃ pṛcchāmaḥ.

UBHE: ⌜ayya! aṇuggahe bi abbhatthaṇā.⌟

RĀJĀ: bhagavān Kāśyapaḥ śāśvate brahmaṇi vartate. iyaṃ ca vāṃ sakhī tad|ātmaj" êti. katham etat?

I.135 ANASŪYĀ: ⌜suṇādu ayyo. atthi Kosio tti gotta|ṇāmaheo maha|ppahāvo rā'|êsī.⌟

RĀJĀ: prakāśas tatra|bhavān.

ANASŪYĀ: ⌜taṃ sahi|aṇe pahavaṃ avagaccha. ujjhia|sarīra|saṃrakkhaṇ'|ādīhiṃ uṇa tāda|Kassavo se pidā.⌟

RĀJĀ: «ujjhita|śabdena» janitaṃ me kutūhalam. tad ā mūlāc chrotum icchāmi.

ANASŪYĀ: ⌜purā kila tassa Kosiassa rā'|êsiṇo ugge tavasi vaṭṭamāṇassa kiṃ pi jāda|saṅkehiṃ devehiṃ Meṇaā ṇāma accharā ṇiama|viggha|kāriṇī pahidā.⌟

I.140 RĀJĀ: asty etad anya|samādhi|bhīrutvaṃ devānām. tatas tataḥ?

BOTH: Then he would satisfy this visitor with the very treasure of his life. 1.130

SHAKÚNTALA: *(angrily)* Pah! Go away! You are just prattling after making up some fantasy in your hearts. I'm not listening. *(Turns away and stays so.)*

KING: For my part, I too would like to question you two concerning your friend.

BOTH: Lord! Your request amounts to a favor.

KING: The reverend Káshyapa abides in constant celibacy, and your friend here is supposed to be his daughter. How can this be?

ANASÚYA: Listen, lord! There is a mighty royal sage of the patriline known as Káushika.* 1.135

KING: His reverence is well known.

ANASÚYA: Know him to be the begetter of our friend. Father Káshyapa is her parent by virtue of protecting her, etc., after she was abandoned.

KING: The word "abandoned" arouses my curiosity. I would like to hear this from the beginning.

ANASÚYA: Long ago, when the royal sage Káushika was enduring severe penances, the gods became mightily alarmed and dispatched the nymph Ménaka to thwart his observances.

KING: The Gods indeed fear the deep concentration of others. What happened then? 1.140

ANASŪYĀ: ⌜tado vasant'|ôdaa|samae tāe unmādayitta rūvaṃ pekkhia. . .⌟ *(ity ardh'|ôkte lajjayā viramati.)*

RĀJĀ: bhavatu! purastād avagamyata eva. . . apsaraḥ|sambhav" âiṣā!

ANASŪYĀ: ⌜adha|iṃ?⌟

RĀJĀ: yujyate.

I.145 mānuṣīṣu kathaṃ vā syād
asya rūpasya saṃbhavaḥ?
na prabhā|taralaṃ jyotir
udeti vasudhā|talāt.

ŚAKUNTALĀ: *(adho|mukhī tiṣṭhati.)*

RĀJĀ: *(sva|gatam)* labdh'|âvakāśo me mano|rathaḥ! kiṃ tu sakhyā parihās'|ôdāhṛtāṃ vara|prārthanām asyāḥ śrutv" âpi na śraddhatte me kātaraṃ manaḥ.

PRIYAṂVADĀ: *(Śakuntalāṃ sa|smitaṃ vilokya nāyak'|âbhimukhī)* ⌜puṇo via vattukāmo ayyo.⌟

ŚAKUNTALĀ: *(sakhīm aṅgulyā tarjayati.)*

I.150 RĀJĀ: samyag upalakṣitaṃ bhavatyā. asti naḥ sac|carita|śravaṇa|lobhād anyat praṣṭavyam.

PRIYAṂVADĀ: ⌜teṇa hi viārideṇa alaṃ. ṇiantaṇ'|âṇuyoggo tavassi|aṇo.⌟

RĀJĀ: upapadyate bhavati! sakhīṃ te jñātum icchāmi:

ANASÚYA: Then, when spring had just begun, he beheld her intoxicating figure. . . *(stops bashfully in mid-sentence.)*

KING: Say no more! The rest can be inferred. . . she is born from a nymph!

ANASÚYA: That's it.

KING: It makes sense.

> How could such a form 1.145
> be born among mortals?
> The flash that flickers
> with unsteady brilliance
> does not arise from the earth.

SHAKÚNTALA: *(remains looking at the ground.)*

KING: *(to himself)* My desire is within reach! But even though I heard her friend wish her a bridegroom in jest, my faint heart cannot believe it.

PRIYAM·VADA: *(after looking at Shakúntala with a smile, to the hero)* His lordship seems inclined to say something more.

SHAKÚNTALA: *(threatens her friend with her finger.)*

KING: You perceive correctly. Out of a desire to hear of the deeds of the virtuous, I would like to ask another question. 1.150

PRIYAM·VADA: Then do not hesitate. Ascetics are equal to being retained.

KING: Of course, my lady. I would like to know your friend:

vaikhānasaṃ kim anayā vratam ā pradānāt
  vyāpāra|rodhi Madanasya niṣevitavyam,
atyantam ātma|sadṛś'|ēkṣaṇa|vallabhābhiḥ
  āho nivatsyati samaṃ hariṇ'|âṅganābhiḥ?

PRIYAṂVADĀ: ⌜ayya! dhamma|caraṇe vi eso par'|ādhīṇo jaṇo, guruṇo uṇa se aṇurūva|vara|paḍivādaṇe saṅkappo.⌟

I.155 RĀJĀ: na khalu durlabh" âiṣā prārthaṇā. *(ātmagatam)*

bhava hṛdaya s'|âbhilāṣaṃ.
  samprati saṃdeha|nirṇayo jātaḥ.
āśaṅkase yad agniṃ
  tad idaṃ sparśa|kṣamaṃ ratnam.

ŚAKUNTALĀ: *(sa|roṣam iva)* ⌜Aṇasūe! gamissaṃ ahaṃ.⌟

ANASŪYĀ: ⌜kiṇ|ṇimittaṃ?⌟

ŚAKUNTALĀ: ⌜imaṃ asambaddh'|ālaviṇiṃ Piaṃvadaṃ ayyāe Godamīe ṇivedaïssaṃ.⌟ *(ity uttiṣṭhati.)*

I.160 ANASŪYĀ: ⌜sahi! ṇa juttaṃ assama|vāsiṇo jaṇassa akida|sak|kāraṃ adidhi|visesaṃ ujjhia sacchandado gamaṇam.⌟

ŚAKUNTALĀ: *(na kiñ cid uktvā prasthit" âiva.)*

RĀJĀ: *(apavārya)* katham? gacchati? *(grahītum icchan punar ātmānaṃ nigṛhya)* aho ceṣṭā|pratirūpikā kāmino mano|vṛttiḥ. ahaṃ hi

Will she observe her hermit's vow,
frustrating the work of the God of love,
until she is given in marriage,
or will she dwell for good with the does,
her favorites because their eyes resemble hers?

PRIYAM·VADA: Lord! Even in her religious duties she is dependent on another. Her preceptor has made up his mind to give her to a worthy groom.

KING: This wish will not be difficult to fulfill. *(to himself)*

Be full of expectation, heart,
the doubt has unravelled.
That which you feared to be fire
is a jewel that may be touched.

SHAKÚNTALA: *(appearing angry)* Anasúya! I am going!

ANASÚYA: What's wrong?

SHAKÚNTALA: I will go and tell the venerable Gáutami that Priyam·vada is prattling incoherently. *(With this, she stands up.)*

ANASÚYA: My friend! It is not proper for a person living in a hermitage to leave a distinguished guest who has not been properly attended to, and go as they please.

SHAKÚNTALA: *(Sets off without a word.)*

KING: *(aside)* What? Is she leaving? *(wishes to detain her, then checks himself)* Ah! A lover's inclinations are mirrored in his bodily movements. For I,

anuyāsyan muni|tanayāṃ
sahasā vinayena vārita|prasaraḥ.
sthānād anuccalann api
gatv" êva punaf pratinivṛttaḥ.

PRIYAṂVADĀ: *(Śakuntalām upasṛtya)* ⌜halā caṇḍi! ṇa de juttaṃ gacchiduṃ.⌟

I.165 ŚAKUNTALĀ: *(parivṛtya, sa|bhrū|bhedam)* ⌜ki·tti?⌟

PRIYAṂVADĀ: ⌜rukkha|seaṇae due me dhāresi. tehi dāva attāṇaaṃ moehi, tado gamissasi.⌟ *(balād enāṃ nivārayati.)*

RĀJĀ: bhadre! vṛkṣa|secanakād eva pariśrāntām atra|bhavatīṃ lakṣaye. tathā hy asyāḥ

srast'|âṃsāv atimātra|lohita|karau
bāhū ghaṭ'|ôtkṣepaṇāt
ady' âpi stana|vepathuṃ janayati
śvāsaf pramāṇ'|âdhikaḥ
baddhaṃ karṇa|śirīṣa|rodhi vadane
gharm'|âmbhasāṃ jālakaṃ
bandhe sraṃsini c' âika|hasta|yamitāḥ
paryākulā mūrdha|jāḥ.

tad aham enām an|ṛṇāṃ karomi tvayi. *(sv'|âṅgulīyaṃ prayacchati.)*

I.170 UBHE: *(nāma|mudr"| âkṣarāṇy anuvācya paras|paraṃ mukham avalokayataḥ.)*

RĀJĀ: alam asmākam anyathā|sambhāvitena. rājñaf parigraho 'yam.

About to pursue the sage's daughter,
my motion has suddenly been held back
by decorum.
Though I did not move from my place,
it is as if I had gone and returned.

PRIYAM·VADA: *(approaching Shakúntala)* Hey! Angry girl! It is not right for you to leave.

SHAKÚNTALA: *(turns around, knits her eyebrows)* Why not?

PRIYAM·VADA: You owe me two tree waterings. Acquit yourself first of these, then you may go. *(Detains her by force.)*

KING: Good lady! I perceive that she is wearied by watering trees. For her

Shoulders are slack,
the hands of her arms are intensely red
from emptying the watering pot,
even now her breath is still heavier than usual,
making her breasts quiver,
a web of perspiration adheres to her face,
hindering the play of the *shirísha* blossoms
on her ear,
and as the band slips,
she holds in check her unruly hair with one hand.

Therefore let me settle her debt with you. *(Offers his ring.)*

BOTH: *(Reading out the letters on the name-seal, they look at each other's faces.)*

KING: Do not take me for what I am not. This is a gift from the king.

PRIYAMVADĀ: ⌜teṇa hi ṇ' ârahadi idaṃ a raṇṇo aṅgulīaaṃ vioa|kāriaṃ. ayyassa tuva vaaṇeṇa ṇāma esā ariṇā eva mama.⌟ *(parivṛty' âpavārya)* ⌜halā Saüntale! moid" âsi aṇukampiṇā ayyeṇa. ahavā mah"|âṇubhāveṇa. kida|ṇṇā dāṇiṃ hohisi.⌟

ŚAKUNTALĀ: *(apavārya niḥśvasya)* ⌜ṇa idaṃ visumarissadi jadi attaṇo pahave.⌟

PRIYAMVADĀ: ⌜halā! kiṃ dāṇiṃ saṃpadaṃ ṇa gacchasi?⌟

1.175 ŚAKUNTALĀ: ⌜idāṇim pi tae kiṃ kattavvaṃ? jadā roissadi me tadā gamissaṃ.⌟

RĀJĀ: *(Śakuntalāṃ vilokayan sva|gatam)* kiṃ nu khalu yathā vayam asyām evam iyam apy asmān prati syāt? atha vā labdha|gādhā me prārthanā. kutaḥ?

vācaṃ na miśrayati yady api mad|vacobhiḥ
  karṇaṃ dadāty avahitā mayi bhāṣamāṇe
kāmaṃ na tiṣṭhati mad|ānana|saṃmukh" îyaṃ
  bhūyiṣṭham anya|viṣayā na tu dṛṣṭir asyāḥ.

NEPATHYE: bhoḥ! bhoḥ! tapasvino 'vahitās tapo|vane sattva|rakṣāyai bhavantu bhavantaḥ. paryāplutaṃ strī|kumāram! pratyāsannaḥ khalu mṛgayā|vihārī pārthivaḥ!

turaga|khura|hatas tathā hi reṇur
  viṭapa|viṣakta|jal'|ârdra|valkaleṣu
patati pariṇat'|âruṇa|prakāśaḥ
  śalabha|samūha iv' āśrama|drumeṣu.

PRIYAM·VADA: Well, then this ring of the king must not be separated from you. On your lordship's word her debt to me has been cancelled. *(turning, aside)* Dear Shakúntala! You have been released by the compassionate lord. Or, rather, by His Majesty. You are indebted to him from now on.

SHAKÚNTALA: *(sighs, aside)* This will not be forgotten if I regain my independence.

PRIYAM·VADA: My dear! Why are you not going now?

SHAKÚNTALA: Who are you to command me now? I will go I.175
when it pleases me.

KING: *(looking at Shakúntala, to himself)* Can it be that she feels toward me as I feel toward her? No, rather, my hope has found a shallow ford. Why?

> Even if she does not mingle her words
> with my words,
> she attentively lends an ear when I speak.
> Granted she will not face me,
> but her eyes are not, on the whole,
> fixed on anything else.

OFFSTAGE: Ye hermits! Be alert to protect the animals in the penance grove. Women and children are in peril! The king is hunting nearby!

> For the dust raised up by the hooves of his horses,
> shining as red as the evening twilight,
> falls like a swarm of locusts
> upon the hermitage trees
> to whose boughs clings damp bark-cloth.

I.180 aho dhik! eṣa khalu nibhṛta|cārī bhūtvā

tīvr'|āpāta|pratihata|taru|
skandha|lagn'|âika|dantaḥ
prauḍh'|āsakta|vratati|valay'|ā-
saṅga|saṃjāta|pāśaḥ
mūrto vighnas tapasa iva no
bhinna|sāraṅga|yūtho
dharm'|âraṇyaṃ virujati gajaḥ
syandan'|āloka|bhītaḥ.

RĀJĀ: *(sva|gatam)* aho dhik! pramādaḥ! mad|anveṣiṇaḥ sainikās tapo|vanam uparundhanti. tad aparāddhaṃ tapasvināṃ asmābhiḥ. bhavatu! gamiṣyāmi tāvat.

ANASŪYĀ: *(sa|saṃbhramam)* ⌜ayya! imiṇā akkandideṇa payyāülamha. tā aṇujāṇīhi ṇo uḍaa|gamaṇāa.⌟

RĀJĀ: *(sa|saṃbhramam)* gacchantu bhavatyaḥ. āśrama|bādhā yathā na bhaviṣyati tathā prayatiṣyāmahe.

I.185 SAKHYAU: ⌜asambhāvida|sak|kāraṃ bhūyo vvi dāva paccavekkhaṇā|ṇimittaṃ lajjāmo ayyaṃ viṇaveduṃ. vidida|bhūyiṭṭho si ṇo sampadaṃ jaṃ dāṇiṃ uvaāra|majjhatthadāe avaraddhamha taṃ marisesi.⌟

RĀJĀ: mā m" âivam! darśanena bhavatīnāṃ puras|kṛto 'smi.

UBHE: ⌜halā Saüntale! ehi sigghadaraṃ! āülā ayyā Godamī bhavissadi.⌟

Woe, alas! This solitary 1.180

> Elephant, frightened
> by the appearance of a chariot,
> one tusk stuck in a chunk of a tree
> struck with a massive blow,
> with fetters formed from a tangle
> of mighty *vrátati* coils clinging to him
> is tearing up the sacred forest scattering
> the herd of antelopes,
> like an incarnate obstacle to our penance.

KING: *(to himself)* Alas! How careless. Soldiers searching for me are disturbing the penance grove. So I have committed an offence against the ascetics. Very well, I must go!

ANASÚYA: *(perturbed)* Lord! We are frightened by this shouting. Permit us to retire to the leaf-hut.

KING: *(agitated)* Go, ladies. I will see to it that no harm befalls the hermitage.

FRIENDS: Without having completed the rites of welcome, 1.185
we feel shame to petition his lordship for another meeting. We now consider you well-nigh an acquaintance, so being tolerant of our conduct you might put up with our offense.

KING: Not at all, not at all! I have been hospitably welcomed by seeing you ladies.

BOTH: Dear Shakúntala! Come quickly! The noble Gáutami will be worried.

ŚAKUNTALĀ: *(sa|vyāja|vilaṃbitaṃ kṛtv" ātma|gataṃ)* ⌜haddhī! ūru|tthambeṇa viala mhi saṃvuttā.⌟

RĀJĀ: svairaṃ svairaṃ gacchantu bhavatyaḥ! vayam āvega|hetum āśramasy' âpaneṣyāmaḥ.

I.190 ŚAKUNTALĀ: *(sa|vyāja|vilambitaṃ kṛtvā parikramya sakhībhyāṃ saha niṣkrāntā.)*

RĀJĀ: *(utthāya sa|khedam)* mand'|âutsukyo 'smi nagaraṃ prati. yāvad anuyātrika|janaṃ sametya n' âtidūre tapo|vanasya niveśayāmi. na khalu śaknomi Śakuntalā|vyāpārād ātmānaṃ nivartayitum. mama hi

gacchati puraḥ śarīraṃ
  dhāvati paścād asaṃvṛtaṃ cetaḥ
cihn'|âṃśukam iva ketoḥ
  prativātaṃ nīyamānasya.

(sa|cintaḥ skhalitāni padāni dattvā niṣkrāntaḥ.)

iti mahā|kavi|Kālidāsa|viracite
Śakuntalā|nāmani nāṭake
prathamo 'ṅkaḥ.

SHAKÚNTALA: *(Delays under a pretext, to herself)* Oh dear! I am crippled by a cramp in my thigh.

KING: Carefully, go carefully. I will draw away the source of perturbation from the hermitage.

SHAKÚNTALA: *(delays under some pretext, walks around and* I.190
then exits with her friends.)

KING: *(arises, grieved)* My eagerness to return to the city has slackened. I will join my retinue and encamp not too far from the penance grove. I am not able to turn myself away from preoccupation with Shakúntala. For my

> Body moves ahead, while my heart lags behind,
> not enclosed by it
> like the marked cloth of a banner
> carried into the wind.

(Exits pensively with faltering steps.)

The first act in the play called "Shakúntala,"
composed by the great poet
Kali·dasa.

ACT TWO:
THE SECRET

tataf praviśati pariśrānto vidūṣakaḥ.

VIDŪṢAKAḤ: *(śramaṃ nāṭayati, niḥśvasya)* ⌐bho diḍho 'mhi! edassa miaā|śīlassa raṇṇo vayassa|bhāveṇa ṇiviṇṇo. «aaṃ mio! aaṃ varāho!» tti. majjhaṃ|diṇe vi gimha|virala|pādava|cchāāsu vaṇa|rāīsu āphaṇḍīadi. patta|saṅkara|kasāāiṃ pīante kaḍuāiṃ uṇhāiṃ giri|ṇadī|jalāiṃ. aṇiada| velaṃ sūla|māṃsaṃ saüṇa|māṃsa|bhūïṭṭhaṃ aṇhīadi. tura'|āṇa|kaṇṭhaïda|sandhi|bandhaṇānaṃ aṅgāṇaṃ rattiṃ pi ṇatthi pakāmaṃ saïdavvam. tado mahanti yyeva paccūse dāsīe|puttehiṃ Saüṇa|luddhaehiṃ kaṇṇa|ghādiṇā vaṇa|gahaṇa|kolāhaleṇa paḍibodhīāmi. *(vicintya)* ettieṇa vi me pāṇā ṇa ṇikkantā. *(s'/âsūyaṃ vihasya)* tado gaṇḍ'|ôvari piḍiā saṃvuttā. hio kila amhesu ohīṇesu tattha|bhavado mi'|âṇusāreṇa assama|padaṃ paviṭṭhassa kila tāvasa|kaññaā Saüntalā ṇāma mama adhaññadāe daṃsidā. saṃpadaṃ ṇaara|gamaṇassa saṅkadhaṃ pi ṇa karedi. ajjha taṃ yeva saṃcintaantassa vibhādaṃ acchīsu. tā kā gadī? jāva ṇaṃ kid'|ācāra|parikammaṃ kahiṃ bi pekkhāmi. *(mandaṃ parikramya vilokya ca)* eso rāā bāṇ'|āsaṇa|hatthāhiṃ javaṇīhiṃ parivudo vaṇa|puppha| mālā|dhārī ido yyev' āgacchadi. tā jāva ṇaṃ ubasappāmi. *(kiṃ cid upasṛtya)* bhodu aṅga|sammaḍḍa|vihalo dāṇiṃ bhavia idha yyeva ciṭṭhissaṃ jado evaṃ pi dāva vīsāmaṃ lahemi.⌐ *(daṇḍa|kāṣṭham avalambya tiṣṭhati.)*

Enter the buffoon, exhausted.

BUFFOON: *(acting fatigue, sighing)* I'm immobilized! I'm sick of being a sidekick to this hunt-mad king. "Here's an antelope! There's a boar!" and even at midday we charge along forest tracks where the shade cast by trees is sparse in summer. We drink lukewarm, acrid water from mountain-streams, bitter by contamination with leaves. At odd hours we eat spit-roast meat—mostly fowl. Even at night I may not rest my limbs at will, for their joints are knocked out by the horse-cart. Then, at the crack of dawn, I am woken up by the ear-splitting din of fowlers taking to the forest, sons of bitches! *(reflects)* Despite all of this, my vital breaths have not departed. *(laughs with malice)* And now a pimple crowns the boil. Just yesterday, as I lagged behind, His Majesty, chasing some antelope, entered a hermitage and was, by my ill fate, shown an ascetic's daughter called Shakúntala. Now he will not even talk of going back to the city. Today he reminisced about her until dawn. What can be done? I will track him down somewhere when he has performed his usual toilet. *(saunters about and looks around)* The king is coming this way, wearing a garland of forest flowers, encircled by his bodyguard of Ionian women bearing bows. So I will confront him. *(approaching a bit)* That's far enough! Now that I am crippled by the crushing of my limbs I will stay right here. At least in this way I might gain some rest. *(Stands leaning on his staff.)*

Tataf praviśati yathā|nirdiṣṭa|parivāro rājā.

RĀJĀ: *(sa|cintaṃ niḥśvasy' ātma|gatam)*

2.5 kāmaṃ priyā na sulabhā
manas tu tad|bhāva|darśan'|āśvāsi.
akṛt'|ârthe 'pi manasi|je
ratim ubhayaṃ prārthanā kurute.

(smṛtim abhinīya vihasya) evam ātm'|âbhiprāya|sambhāvit'|êṣṭa|jana|citta|vṛttif prārthayitā viḍambyate. kutaḥ?

snigdhaṃ vīkṣitam anyato 'pi nayane
yat prerayantyā tayā
yātaṃ yac ca nitambayor gurutayā
mandaṃ vilāsād iva.
«mā gā» ity avaruddhayā yad api sā
s'|âsūyam uktā sakhī
sarvaṃ tat kila mat|parāyaṇam aho
kāmaḥ svatāṃ paśyati.

(parikrāmati.)

VIDŪṢAKAḤ: *(tathā|sthita eva.)* ⌜bho rāaṃ! ṇa me hattho pasaradi vāā|mettaeṇa jaāvīasi. jaadu jaadu bhavaṃ!⌟

2.10 RĀJĀ: *(vilokya sa|smitam.)* vayasya! kuto 'yaṃ gātr'|ôpaghātaḥ?

VIDŪṢAKAḤ: ⌜kudo kila! saaṃ yeva acchī āülīkadua aṃsu|kāraṇaṃ pucchasi!⌟

Enter the king, attended as described.

KING: *(sighs pensively, to himself)*

Granted, my love is not easily won, 2.5
but my heart takes comfort
in perceiving her feelings.
Though love be not satisfied,
mutual longing gives pleasure.

(mimes recollection and smiles) In this way, the longing lover, imagining the feelings of his beloved according to his own intentions, is duped. How so?

That tender look,
even when her eyes glanced elsewhere,
that gait, slowed by the heaviness of her buttocks,
as if deliberately teasing,
that angry outburst at her friend
who had detained her,
saying: "You may not leave!"
—All this was really aimed at me!
Ah! Love perceives all as its own.

(Walks about.)

BUFFOON: *(remaining where he is)* Lord King! My hand will not extend, so I hail you with words alone. Victory! Victory, sir!

KING: *(looks on, smiling)* My friend! Whence this bodily paralysis? 2.10

BUFFOON: Whence indeed! You poke me in the eye then ask why these tears!

RĀJĀ: vayasya! na khalv avagacchāmi.

VIDŪṢAKAḤ: *(sa|roṣam iva)* ⌜bho! tae ṇāma rāa|kayyāiṃ ujjhia tādise a kīḷā|pasāde vaṇ'|âr'|ekka|vuttiṇā hodavvaṃ? jaṃ saccaṃ paccahaṃ sāvada|saüṇ'|âṇugāmaṇehiṃ saṅkhohida|sandhi|bandhaṇānaṃ aṅgāṇaṃ aṇīso 'mhi saṃvutto.⌟ *(sa|praṇayaṃ.)* ⌜tā pasīda! maṃ vajjehi. ekk'|âhaṃ pi dāva vīsamīadu.⌟

RĀJĀ: *(ātma|gatam)* ayam evam āha, mam' âpi Kāśyapa|sutām anusṛtya mṛgayā|viklavaṃ cetaḥ. kutaḥ?

2.15 na namayitum adhijyam asmi śakto
dhanur idam āhita|sāyakam mṛgeṣu.
saha|vasatim upetya yaif priyāyāḥ
kṛta iva mugdha|vilok'|ôpadeśaḥ.

VIDŪṢAKAḤ: *(rājño mukhaṃ vilokya)* ⌜bho! attha|bhavaṃ hiaeṇa kiṃ pi mantedi. araṇṇe mae rudidaṃ.⌟

RĀJĀ: *(sa|smitam iva)* kim anyat? anatikramaṇīyaṃ me suhṛd|vākyam iti sthito 'smi.

VIDŪṢAKAḤ: ⌜ciraṃ jīva!⌟

RĀJĀ: tiṣṭha. s'|âvaśeṣaṃ me vacaḥ.

2.20 VIDŪṢAKAḤ: ⌜āṇavedu bhavaṃ.⌟

RĀJĀ: viśrāntena bhavatā mam' ânyasminn anāyāse karmaṇi sahāyena bhavitavyam.

KING: My friend! I really do not follow.

BUFFOON: *(as if angry)* Sir! Have you given up your royal duties, and an exquisite life of luxury, to become no better than a forest ranger? So that, truth be known, with running after wild beasts and birds every day, I am no longer master of my limbs whose joints are knocked out. *(pleading)* Have mercy now! Give me a break! Rest just one day.

KING: *(to himself)* My friend urges me like this, and my heart, too, preoccupied with the daughter of Kanva, is averse to hunting. Why?

I am no longer able to bend this strung bow,
with arrow laid upon it, against fawns, who,
dwelling with my beloved, have given
her instruction, as it were,
in innocent glances.

BUFFOON: *(looking at the king's face)* Sir! You are mulling something over in your heart. I am crying in the wilderness.

KING: *(with a slight smile)* How could it be any other way? I would never defy the words of a friend. I will stay here.

BUFFOON: Live long!

KING: Stay! I have more to say.

BUFFOON: Command, Your Majesty!

KING: When you have rested you must assist me in another undemanding matter.

VIDŪṢAKAḤ: *(s'|âbhilāṣena.)* ⌜avi modaa|khajjiāe?⌟

RĀJĀ: yatra vakṣyāmi. . .

VIDŪṢAKAḤ: ⌜gahido khaṇo.⌟

RĀJĀ: kaḥ ko 'tra bhoḥ?

(praviśya) DAUVĀRIKAḤ: ⌜āṇavedu bhaṭṭā.⌟

RĀJĀ: Revaka! senā|patis tāvad āhūyatām.

DAUVĀRIKAḤ: ⌜jaṃ bhaṭṭā āṇavedi.⌟ *(iti niṣkrāntaḥ.)*

tataf praviśati SENĀ|PATIR DAUVĀRIKAŚ *ca.*

SENĀ|PATIḤ: *(rājānaṃ vilokya)* dṛṣṭa|doṣ" âpi svāmini mṛgayā khalu guṇāy' âiva saṃvṛttā. tathā hi,

anavarata|dhanur|jyā|sphālana|krūra|pūrvaṃ
ravi|kiraṇa|sahiṣṇuḥ sveda|leśair abhinnaḥ.
apacitam api gātraṃ vyāyatatvād alakṣyaṃ
giri|cara iva nāgaf prāṇa|sāraṃ bibharti.

DAUVĀRIKAḤ: ⌜eso kkhu aṇuvaaṇa|diṇṇa|kaṇṇo ido diṇṇa|diṭṭhī yeva bhaṭṭā tumaṃ paḍivāledi. tā uvasappadu ayyo.⌟

SENĀ|PATIḤ: *(upasṛtya sa|praṇāmam.)* jayatu jayatu svāmī! pracāra|sūcita|gṛhīta|śvāpadam araṇyam. kim anyad avasthīyate?

BUFFOON: *(greedily)* Tasting some cakes?

KING: I will tell you what it is. . .

BUFFOON: Take your time.*

KING: Who is here?

(Enter) DOOR-KEEPER: Command, master!

KING: Révaka! Summon the general at once.

DOOR-KEEPER: As you command, master. *(With this he exits.)*

Enter the general and the door-keeper.

GENERAL: *(looking at the king)* Though considered a vice, hunting, in fact, has proved beneficial for our Commander. For

With his body, its forefront raw
from the ceaseless impact of the bowstring,
withstanding the sun's rays
without breaking into sweat,
though it has lost weight this is not noticeable
because of its muscular development,
he exhibits a vital force
like a mountain-roving elephant!

DOOR-KEEPER: There is the master, listening to a conversation, casting his glance hither, expecting you. Approach, sir!

GENERAL: *(approaches with a bow)* Be victorious, be victorious, Commander! The forest's beasts of prey are hemmed in, it is fit for roaming in. What are we waiting for?

RĀJĀ: mand'|ôtsāhaḥ kṛto 'smi mṛgay"|âpavādinā Mādhavyena.

2.35 SENĀ|PATIḤ: *(jan'|ântikam)* Mādhavya! sthira|pratibandho bhava. ahaṃ tāvat svāminaś citta|vṛttim anuvartiṣye. *(prakāśam)* deva! pralapaty eṣa vaidheyaḥ. nanu prabhur eva nidarśanam mṛgayā|guṇānām.

medaś|cheda|kṛś'|ôdaraṃ laghu bhavaty
    utthāna|yogyaṃ vapuḥ
  sattvānām api lakṣyate vikṛtimac
    cittaṃ bhaya|krodhayoḥ.
utkarṣaḥ sa ca dhanvināṃ yad iṣavaḥ
    sidhyanti lakṣye cale
  mithy" âiva vyasanaṃ vadanti mṛgayām.
    īdṛg vinodaḥ kutaḥ?

VIDŪṢAKAḤ: *(sa|kṛtaka|roṣaṃ)* ⌜attha|bhavaṃ dāva païdiṃ āvaṇṇo. tumaṃ puṇo aḍavīdo aḍaviṃ āhiṇḍa jāva sīsa|siālo via juṇṇa|rikkhassa muhe paḍissasi.⌟

RĀJĀ: bhadra senāpate! āśrama|saṃnikarṣe vartāmahe. atas te vaco n' âbhinandāmi. adya tāvat,

KING: My enthusiasm has been dampened by Madhávya, who is denouncing hunting.

GENERAL: *(aside)* Madhávya! Remain steadfast in your opposition! I will probe the Commander's frame of mind.* *(aloud)* Commander! This dolt prattles nonsense. Why, Your Majesty is yourself an advertisement for the virtues of hunting. 2.35

The body, slim-waisted and trim,
becomes light and fit for intrepid adventure;
the temperament of the wild animals, too,
is seen altered by fear and rage;
and then there is that exaltation for the archer,
that his arrows should strike a fleeting target;
It is plain false, that they should decry
hunting as a vice;
whence else derives such recreation?

BUFFOON: *(feigning anger)* His Majesty has come to his senses. You can carry on blundering from thicket to thicket until, like a lead jackal, you stumble into the jaws of an old bear.

KING: My good general! We are in the proximity of a hermitage. Therefore I do not applaud your words. For today,

gāhantāṃ mahiṣā nipāna|salilaṃ
  śṛngair muhus tāḍitam
chāyā|baddha|kadambakaṃ mṛga|kulaṃ
  romantham abhyasyatu
viśvastaiḥ kriyatāṃ varāha|patibhir
  mustā|kṣatif palvale
viśrāntiṃ labhatām idaṃ ca śithila|
  jyā|bandham asmad|dhanuḥ.

2.40 SENĀ|PATIḤ: yat prabhaviṣṇave rocate.

RĀJĀ: tena hi nivartyantāṃ vana|grāhiṇaḥ. yathā ca sainikās tapo|vanaṃ dūrāt pratiharanti tathā niṣeddhavyāḥ. paśya,

śama|pradhāneṣu tapo|dhaneṣu
  gūḍhaṃ hi dāh'|ātmakam asti tejaḥ.
sparś'|ânukūlā iva sūrya|kāntās
  tad anya|tejo 'bhibhavād vamanti.

SENĀ|PATIR: yad ājñāpayati devaḥ.

VIDŪṢAKAḤ: ⌜gaccha saṃpadaṃ dāsīe putta!⌟

2.45 *niṣkrāntaḥ senā|patiḥ.*

RĀJĀ: *(parijanam avalokya)* apanayantu bhavanto mṛgayā|veṣam. Revaka! tvam api sva|niyogam aśūnyaṃ kuru.

PARIJANO: ⌜jaṃ bhaṭṭā āṇavedi.⌟ *(iti niṣkrāntaf parijanaḥ.)*

VIDŪṢAKAḤ: ⌜kado bhavatā ṇiddhūmao daṃsa|paḍīāro. tā saṃpadaṃ edassiṃ āvāsa|pādava|chāā|parivude vidāṇaa|saṇādhe āsaṇe jadhā|suhaṃ uvavisadu bhavaṃ, jāva ahaṃ pi suh'|āsana|ttho homi.⌟

Let the water buffaloes plunge
  into the water of pools
  repeatedly battered by their horns;
let the herd of deer band together in the shade
  to chew the cud;
let the leading boars tear up the *musta* weed
  in the ponds unworried;
and may this my bow take rest
  with its string loosened.

GENERAL: As it pleases the mighty one. 2.40

KING: Then recall the forest rangers. Issue an interdict so that my soldiers are kept far from the penance grove. Behold,

There is burning brilliance hidden in ascetics,
  who are usually pacific;
Like sun-crystals, pleasing to touch, they emit it
  when assailed by a hostile effulgence.

GENERAL: As His Majesty commands.

BUFFOON: Leave now, you son of a slave!

Exit the general. 2.45

KING: *(looking at his retinue)* Remove your hunting dress. Révaka! You too should not allow your post to be unoccupied.

RETINUE: As His Majesty commands. *(Exit the retinue)*

BUFFOON: You have driven off the parasites without using fumigants. So now be seated at ease on this seat provided with a canopy, surrounded by the shade of *avása* trees, so that I, too, may repose in comfort.

RĀJĀ: gaccha gacch' âgrataḥ! *(parikramya.)*

2.50 *ubhāv upaviṣṭau.*

RĀJĀ: sakhe Mādhavya! anavāpta|cakṣuh|phalo 'si yena tvayā darśanīyaṃ na dṛṣṭam!

VIDŪṢAKAḤ: ⌜ṇaṃ bhavaṃ aggado me ciṭṭhadi.⌟

RĀJĀ: sarvaḥ kāntam ātmānaṃ paśyati. kiṃ tu tām ev' âham āśrama|lalāma|bhūtāṃ Śakuntalām adhikṛtya bravīmi.

VIDŪṢAKAḤ: *(apavārya)* ⌜bhavadu! ṇa se pasaraṃ vaḍḍhaïssaṃ⌟ *(prakāśam)* ⌜jadā dāva sā tāvasa|kaṇṇaā appatthaṇīā tā kiṃ tāe diṭṭhāe.⌟

2.55 RĀJĀ: mūrkha! parihārye 'pi vastuni Duṣyantasya manaf pravartate?

VIDŪṢAKAḤ: ⌜tā kadhaṃ edaṃ?⌟

RĀJĀ:

Lalitānya|sambhavaṃ kila
   muner apatyaṃ tad|ujjhit'|âdhigatam.
arkasy' ôpari śithilaṃ
   cyutam iva nava|mālatī|kusumam.

VIDŪṢAKAḤ: ⌜jaï vi ṇa Kassavassa mah"|êsiṇo orasā dhūdā tadhā vi kiṃ tāe diṭṭhāe?⌟

2.60 RĀJĀ: aviśeṣa|jña!

KING: Lead the way! *(They walk about.)*

Both sit down. 2.50

KING: Friend Madhávya! You have not attained the fruit of sight, for you have not beheld that which is truly worth seeing!

BUFFOON: But surely you are right before me?

KING: Everyone thinks himself attractive. But I speak of Shakúntala, the ornament of the hermitage.

BUFFOON: *(aside)* Ha! I will give him no chance. *(aloud)* If, in fact, she is the daughter of an ascetic, and cannot be wed, then what is the point of looking at her?

KING: Fool! Can Dushyánta's heart crave a forbidden thing? 2.55

BUFFOON: Then what is going on?

KING:

> It is said the sage's child was born from Lalitánya,
> then taken in when deserted by her,
> just like a loose jasmine blossom fallen
> upon an *arka* shrub.

BUFFOON: Even if she is not the natural child of the great sage Káshyapa, still, what is the point of looking at her?

KING: Ignoramus! 2.60

ciraṃ gata|nimeṣābhir netra|paṅktibhir unmukhaḥ
navāṃ indu|kalāṃ lokaḥ kena bhāvena paśyati?
na ca sā mādṛśā nāma prārthanīyā samāsataḥ
samin|madhya|gata|kāḷāguru|khaṇḍavad ujjvalā.

VIDŪṢAKAḤ: *(vihasya)* ⌜bhoḥ! jadhā kass' âvi piṇḍa|kajjūrīhiṃ uvvejidassa tintiliāṇaṃ ahilāso bhodi tadhā itthī|raaṇa|paribhāviṇo bhavado iaṃ patthaṇā.⌟

RĀJĀ: na tāvad enāṃ paśyasi yena tvam evaṃ|vādī.

VIDŪṢAKAḤ: ⌜taṃ khu ramaṇīaṃ ṇāma jaṃ bhavado vi vimhaaṃ jaṇaadi!⌟

2.65 RĀJĀ: vayasya! kiṃ bahunā?

citre niveśya parikalpita|sattva|yogā?
  rūp'|ôccayena vihitā manasā kṛtā nu?
strī|ratna|sṛṣṭir aparā pratibhāti sā me
  dhātur vibhutvam anucintya vapuś ca tasyāḥ.

VIDŪṢAKAḤ: *(sa|vismayam)* ⌜paccādeso dāṇiṃ rūvavatīnaṃ!⌟

RĀJĀ: idaṃ ca me manasi vartate.

With what melancholy does the world gaze up
  at length at the first digit of the moon
  with unwinking rows of eyes?
And, for a man such as me
  she, ablaze like a fragment of dark aloe
  fallen among kindling,
is utterly beyond reach.

BUFFOON: *(laughing)* Ha! Just as someone who is fed up with sweet dates might crave sour tamarind, so you, scorning the most exquisite of women, have this yearning.*

KING: You have not seen her, that you can prattle like this.

BUFFOON: That must indeed be lovely which amazes even you!

KING: My friend! Why go on? 2.65

Was she painted and then infused with life?
Or was she visualized by assembling
  alluring forms?
When I contemplate the power of the creator
  her body appears to me like a second creation
  of Lakshmi, jewel among women.

BUFFOON: *(astonished)* Now the fairest are usurped!

KING: And this is lodged in my heart:

an|āghrātaṃ puṣpaṃ
  kisalayam a|lūnaṃ kara|ruhair
an|āmuktaṃ ratnaṃ
  madhu navam an|āsvādita|rasam.
a|khaṇḍaṃ puṇyānāṃ
  phalam iva ca tad|rūpam an|aghaṃ
na jāne bhoktāraṃ
  kam iha samupasthāsyati bhuvi.

2.70 VIDŪṢAKAḤ: ⌜teṇa hi lahu pariṇaadu bhavaṃ mā kassa vi tavassiṇo iṅgudī|tella|cikkaṇa|sīsassa āraṇṇaassa hatthe paḍissadi.⌟

RĀJĀ: paravatī khalu tatra|bhavatī, na ca saṃnihita|guru|janā.

VIDŪṢAKAḤ: ⌜adha bhavantaṃ antareṇa kīdiso se citt'|âṇurāo?⌟

RĀJĀ: sakhe! svabhāvād apragalbhas tapasvi|kanyakā|janaḥ. tath" âpi tu

abhimukhaṃ mayi samhṛtam īkṣitaṃ
  hasitam anya|nimitta|kath"|ôdayam.
vinaya|bādhita|vṛttir atas tayā
  na vivṛto madano na ca saṃhṛtaḥ.

2.75 VIDŪṢAKAḤ: *(vihasya)* ⌜kiṃ khu sā bhavado diṭṭha|mettassa yyeva aṅkaṃ ārohadu.⌟

RĀJĀ: sakhe! sakhībhyāṃ mithaf prasthāne śālīnay" âpi tatra|bhavatyā mayi bhūyiṣṭham āviṣkṛto bhāvaḥ. tadā khalu,

A flower unsmelled,
a frond not plucked off by fingernails,
a jewel not set,
new wine as yet unsavored.
I do not know what enjoyer of this faultless form,
  the full reward of merits, as it were,
  might arise on this earth.

BUFFOON: Then you must marry her at once, lest she fall into the hands of some rustic ascetic whose head is slimy with *íngudi* oil! 2.70

KING: She is a dependent, and her parent is absent.

BUFFOON: Well, what does her heart feel toward you?

KING: Friend! The daughters of ascetics are naturally coy. Nevertheless

When I faced her she withdrew her eyes,
her smile was feigned
  to arise from some other cause.
Therefore, restrained by decorum,
her passion was neither displayed nor concealed.

BUFFOON: *(laughing)* Was she to have climbed onto your lap the moment she laid eyes on you? 2.75

KING: My friend! When she departed with her two companions, she, though modest, did to some extent betray her feelings for me. For then,

«darbh'|âṅkureṇa caraṇaḥ kṣata ity» akāṇḍe
tanvī sthitā kati cid eva padāni gatvā
āsīd vivṛtta|vadanā ca vimocayantī
śākhāsu valkalam a|saktam api drumāṇām.

VIDŪṢAKAḤ: ⌜bho! gahida|pādheo hosi. kadhaṃ puṇo uṇa tavo|vaṇa|gamaṇaṃ ti pekkhāmi.⌟

RĀJĀ: sakhe! cintaya tāvat ken' ôpāyena punar āśrama|padaṃ gacchāmaḥ.

2.80 VIDŪṢAKAḤ: ⌜eso cintemi. . . mā khu me alīa|paridevidehiṃ samādhiṃ bhañjihisi.⌟ *(cintayitvā)* ⌜bho! ko aṇṇo uvāo? ṇaṃ bhavaṃ rāā?⌟

RĀJĀ: tataḥ kim?

VIDŪṢAKAḤ: ⌜nīvāra|cchab|bhāaṃ dāva sāmī uvatti.⌟

RĀJĀ: mūrkha! anyam bhāgam ete rakṣiṇe nirvapanti ratna|rāśīn api vihāy' âbhinandyam. paśya

yad uttiṣṭhati varṇebhyaḥ
nṛpāṇāṃ kṣayi tat phalam.
tapaḥ|ṣaḍ|bhāgam akṣayaṃ
dadāty āraṇyako janaḥ.

2.85 NEPATHYE: hanta! siddh'|ârthau svaḥ!

RĀJĀ: *(karṇaṃ dattvā)* aye! dhīra|praśānta|svarais tapasvibhir bhavitavyam.

When she had gone but a few paces
the slender woman stopped all of a sudden, saying:
  "My foot is pierced by a *darbha* shoot!"
And she turned back her face
  as she freed her bark-cloth,
  which was not really snagged
  in the tree's branches.

BUFFOON: Well, then! You have your provisions for the journey. I foresee, somehow, many more trips to the penance-grove.

KING: My friend! Think of some pretext to get us back into the hermitage grounds.

BUFFOON: I am thinking. . . don't interrupt my cerebration with your irritating whining. *(thinking)* Ha! What other pretext? Are you not the king?

KING: So what?

BUFFOON: The ruler can claim one sixth part of the harvest.

KING: Idiot! These hermits offer a different tribute to their protector, more valuable than heaps of jewels. Look,

That tribute which accrues to kings
  from the castes is perishable.
Foresters offer the imperishable sixth part
  of their penance.

OFFSTAGE: Good! We have found him!

KING: *(listening)* Ah! With such steady and calm voices—it must be hermits.

DAUVĀRIKAḤ *(praviśya)*: ⌜jaadu jaadu bhaṭṭā! ede duve isi|kumāraā paḍihāra|bhūmiṃ uvatthidā.⌟

RĀJĀ: avilambitaṃ praveśaya.

DAUVĀRIKAḤ: ⌜aaṃ pavesaāmi.⌟ *(iti niṣkrāntaḥ.)*

2.90 *tataf praviśatas tāpasau dauvārikaś ca.*

DAUVĀRIKAḤ: ⌜ido ido bhavantā.⌟

TĀPASAU: *(rājānaṃ dṛṣṭvā)* aho dīptimato 'pi viśvasanīyatā vapuṣaḥ. atha vā, upapannam etad asminn ṛṣi|kalpe rājani. tathā hi,

adhyākrāntā
vasatir amun" âpy āśrame sarva|bhogye
rakṣā|yogād
ayam api tapaf pratyahaṃ saṃcinoti,
asy' âpi dyāṃ
spṛśati vaśinaś cāraṇa|dvandva|gītaḥ
puṇyaḥ śabdo
«munir» iti muhuḥ kevalaṃ rāja|pūrvaḥ.

DVITĪYAḤ: Gautama! ayaṃ sa Balabhit|sakho Duṣyantaḥ.

2.95 PRATHAMAḤ: atha kim?

DVITĪYAḤ: tena hi,

DOOR-KEEPER *(entering)*: Victory, victory, lord! These two young hermits have arrived at the gate.

KING: Show them in without delay.

DOOR-KEEPER: I will bring them. *(Exit.)*

Enter two ascetics and the door-keeper. 2.90

DOOR-KEEPER: This way, this way, sirs.

ASCETICS: *(seeing the king)* Oh! What confidence his person, though majestic, inspires. But that is quite natural in a king who is like a sage. For,

> He too now abides in that stage of life
> which benefits all.
> Through the protection he affords,
> he too accumulates
> the merit of penance day by day,
> and the sacred appellation "sage," for him too,
> who has mastered himself, reaches up to heaven,
> chanted by pairs of minstrels,
> —but prefixed by "royal."

SECOND: Gáutama! This is Dushyánta, the friend of Indra.

FIRST: What of it? 2.95

SECOND: That is why

n' âitac citraṃ yad ayam udadhi|
śyāma|sīmāṃ dharitrīm
ekaḥ kṛtsnāṃ nagara|parigha|
prāṃśu|bāhur bhunakti.
āśaṃsante Sura|samitayaḥ
śakta|vairā hi daityaiḥ
asy' âdhijye dhanuṣi vijayaṃ
Paurahūte ca vajre.

UBHAU: *(upasṛtya)* svasti bhavate! *(phalāny upanayataḥ.)*

RĀJĀ: *(s'|ādaram utthāya)* abhivādaye bhavantau. *(sa|praṇāmaṃ gṛhīt'|āsana upaviśya)* kim ājñāpayato bhavantau?

2.100 ṚṢĪ: vidito bhavān āśrama|vāsināṃ iha|sthaḥ. tena bhavantam abhyārthayante.

RĀJĀ: kim ājñāpayanti?

UBHAU: tatra|bhavataḥ Kāśyapa|muner asāṃnidhyād rakṣāṃsi parāpatiṣyanti. tat katipaya|rātraṃ sārathi|dvitīyena bhavatā sanāthīkriyatām āśrama iti.

RĀJĀ: anugṛhīto 'smi.

VIDŪṢAKAḤ: *(apavārya)* ⌜aaṃ dāṇiṃ aṇuūla|gala|hattho.⌟

2.105 RĀJĀ: Revaka! mad|vacanād ucyatāṃ sārathiḥ: «sa|bāṇa|kārmukaṃ ratham upanay' êti.»

DAUVĀRIKAḤ: ⌜jaṃ bhaṭṭā āṇavedi.⌟ *(iti niṣkrāntaḥ.)*

It is no wonder that he alone,
whose arm is as long as the bar of a city gate,
enjoys the whole earth bounded
by the dark ocean.
For the Gods' wars, vehement in their hostility,
fought with the demons, depend for victory
on his strung bow and
on the thunderbolt of Indra.

BOTH: *(approaching)* Hail to His Majesty! *(They offer fruit.)*

KING: *(stands up respectfully)* I salute you both. *(accepts a seat with a bow and sits)* What do you command?

SEERS: It has become known to the hermitage inmates that you are here. Therefore they beseech Your Majesty. 2.100

KING: What do they command?

BOTH: Because his reverence the sage Káshyapa is not present we are pressed by demons. Therefore, accompanied by your charioteer, deign to ensure the protection of the hermitage for a few nights.

KING: I am honored.

BUFFOON: *(aside)* Now, this is a welcome hand throttling your throat.

KING: Révaka! Command the charioteer in my name: "Bring the chariot with bow and arrows!" 2.105

DOOR-KEEPER: As the lord commands. *(Exit.)*

ṚṢĪ: *(sa|harṣam)*

anukāriṇi pūrveṣāṃ yukta|rūpam idaṃ tvayi.
āpann'|âbhaya|sattreṇa dīkṣitāḥ khalu Pauravāḥ.

RĀJĀ: gacchatāṃ puro bhavantau. aham apy anupadam āgata eva.

2.110 ṚṢĪ: vijayasva! *(ity utthāya niṣkrāntau.)*

RĀJĀ: Mādhavya! apy asti Śakuntalā|darśana|kautukam?

VIDŪṢAKAḤ: ⌜pradhamaṃ aparibādhaṃ āsi.⌟ *(sa|bhayam.)* ⌜rakkhasa|vutt'|ânteṇa uṇa saṃpadaṃ visāda|daṃsiṇā visesidaṃ.⌟

RĀJĀ: mā bhaiṣīḥ! nanu mat|samīpe bhaviṣyasi.

VIDŪṢAKAḤ: ⌜eso *cakkākī* bhūdo 'mhi!⌟

2.115 *(praviśya)* DAUVĀRIKAḤ: ⌜bhaṭṭā! sajjo radho bhaṭṭiṇo vijaa|patthāṇaṃ udikkhadi. eso uṇa ṇaarādo devīṇaṃ saāsādo Karabhao uvatthido.⌟

RĀJĀ: *(s'|ādaram)* kim ajjūbhif preṣitaḥ.

DAUVĀRIKAḤ: ⌜adha|iṃ?⌟

RĀJĀ: praveśyatām.

SEERS: *(joyfully)*

> This befits you, who follows the path
> of your predecessors;
> the descendents of Puru
> are indeed consecrated
> for the sacrifice of allaying the fear
> of the oppressed.

KING: Go ahead, sirs! I too will follow shortly.

SEERS: Be victorious! *(With this they arise and exit.)* 2.110

KING: Madhávya! Are you curious to see Shakúntala?

BUFFOON: At first my curiosity knew no bounds. *(fearfully)* But now it has been put in perspective by this news of demons, making it dubious.

KING: Fear not! Surely you will stand by my side.

BUFFOON: I'd be *your wheel-guard : a sitting duck!**

(entering) DOOR-KEEPER: Lord! The readied chariot awaits 2.115
the lord's victorious advance. But Kárabhaka here has arrived from the city and the entourage of the Queen Mother.

KING: *(respectfully)* What? despatched by Mama?*

DOOR-KEEPER: What now?

KING: Show him in!

DAUVĀRIKAḤ: ⌜jaṃ bhaṭṭhā āṇavedi.⌟ *(iti niṣkrāntaḥ.)*

2.120 *tataf praviśati* DAUVĀRIKEṆA *saha* KARABHAKAḤ.

KARABHAKAḤ: *(upasṛtya)* ⌜jaadu jaadu bhaṭṭā! devīo āṇaventi jadhā āgamiṇi caütthe diase «putta|piṇḍao dāṇao» ṇāma uvavāso bhavissadi tattha dīhāüṇā avassaṃ saṇṇihideṇa hodavvaṃ.⌟

RĀJĀ: *(saṅkulam)* Mādhavya! itas tapasvi|kāryam, ito guru|jan'|ājñā, ubhayam apy anullaṅghanīyaṃ mayā. katham atra pratividheyam.

VIDŪṢAKAḤ: ⌜Tisaṅkū via antare ciṭṭha!⌟

RĀJĀ: satyam ākulo 'smi.

2.125 kṛtyayor bhinna|deśatvād
dvaidhībhavati me manaḥ.
puraf pratihataṃ śaile
srotaḥ sroto|vaho yathā.

(sa|khedaṃ cintayitvā.) sakhe Mādhavya! tvam ajjūbhif putra iti pratigṛhītaḥ. tad bhavān itaf pratinivṛtya tatra|bhavatīnāṃ putra|kāryam anuṣṭhātum arhati. «tapasvi|kārya|vyagritāḥ smaḥ» ity āvedaya.

VIDŪṢAKAḤ: *(sa|garvam.)* ⌜sādhu! rakkhasa|bhīruaṃ maṃ gaṇaïssadi!⌟

DOOR-KEEPER: As His Majesty commands. *(Exit.)*

Enter KÁRABHAKA *with the* DOOR-KEEPER.

KÁRABHAKA: *(approaching)* Victory! Victory, Your Majesty! The Queen lets it be known that: "On the coming fourth lunar day* there will take place the ceremony known as the 'offering ensuring the birth of a son.' On this occasion Your Majesty must be present."

KING: *(perturbed)* Madhávya! On the one hand, there is my obligation to the ascetics, on the other hand, there is the command of my venerable parent. Neither may I transgress. What should I do in this case?

BUFFOON: Stay in the middle like Tri·shanku.*

KING: Truly I am confounded.

My mind is divided
  because the two duties must be carried out
  in different places;
just like the stream of a river
  branching because of a rock in its path.

(reflecting, troubled) My friend Madhávya! You have been welcomed by Mama like a son. Therefore you must please return from here and stand in for the duty of a son. Tell her that I have been detained by obligations to ascetics.

BUFFOON: *(haughtily)* Oh, I get it! You think I am afraid of these demons.

RĀJĀ: *(sa|smitam)* mahā|brāhmaṇa! katham etad bhavati sambhāvyate.

VIDŪṢAKAḤ: ⌜teṇa hi jadhā *rā'|âṇurāeṇa* gantavvaṃ, tadhā gamissaṃ.⌟

2.130 RĀJĀ: nanu tapo|van'|ôparodhaf pariharaṇīya iti sarvān ānuyātrikān tvay" âiva saha prasthāpayāmi.

VIDŪṢAKAḤ: *(sa|garvam.)* ⌜teṇa hi jua|rāā khu amhi saṃvutto.⌟

RĀJĀ: *(sva|gatam)* capalo 'yaṃ baṭuḥ. kadā cid asmat|prārthanām antaḥ|purebhyaḥ kathayet. bhavatu. evaṃ tāvad vakṣye... *(prakāśaṃ, vidūṣakaṃ haste gṛhītvā)* vayasya! ṛṣi|gauravād āśramaṃ gacchāmi. na khalu satyam eva tāpasa|kanyakāyāṃ mam' âbhilāṣaḥ. paśya

kva vayaṃ kva parokṣa|manmatho
  mṛga|śāvaiḥ samam edhito janaḥ.
parihāsa|vikalpitaṃ sakhe
  param'|ârthena na gṛhyate vacaḥ!

VIDŪṢAKAḤ: ⌜evaṃ ṇ' êdaṃ!⌟

2.135 *iti niṣkrāntāḥ sarve.*

iti mahā|kavi|Kālidāsa|viracite
Śakuntalā|nāmani nāṭake
dvitīyo 'ṅkaḥ.

KING: *(smiling)* Great brahmin! In your case that is inconceivable.

BUFFOON: Since, then, I must go *because of love of the king,* I shall do so.

KING: Surely, to prevent disturbance to the penance grove I will dispatch the entire train with you. 2.130

BUFFOON: *(puffed up)* Now I have become a crown prince.

KING: *(to himself)* This fellow is a chatterbox. He might reveal my dalliance to the ladies in the inner apartments of the palace. Well, then, I will tell him this... *(aloud, taking the buffoon by the hand)* My friend! I go to the hermitage out of respect for the seers. There is nothing to that affection of mine for the ascetic's daughter. Look,

> Where, on the one hand, stand we,
> and where that person raised with fawns,
> unacquainted with love.
> Friend, do not take as a declaration of truth
> what was made up as a jest!

BUFFOON: Why, of course!

All withdraw. 2.135

The end of the second act
in the play called "Shakúntala,"
composed by the great poet Kali·dasa.

ACT THREE: THE PASSION

tataf praviśati yajamāna|śiṣyaḥ.

ŚIṢYAḤ: *(kuśān ādāya)* aho mahā|prabhāvo Duṣyantaḥ! praviṣṭa|mātra eva sārathi|dvitīye tatra|bhavat' îdam āśrama|padaṃ nirvṛtta|rakṣo|vighnaṃ saṃvṛttaṃ nirupaplavāṇi ca naḥ karmāṇi siddhāni.

kā kathā bāṇa|saṃdhāne?
  jyā|śabden' âiva dūrataḥ
huṃ|kāreṇ' êva dhanuṣaḥ
  sa hi vighnān apohati.

yāvad imān vedi|saṃstaraṇ'|ârthaṃ darbhān ṛtvigbhya upaharāmi. *(parikramy' ākāśe)* Priyaṃvade! kasy' êdam uśīr'|ânulepanaṃ mṛṇāla|valayavanti ca kamalinī|patrāṇi nīyante? *(śrutim abhinīya)* kiṃ bravīṣi? «ātapa|laṅghanād balavad asvasthā Śakuntalā. tasyā dāhe nirvāpaṇāy' êti.» aho yatnād upakramyatām sakhī. yatas tatra|bhavataḥ kula|pater ucchvasitam. aham api tāvad vaitānika|śānty|udakam asyai Gautamī|haste praheṣyāmi. *(iti niṣkrāntaḥ.)*

3.5 *praveśakaḥ.*

tataf praviśati kāmayān'|âvastho rājā.*

RĀJĀ: *(sa|vitarkam)*

jāne tapaso vīryaṃ
  sā bālā paravat" îti me viditam
alam asmi tato hṛdayaṃ
  tath" âpi n' êdaṃ nivartayitum.

Enter the disciple of the sacrificial priest.

DISCIPLE: *(bearing* kusha *grass)* Lo! How mighty is Dushyánta! No sooner had His Majesty entered the hermitage grounds with his charioteer than we were rid of the demon menace, and our rites succeed without distractions.

What need of fitting an arrow?
For he drives out troublemakers
  simply with the twang
  of his bowstring from afar,
  as if it were by the threatening growl of his bow.

I must bring this *darbha* grass to the priests so they can strew the altar. *(proceeds, offstage)* Priyam·vada! For whom are you fetching *ushíra* salve and lotus leaves wrapped in filaments? *(Mimes listening.)* What do you say? "Shakúntala is gravely ill with a heatstroke; to quench her fever." Ah! Nurse your friend with care, for she is the life-breath of our patriarch. I, too, will at once send soothing, consecrated water to her by the hand of Gáutami. *(Exit.)*

End of the prelude. 3.5

Enter the infatuated king.

KING: *(pensively)*

I know the potency of penance,
  and realize the girl is a dependent,
despite this I am not able to turn my heart
  away from her.

(sa|dainyam) bhagavan Kāma! evam apy upapadyate na te mayy anukrośaḥ. kutaś ca te kusum'|āyudhasya satas tīkṣṇatvam? *(vicintya)* āṃ jñātam,

3.10 ady' âpi nūnaṃ Hara|kopa|vahnis
tvayi jvalaty aurva iv' âmbu|rāśau;
tvam anyathā, Manmatha! mad|vidhānāṃ
bhasm'|âvaśeṣaḥ katham evam uṣṇaḥ?

(s'|âsūyam) Kusum'|āyudha! tvayā candramasā ca viśvasanīyābhyām abhisaṃdhīyate kāmi|jana|sārthaḥ katham iti?

tava kusuma|śaratvaṃ śīta|raśmitvam indoḥ
dvayam idam a|yath"|ârthaṃ dṛśyate mad|vidheṣu
visṛjati hima|garbhair agnim indur mayūkhais
tvam api kusuma|bāṇān vajra|sārīkaroṣi!

(sa|khedam) kva nu khalu saṃsthite karmaṇi sadasyair anujñāta|viśrāntiḥ klāntam ātmānaṃ vinodayāmi? *(niḥśvasya)* kiṃ nu khalu me priyā|darśanād ṛte śaraṇam anyat? yāvad enām anviṣye. *(sūryam avalokya)* imām ugr'|ātapāṃ velāṃ prāyeṇa latā|valayavatsu Mālinī|tīreṣu tatra|bhavatī sa|sakhī|janā gamayati. tatr' âiva tāvad gamiṣyāmi. *(parikramya s'|āhlādaṃ vāyu|sparśaṃ nirūpayan.)* aho pravāta|subhago 'yam uddeśaḥ.

(dejected) Lord Cupid! Despite this you show me no pity. And how can you, bearing flowers as weapons, be so fierce? *(reflects)* Yes, I understand,

Even now, surely, the flame of Shiva's wrath 3.10
still smolders within you,
like the submarine fire in the ocean;
How else, O Shaker, could you,
reduced to ashes, be so ferocious
to those like me?

(with malice) God of the flower bow! Why do you and the moon, who ought to be trustworthy, assail the caravan-train of lovers?

That your arrows should be flowers
and that the moon's rays should be cool
—both of these are evidently false
for those like me:
the moon spews fire with his icy rays,
and you make your flower-arrows adamantine!

(dejected) Now that the priests have concluded their rites, where may I, granted some respite, rest my weary soul? *(sighing)* What other refuge is there for me but the sight of my beloved? I must seek her. *(observes the sun)* She is wont to pass this period of severe heat with her friends on the Málini's banks, which are wreathed in vine bowers. That is where I will go. *(advances, acting the delightful touch of the wind)* Ah! This spot is pleasant with a fresh breeze.

śakyo 'ravinda|surabhiḥ
kaṇa|vāhī Mālinī|taraṅgāṇām
madana|glānair aṅgaiḥ
pīḍitam āliṅgituṃ pavanaḥ.

3.15 *(parikramy' âvalokya ca)* asmin vetasa|parikṣipte latā|maṇḍape Śakuntalayā bhavitavyam. tathā hi *(adho 'valokya)*

alpa|nihitā purastād avagāḍhā jaghana|gauravāt paścāt
dvāre 'sya pāṇḍu|sikate pada|paṅktir dṛśyate 'bhinavā.

yāvad viṭap'|ântareṇ' âvalokayāmi. *(tathā kṛtvā, sa|harṣam)* aye! labdhaṃ khalu netra|nirvāpaṇam. eṣā mano|ratha|bhūmif priyatamā me sa|kusum'|āstaraṇaṃ śilā|paṭṭam adhiśayānā sakhībhyām anvāsyate. bhavatu. latā|vyavahitaḥ śroṣyāmi tāvad āsāṃ viśrambha|kathitāni. *(avalokayan sthitaḥ.)*

tataf praviśati yathā|nirdiṣṭā Śakuntalā sakhyau ca.

SAKHYAU: *(upavījya)* ⌜sahi Saüntale! avi suhāadi de ṇaliṇī|vatta|vādo?⌟

3.20 ŚAKUNTALĀ: *(vedanaṃ nāṭayitvā)* ⌜kiṃ vā vījaanti maṃ sahīo?⌟

ubhe sa|viṣādaṃ mukham anyonyaṃ paśyataḥ.

ŚAKUNTALĀ: *(sa|khedaṃ niḥśvasati.)*

RĀJĀ: balavad asvasthā khalv atra|bhavatī. *(sa|vitarkam)* kim atr' âyam ātapa|doṣaḥ syād, uta yathā me manasi vartate? *(s'|âbhilāṣaṃ nirvarṇya)* athavā kṛtaṃ saṃdehena!

I am able to embrace closely
the lotus-fragranced wind, bearing the spray
of the Málini's ripples, with my limbs
languid with passion.

(wanders around and observes) Shakúntala must be in this 3.15
bower of shrubs surrounded by reeds. For, *(looking down)*

At its entrance, in the pale sand is seen
a line of fresh footprints,
shallow at the front,
depressed at the back with the weight of her
hips.

I will peer through the branches. *(does so, joyfully)* Ah! My eyes have received their alms. My darling, the ground of my love, lies upon a flower-strewn stone slab, together with her two friends. Good. Concealed by vines, I will eavesdrop on their private conversation. *(Watches.)*

Then enters Shakúntala and her two friends as described.

FRIENDS: *(fanning, affectionately)* Dear Shakúntala! Does the breeze of the lotus leaves relieve you?

SHAKÚNTALA: *(acts anguish)* Oh? Are my friends fanning 3.20
me?

Both look sorrowfully at each other's face.

SHAKÚNTALA: *(sighs dejectedly.)*

KING: Her ladyship is gravely indisposed. *(pondering)* Might this be a symptom of the heat, or is it as I suspect? *(longingly)* Enough of this doubt!

stana|nyast'|ôśīraṃ praśithila|mṛṇāl'|âika|valayam
priyāyāḥ s'|ābādhaṃ tad api kamanīyaṃ vapur idam
samas tāpaḥ kāmaṃ manasi|ja|nidāgha|prasarayoḥ
na tu grīṣmasy' âivaṃ subhagam aparādhaṃ yuvatiṣu.

3.25 ANASŪYĀ: ⌜halā Saüntale! aṇantara|ṇṇā amhe maaṇa|gadassa vuttantassa. tadhā vi jādisī idihāsa|gadesu maaṇa|vuttantesu kāmaamāṇassa avatthā suṇīadi tādisaṃ ca lakkhamha. tā kadhehi kiṇ|ṇimittaṃ de aaṃ āāso. viāraṃ khu param'|atthado aāṇia aṇārambho paḍīārassa.⌟

RĀJĀ: Anasūyay" âpy anugato madīyas tarkaḥ!

ŚAKUNTALĀ: *(ātma|gatam)* ⌜balavaṃ ca me ahiṇiveso. na a sakkaṇomi sahasā ṇivvaridum.⌟

PRIYAṂVADĀ: ⌜sahi! suṭṭhu esā bhaṇādi. kiṃ ṇ' êdaṃ attaṇo uvaddavaṃ nigūhasi? aṇudiasaṃ ca parihīasi aṅgehim. kevalaṃ lāvaṇṇamaī chāā tumaṃ ṇa muñcadi.⌟

This figure of my beloved,
her breasts anointed with *ushíra* salve,
her only bracelet of lotus filaments hanging loose,
though pained, is still desirable.
Admittedly, the inflammation
arising from love
and the heat appears the same,
yet the injury wrought by summer
upon young women
is not as lovely as this.

ANASÚYA: Dear Shakúntala! We may not be familiar with affairs of love. Even so, we can see that your state is like that of a lover described in historical romances. Please do tell what is the cause of your malady. Without knowing for sure what is the source of a disease, no remedy can be found. 3.25

KING: Anasúya, too, shares my suspicion!

SHAKÚNTALA: *(to herself)* My yearning is intense, and I am not able to ward it off just like that.

PRIYAM·VADA: Dear Shakúntala! What she says is right. Why should you conceal your sorrow? Day by day your limbs waste away, all that remains is your lovely aura.

RĀJĀ: avitatham āha Priyamvadā. tathā hy asyāḥ

3.30 kṣāma|kṣāma|kapolam ānanam, uraḥ
kāṭhinya|mukta|stanam,
madhyaṃ klāntataraṃ, prakāma|vinatāv
aṃsau, chavif pāṇḍurā
śocyā ca priya|darśanā ca madana|
kliṣṭ" êyam ālakṣyate
pattrāṇām iva śoṣaṇena marutā
spṛṣṭā latā mādhavī.

ŚAKUNTALĀ: ⌜kassa vā aṇṇassa idaṃ kadhaïdavvaṃ? āāsaïttiā dāṇiṃ vo bhavissaṃ.⌟

UBHE: ⌜ado yyeva ṇo ṇibbandho. saṃvibhaṭṭaṃ khu duḥkhaṃ sajjha|veaṇaṃ bhodi.⌟

RĀJĀ:

pṛṣṭā janena sama|duḥkha|sukhena bālā
n' êyaṃ na vakṣyati mano|gatam ādhi|hetum.
dṛṣṭo vivṛtya bahuśo 'py anayā sa|hāvam
atr' ântaraṃ śravaṇa|kātaratāṃ gato 'smi.

3.35 ŚAKUNTALĀ: *(sa/lajjam)* ⌜jado pahudi so tavo|vaṇa|rakkhidā rā'|êsī me daṃsaṇa|padhaṃ gado, tado ārabhia uggadeṇa ahilāseṇa edavatthā mhi saṃvuttā.⌟

KING: Priyam·vada speaks the truth. For her

Face has deeply sunken cheeks, 3.30
her bosom has lost the firmness of her breasts,
her waist has grown thin,
her shoulders droop limp, her skin is pale;
tormented by love,
she appears both pitiful and lovely to behold,
just like a *mádhavi* vine,
touched by a wind that withers its leaves.

SHAKÚNTALA: Whom else could I confide this to? But now I will bring you sorrow.

BOTH: That is why we are so insistent, for grief, shared, becomes sorrow that can be borne.

KING:

The girl, questioned by someone
who shares her joy and grief,
cannot fail to divulge the cause
of her secret sorrow.
Though she looked at me, turning back repeatedly,
suggestively,* I have, by now,
become fainthearted
to hear her answer.

SHAKÚNTALA: *(coyly)* Since that royal sage, the protector of 3.35
the penance grove, strayed into the path of my sight, from that moment onward, in love with him, I have been reduced to this plight.

RĀJĀ: *(sa|harṣam)* śrutaṃ śrotavyam!

Smara eva tāpa|hetur
  nirvāpayitā sa eva me jātaḥ;
divasa iv' âbhra|śyāmas
  tap'|âtyaye jīva|lokasya.

ŚAKUNTALĀ: ⌜evaṃ jaï vo aṇumadaṃ taṃ tadhā mantedhaṃ maṃ jadhā tassa rā'|êsiṇo aṇukampaṇīā homi. aṇṇadhā māṃ siñcadha dāṇiṃ sānt'|udaeṇa.⌟

RĀJĀ: vimarśa|chedi vacanam etāvat kāma|phalaṃ, yatna|phalam anyat.

3.40 PRIYAṂVADĀ: *(apavārya)* ⌜Aṇasūe! dūre|gada|mammadhā iaṃ akkhamā kāla|haraṇassa. jassiṃ baddha|bhāvā esā, so vi lalāma|bhūdo Poravāṇaṃ. tā turaïdaṃ yyeva se ahilāsaṃ aṇuvattiduṃ.⌟

ANASŪYA: *(apavārya)* ⌜jadhā bhaṇāsi! *(prakāśam)* sahi! diṭṭhiā aṇurūvo se ahilāso. sāaraṃ vajjia kahim vā mahā|ṇaïe gantavvaṃ?⌟

PRIYAṂVADĀ: ⌜ko dāṇiṃ saha|āraṃ adimutta|ladāe pallaviduṃ ṇa icchadi?⌟

RĀJĀ: kim atra citraṃ, yadi citra|viśākhe śaś'|âṅka|lekhām anuvartete? ayam atra|bhavatībhyāṃ krīto janaḥ.

ANASŪYA: ⌜ko uṇa uvāo bhave jeṇa sahīe avilambidaṃ ṇigūḍhaṃ maṇo|radhaṃ sampādemha?⌟

3.45 PRIYAṂVADĀ: ⌜«ṇiuṇaṃ paadidavvaṃ ti» cintaṇīaṃ bhave. «sigghaṃ ti» ṇa dukkaraṃ.⌟

KING: *(joyfully)* I have heard what I needed to hear!

> Love alone is the source of the fever,
> Love alone has come to quench it for me;
> just as at the end of the hot season, a day,
> dark with clouds, does for the world.

SHAKÚNTALA: Now if you approve, then tell me what I must do to make the royal sage take pity on me. Otherwise, sprinkle me now with funerary libations.

KING: These words, cutting through my doubts, are the fruit of love; the fruit of effort is another matter.

PRIYAM·VADA: *(aside)* Anasúya! Her lovesickness is far ad- 3.40
vanced and will not brook any delay! He upon whom she has fixed her heart is no less than the scion of the Páuravas. We must hurry to court his affection.

ANASÚYA: *(aside)* As you say! *(aloud)* My friend! Happily, her desire is worthy. If not to the sea, where else should a great river flow?

PRIYAM·VADA: Who, now, would not wish the mango tree to bloom with the *atimúkta* vine?

KING: Is it surprising that the two bright stars of the constellation Vishákha should follow the lunar crescent? I am beholden to you.

ANASÚYA: Now, with what stratagem can we secretly fulfill our friend's desire without delay?

PRIYAM·VADA: "To get it done secretly" requires some effort; 3.45
"quickly" is no problem.

ANASŪYA: ⌜kadhaṃ via?⌟

PRIYAMVADĀ: ⌜so rā'|êsi imāe siṇiddha|diṭṭhi|sūid'|âhilāso imāiṃ divasāiṃ paāara|kiso via lakkhīadi.⌟

RĀJĀ: satyam itthaṃ|bhūto 'smi. tathā hi

idam aśiśirair antas|tāpāir vivarṇa|maṇīkṛtam
niśi niśi bhuja|nyast'|âpāṅga|prasāribhir aśrubhiḥ
anabhilulita|jyā|ghāt'|âṅkān muhur maṇi|bandhanāt
kanaka|valayaṃ srastaṃ srastaṃ mayā pratisāryate.

3.50 PRIYAMVADĀ: *(vicintya)* ⌜Aṇasūe! maaṇa|leho dāṇiṃ karīadu. taṃ sumaṇo|govidaṃ kadua deva|ses'|âpadeseṇa tassa raṇṇo hatthe pāḍaïssaṃ.⌟

ANASŪYA: ⌜roadi me sukumāro paoo vi. kiṃ vā Saüntalā bhaṇādi?⌟

ŚAKUNTALĀ: *(sa|lajjam)* ⌜nioo vi vikappīadi.⌟

PRIYAMVADĀ: *(Śakuntalāṃ prati)* ⌜teṇa hi uvaṇṇāsa|puravaṃ attaṇo cintehi kiṃ pi sulalidaṃ pada|bandhaṃ.⌟

ŚAKUNTALĀ: ⌜cintaïssaṃ. avadhīraṇā|bhīruaṃ puṇo vevadi me hiaaṃ.⌟

ANASÚYA: How so?

PRIYAM·VADA: That royal sage, betraying his desire for her by his tender glances, seems to be wasting away these days through sleeplessness.

KING: It is true, so I am. For,

I repeatedly have to pull back
this golden bracelet,
its gems discolored by tears
warmed by my inner fever,
flowing night after night
from the corners of my eyes
resting on my arm,
as it slips again and again from my wrist
without even brushing against the scars
inflicted by the striking of the bowstring.

PRIYAM·VADA: *(thinking)* Anasúya! A love letter is now called 3.50
for. I will deliver it into the king's hand, concealed among flowers, by pretending that they are the ritual leftovers.

ANASÚYA: I like this subtle plan. What does Shakúntala say?

SHAKÚNTALA: *(coyly)* Is a command to be questioned?

PRIYAM·VADA: *(to Shakúntala)* Well, then, just make up some pretty verse beginning with an allusion to yourself.

SHAKÚNTALA: I am thinking, but my heart trembles, fearing rejection.

3.55 RĀJĀ: *(sa|harṣam)*

ayaṃ sa te tiṣṭhati saṃgam'|ôtsuko
viśaṅkase bhīru yato 'vadhīraṇām
labheta vā prārthayitā na vā śriyam,
śriyo durāpaḥ katham īpsito bhavet?

SAKHYAU: ⌜atta|guṇ'|âvamāṇini! ko dāṇiṃ sāradīaṃ joṇhaṃ ādapa|tteṇa vāraïssadi?⌟

ŚAKUNTALĀ: *(sa|smitam)* ⌜nioida mhi!⌟ *(upaviṣṭā cintayati.)*

RĀJĀ: sthāne khalu vismṛta|nimeṣeṇa cakṣuṣā priyām avalokayāmi, yataḥ

3.60 unnamit'|âika|bhrū|latam
ānanam asyāḥ padāni racayantyāḥ
kaṇṭakitena prathayati
mayy anurāgaṃ kapolena.

ŚAKUNTALĀ: ⌜halā! cintidā mae gīdiā. asaṇṇihidāiṃ uṇa leha|sāhaṇāiṃ.⌟

PRIYAMVADĀ: ⌜ṇaṃ imassiṃ suk'|ôdara|suumāre ṇaliṇī|vatte patta|cheda|bhattīe ṇahehiṃ ṇikkhitta|vaṇṇaṃ karehi? tado suṇamha se akkharāṇi.⌟

ŚAKUNTALĀ: *(tathā kṛtvā)* ⌜suṇadha dāva ṇaṃ saṅgad'|atthā ṇa va tti.⌟

UBHE: ⌜avahida 'mha!⌟

KING: *(joyfully)* 3.55

He from whom you, timid girl,
fear rejection stands here
  pining to make love with you!
The seeker may or may not find fortune.
But how could fortune find it difficult
  to attain what it wants?

FRIENDS: O belittler of your own virtues! Who would ward off autumnal moonlight with a parasol?

SHAKÚNTALA: *(smiling)* I'll do as I'm told! *(Ponders, seated.)*

KING: Justly I gaze upon my beloved with an eye that has forgotten how to wink, since

Her countenance, one eyebrow raised, 3.60
  as she composes her poem,
  reveals her passion for me
  through her horripilating cheek.

SHAKÚNTALA: My dear! I have thought of a verse, but writing materials are not at hand.

PRIYAM·VADA: Can you not just incise the characters on this lily leaf, soft as a parrot's belly, with your fingernails? Then we will appraise your syllables.

SHAKÚNTALA: *(does so)* Listen, then, if it makes sense or not.

BOTH: We're ready.

3.65 ŚAKUNTALĀ: *(paṭhati)*

⌜tujjha ṇa āṇe hiaaṃ
  mama uṇa kāmo divā a rattiṃ ca
ṇikkiva taveï baliaṃ
  tuha hutta|maṇo|rahāï aṅgāiṃ.⌟

RĀJĀ: *(sa|harṣam upagamya)*

tapati tanu|gātri Madanas
  tvām aniśaṃ māṃ punar dahaty eva
glapayati yathā śaś'|âṅkaṃ
  na tathā hi kumudvatīṃ divasaḥ.

SAKHYAU: *(vilokya sa|harṣam utthāya)* ⌜sāgadaṃ jadhā|cintida|phalassa avalambiṇo maṇo|radhassa.⌟ *(Śakuntalā abhyutthātum icchati.)*

3.70 ŚAKUNTALĀ: *(ātma|gataṃ sa|sādhvasaṃ ca)* ⌜hiaa! tadhā uttammia dāṇiṃ ṇa kiṃ ci paḍivajjasi.⌟ *(ity utthātum icchati.)*

RĀJĀ: alam āyāsena.

saṃspṛṣṭa|kusuma|śayanāny
  āśu|vivarṇita|mṛṇāla|valayāni
guru|saṃtāpāni na te
  gātrāṇy upacāram arhanti.

ANASŪYA: ⌜ido silā|dal'|ekka|desaṃ aṇugeṇhadu vaasso.⌟

RĀJĀ: *(upaviśya)* Priyaṃvade! kac cit sakhīṃ vo n' âtibādhate śarīra|santāpaḥ?

3.75 PRIYAMVADĀ: *(sakhyā sah' ôpaviṣṭā)* ⌜laddh'|âusadho saṃpadaṃ uvasamaṃ gamissadi kāleṇa.⌟

SHAKÚNTALA: *(recites)* 3.65

> Your heart I do not know,
> cruel one,
> but Love day and night painfully inflames
> my limbs, which long for you.

KING: *(approaches joyfully)*

> Love may inflame you incessantly,
> slender girl, but me he consumes;
> day does not wreak havoc on the night-lily pond
> as much as it does on the moon.

FRIENDS: *(looking, stand up happily)* We bid welcome to this wish that is granted without delay by merely thinking of it. *(Shakúntala wants to get up.)*

SHAKÚNTALA: *(to herself, in turmoil)* My heart! Beating like 3.70
this you will not get anything done. *(Tries to stand up.)*

KING: Do not exhaust yourself!

> Your limbs, cleaving to the bed of flowers,
> garlanded with quickly faded lotus fibers,
> acutely inflamed,
> need not observe decorum.

ANASÚYA: May our friend grace this part of the stone slab.

KING: *(sits down)* Priyam·vada! I hope your friend is not too badly afflicted by this inflammation of her body.

PRIYAM·VADA: *(sits down with her friend)* Now that the cure 3.75
is found, it will die down in due course.

ANASŪYĀ: *(jan'|ântikam)* ⌜Priyamvade! «kālena» tti kiṃ? pekkha, meha|ṇād'|āhadaṃ via maūriṃ ṇimes'|antareṇa paccāgadaṃ pia|sahiṃ.⌟

ŚAKUNTALĀ: *(sa|lajjā tiṣṭhati.)*

PRIYAMVADĀ: ⌜mahā|bhāa! doṇhaṃ pi vo aṇṇoṇṇ'|âṇurāo paccakkho, sahī|siṇeho uṇa maṃ puṇar|utta|vādiṇiṃ karedi.⌟

RĀJĀ: ucyatām. vivakṣitaṃ hy anuktam anutāpaṃ janayati.

3.80 PRIYAMVADĀ: ⌜teṇa hi suṇādu mahā|rāo.⌟

RĀJĀ: avahito 'smi.

PRIYAMVADĀ: ⌜iaṃ ṇo sahī tumaṃ yeva uddisia bhaavadā Maaṇeṇa imaṃ īdisaṃ avatth"|antaraṃ ṇīdā. tā arahasi abbhuvattīe se jīvidaṃ avalambiduṃ.⌟

RĀJĀ: anugṛhīto 'smi.

ŚAKUNTALĀ: *(sa|smitam)* ⌜halā! alaṃ vo ante|ura|vihāra|pa-yyussueṇa rā'|êsiṇā uvaruddheṇa!⌟

3.85 RĀJĀ: sundari!

ANASÚYA: *(in private)* Priyam·vada! What do you mean "in due course"? Look! Our dear friend is staring like a peahen revived in a flash by the rumbling sound of clouds.

SHAKÚNTALA: *(Remains bashful.)*

PRIYAM·VADA: Favored lord! Your mutual love is obvious, but affection for my friend makes me want to state the obvious.

KING: Speak up. Not saying what is on your mind leads to regret.

PRIYAM·VADA: Then may the great king lend me an ear. 3.80

KING: I am attentive.

PRIYAM·VADA: This friend of ours has been reduced to this state by the God of love because of you. Therefore you must be so kind as to save her life.

KING: I would be honored.

SHAKÚNTALA: *(smiling)* My friend! Stop making trouble for the royal sage who is restless to enjoy himself in his zenana.

KING: Fair one! 3.85

idam ananya|parāyaṇam anyathā
hṛdaya|saṃnihite hṛdayaṃ mama
yadi samarthayase madir"|ēkṣaṇe
madana|bāṇa|hato 'pi hataf punaḥ.

ANASŪYA: ⌜vaassa! bahu|vallabhā rāāṇo suṇīanti. jadhā ṇo sahī bandhu|aṇe asoaṇīā bhodi tadhā ṇivvāhehi.⌟

RĀJĀ: bhadre!

parigraha|bahutve 'pi
dve pratiṣṭhe kulasya me
dharmeṇ' ôllekhitā Lakṣmīḥ
sakhī ca yuvayor iyam.

3.90 UBHE: ⌜aṇuggahida mha.⌟

ŚAKUNTALĀ: ⌜halā! marisāvedha loa|vālaṃ jaṃ kiṃ ca amhehiṃ uvaār'|âdikkameṇa vīsambha|palāviṇīhiṃ bhaṇidaṃ.⌟

SAKHYAU: ⌜jeṇa taṃ mantidaṃ so marisāvedu. aṇṇassa jaṇassa ko accao? parokkhaṃ ko vā kiṃ ṇa mantedi?⌟

RĀJĀ: *(sa|smitam)*

aparādham imaṃ tataḥ sahiṣye
eyadi rambh'|ōru tav' âṅga|recit'|ârdhe
kusum'|āstaraṇe klam'|âpahaṃ me
sujanatvād anumanyase 'vakāśam.

You whose eyes intoxicate like wine,
you who are sheltered within my heart,
if you should believe this heart of mine
which is intent on no other to be otherwise,
then, already wounded by Love's arrow,
I am wounded again.

ANASÚYA: My friend! We hear that kings have many consorts. Conduct yourself so that our friend is not to be pitied by her kinsfolk.

KING: Fair one!

Though I may take many wives,
two will support my lineage,
the Goddess of fortune made manifest
by righteousness,
and this friend of yours.

BOTH: We are obliged. 3.90

SHAKÚNTALA: Friends! You must plead for the world-protector's pardon, for the things we said, when, overstepping the bounds of courtesy, we chattered in private.

FRIENDS: Only a person with whom one converses can pardon. Who else can be offended? Who might not be saying who knows what behind your back?

KING: *(smiling)*

I can tolerate this transgression, provided,
O smooth-thighed girl, you make some space
for me,
as a friend, on this flower bed half vacated
by your limbs.*

3.95 PRIYAMVADĀ: ⌜ettieṇa uṇa de tuṭṭhī bhave?⌟

ŚAKUNTALĀ: *(sa|roṣam iva)* ⌜virama dullalide! edāvatthāe vi me kīḷasi.⌟

ANASŪYĀ: *(bahir vilokya)* ⌜Piaṃvade, esa mia|podao ido tado diṇṇa|diṭṭhī ussuo ṇūṇaṃ mādaram paribbhaṭṭhaṃ aṇṇesadi. tā saṃjojaïssaṃ dāva eṇaṃ.⌟ *(ity uttiṣṭhati.)*

PRIYAMVADĀ: ⌜ṇaṃ cavalao kkhu eso! eāiṇī ṇiojedum ṇa pāresi. tā ahaṃ pi de aṇuvaṭṭiduṃ karaïssaṃ.⌟ *(ubhe prasthite.)*

ŚAKUNTALĀ: ⌜halā! aṇṇadarā vo gacchadu! aṇṇadhā asaraṇa mhi.⌟

3.100 UBHE: *(sa|smitam)* ⌜jo puhavīe saraṇaṃ so tuha samīve.⌟ *(iti niṣkrānte.)*

ŚAKUNTALĀ: ⌜kadhaṃ gadaṃ yeva?⌟

RĀJĀ: alam āvegena. nanv ayam ārādhayitā janas tava sakhī|bhūmau vartate.

kiṃ śītalaiḥ klama|vinodibhir ārdra|vātān
  sañcālayāmi nalinī|dala|tāla|vṛntaiḥ
aṅke nidhāya caraṇāv uta padma|tāmrau
  saṃvāhayāmi karabh'|ōru yathā|sukhaṃ te?

ŚAKUNTALĀ: ⌜ṇa māṇaṇīe jaṇe attāṇaaṃ avarādhaïssaṃ.⌟ *(avasthā|sadṛśam utthāya prasthitā.)*

PRIYAM·VADA: But will that much be enough to satisfy you? 3.95

SHAKÚNTALA: *(as if angrily)* Stop it, you precocious girl! You poke fun at me even while I am in such a sorry state.

ANASÚYA: *(looking outside)* Priyam·vada! This anxious fawn is casting its eyes here and there. Surely he is looking for his lost mother. I will go and reunite him. *(With this she stands up.)*

PRIYAM·VADA: My, is he not frisky! You'll never catch him alone. I will assist you. *(Both set off.)*

SHAKÚNTALA: My friends! Only one of you must go! Otherwise I am helpless.

BOTH: *(smiling)* He who is the refuge of the world is with 3.100
you. *(With this they exit.)*

SHAKÚNTALA: What, they have just gone?

KING: Do not be alarmed. Have not I, who try to win your favor, taken the place of your friends?

> Shall I stir up moist breezes
> with cool lily-petal fans,
> removing your languor?
> Or shall I, laying your feet, red as lotuses,
> on my lap, rub them to relieve you,
> O smooth-thighed girl?

SHAKÚNTALA: I will not let myself disrespect a person I ought to honor. *(Gets up in a manner befitting her condition and sets off.)*

3.105 RĀJĀ: *(avaṣṭabhya)* sundari! aparinirvāṇo 'yaṃ divasa, iyaṃ ca te 'vasthā.

utsṛjya kusuma|śayanaṃ
  kadalī|dala|kalpita|stan'|āvaraṇā
katham ātape gamiṣyasi
  paripāṇḍura|pelavair aṅgaiḥ?

ŚAKUNTALĀ: ⌜sahī|metta|saraṇā kaṃ vā saraṇaïssam?⌟

RĀJĀ: idānīṃ vrīḍito 'smi.

ŚAKUNTALĀ: ⌜ṇa kkhu ayya|uttaṃ, devvam uvālahāmi!⌟

3.110 RĀJĀ: kim anukūla|kāriṇa upālabhyate daivasya?

ŚAKUNTALĀ: ⌜kadhaṃ dāṇim ṇa uvālabhissaṃ jaṃ attaṇ aṇīsaṃ para|guṇehiṃ maṃ ohāsedi?⌟

RĀJĀ: *(sva|gatam)*

apy autsukye mahati na vara|
    prārthanāsu pratāryāḥ
  kāṅkṣantyo 'pi vyatikara|sukhaṃ
    kātarāḥ sv'|âṅga|dāne
ābādhyante na khalu Madane-
    n' âpi labdh'|āspadatvād
  ābādhante Manasi|jam api
    kṣipta|kālāḥ kumāryaḥ.

KING: *(stopping her)* Fair one! The day is not yet ended, and consider your condition.

How can you venture forth into the heat,
with your delicate limbs so pale,
forsaking your flower bed in this cloister,
shielding your breast with an armor of plantain petals?

SHAKÚNTALA: My sole refuge is my friends. Whom can I turn to for protection?

KING: Now I am shamed.

SHAKÚNTALA: I do not reproach the king,* but fate.

KING: Why should you reproach fate that so favors you?

SHAKÚNTALA: Why should I not reproach that which mocks me, who is not mistress of herself, with the virtues of another?

KING: *(to himself)*

Virgins, though they have a deep yearning,
frustrate the advances of their lovers;
though they crave the bliss of union,
they are fearful of yielding their bodies.
It is not so much that they are troubled by Love
once it has found a foothold, but that they,
wasting time, trouble Love.

Śakuntalā prasthit" âiva.

3.115 RĀJĀ: *(sva/gatam)* katham ātmanaf priyaṃ na kariṣye? *(ut-thāy' ôpasṛtya paṭ'/ântād avalambate.)*

ŚAKUNTALĀ: ⌜Porava! muñca maṃ!⌟

RĀJĀ: bhavati tadā muñcāmi.

ŚAKUNTALĀ: ⌜kadā?⌟

RĀJĀ: yadā surata|jño bhaviṣyāmi.

3.120 ŚAKUNTALĀ: ⌜maaṇ'|âvaṭṭhaḍḍho vi ṇa attaṇo kaṇṇaā|aṇo pahavadi. bhūyo vi dāva sahī|aṇaṃ aṇumāṇaïssaṃ.⌟

RĀJĀ: *(muhūrtam upaviśya)* tato mokṣyāmi.

ŚAKUNTALĀ: *(kṛtaka/kopā)* ⌜Porava, rakkha vinaaṃ! ido tado isīo sañcaranti.⌟

RĀJĀ: *(diśo 'valokya)* kathaṃ prakāśam asmi nirgataḥ? *(sa/sambhramaṃ Śakuntalāṃ muktvā tair eva padair niva-rtate.)*

ŚAKUNTALĀ: *(stokam upagamya s'/âṅga/bhaṅgam)* ⌜Porava! aṇicchā|pūrao vi daṃsaṇa|metta|suha|do ṇa te aaṃ jaṇo visumaridavvo.⌟

3.125 RĀJĀ: sundari,

Shakúntala is about to go.

KING: *(to himself)* Why should I not do what I wish? *(Arises, approaches her and holds on to the hem of her garment.)* 3.115

SHAKÚNTALA: Páurava! Let me go!

KING: Lady, I will let you go.

SHAKÚNTALA: When?

KING: When I have made love to you.

SHAKÚNTALA: Even if overwhelmed by passion, a daughter is not her own mistress. On top of that, I must ask my friends' permission. 3.120

KING: *(sits for a moment)* Then I will let you go.

SHAKÚNTALA: *(feigning anger)* Páurava! Maintain decorum! Seers pass by here.

KING: *(looking around)* What? I have come out into the open? *(Startled, he lets go of Shakúntala and retraces his steps.)*

SHAKÚNTALA: *(approaching a little bit, with her body curved)* Páurava! Though I do not fulfill your desire, giving you only the pleasure of sight, you must not forget me.

KING: O beautiful one! 3.125

tvaṃ dūram api gacchantī
  hṛdayaṃ na jahāsi me;
din'|âvasāna|cchāy" êva
  puro|mūlaṃ vanas|pateḥ.

ŚAKUNTALĀ: *(stokam iva gatvā)* ⌜haddhī ṇa me caraṇā puro|muhā pahavanti. imehiṃ ayya|uttassa kuravaehiṃ vavahidā pacchādo ladā|maṇḍavaassa pekkhissaṃ dāva se bhāv'|ânubandhaṃ.⌟ *(tathā karoti.)*

RĀJĀ: priye! mām evam anurāg'|âika|rasaṃ samutsṛjya prasthit" âiv' âsi nirapekṣaṃ gantum.

anirday'|ôpabhogyasya
  rūpasya mṛdunas tathā
dāruṇaṃ khalu te cetaḥ
  śirīṣasy' êva bandhanam?

3.130 ŚAKUNTALĀ: ⌜imaṃ suṇia ṇa me atthi vihavo gantuṃ.⌟

RĀJĀ: kim ih' âhaṃ samprati priyā|śūnye karomi? gamiṣyāmi. *(prasthito bhūmiṃ vilokya)* hanta! vyāhataṃ me gamanam.

maṇi|bandha|vigalitam idaṃ
  saṅkrānt'|ôśīra|parimalaṃ tasyāḥ
hṛdayasya nigaḍam iva me
  mṛṇāla|valayaṃ sthitaṃ purataḥ
(sa|bahu|mānam ādatte.)

ŚAKUNTALĀ: *(hastam avalokya)* ⌜ammo! dubbala|siḍhiladāe pabbhaṭṭhaṃ pi edaṃ muṇāla|valaaṃ mae ṇa viṇṇādaṃ.⌟

Even though you go far away
you do not leave my heart;
just as the shade of a tree, at the end of the day,
does not leave its eastern root.

SHAKÚNTALA: *(walking a short distance)* Alas! My feet have no power to carry me forward. Concealed from the noble lord by these *kúrabaka* shrubs I will see what becomes of his passion from behind the vine bower. *(Does so.)*

KING: My love! You have forsaken me, whose only pleasure is loving you, to depart indifferently.

The heart within your tender figure,
which may not be enjoyed ruthlessly,
can it be* as hard as the casing of a *shirísha* flower?

SHAKÚNTALA: Hearing this I have no power to leave. 3.130

KING: What use is this place, desolate without my beloved? I will leave. *(sets out, looks at the ground)* Alas! My departure is checked.

This is her bracelet of lotus fibers before me,
fallen from her wrist,
perfumed with *ushíra*,
as if it were a chain for my heart.
(Picks it up reverentially.)

SHAKÚNTALA: *(looking at her hand)* Oh no! I failed to note that my fiber bracelet has fallen off, loosened by my emaciation.

RĀJĀ: *(valay'|ābharaṇam urasi vinyasya)* aho sukha|sparśaḥ!

3.135 anena līl"|ābharaṇena te priye
vihāya kāntaṃ bhujam atra tiṣṭhatā
janaḥ samāśvāsita eṣa duḥkha|bhāg
acetanen' âpi satā na tu tvayā.

ŚAKUNTALĀ: ⌜ado avaraṃ asamattha mhi vilambiduṃ. bhodu, edeṇa yyeva vavadeseṇa se attāṇaaṃ daṃsaïssaṃ.⌟ *(ity upagacchati.)*

RĀJĀ: *(dṛṣṭvā, sa|harṣam)* aye! jīvit'|ēśvarī me prāptā. paridevit'|ânantaraṃ prasāden' ôpakartavyo 'smi khalu daivasya.

pipāsā|kṣāma|kaṇṭhena
yācitaṃ c' âlpa|yācinā
nava|megh'|ôjjhitā c' âsya
dhārā nipatitā mukhe.

ŚAKUNTALĀ: *(rājñaf pramukhe sthitā)* ⌜aṅga! addha|padhe sumaria edassa hattha|bbhaṃsiṇo muṇāla|valaassa kade saṇṇiatta mhi. ācakkhidaṃ via me hiaeṇa tae gahidaṃ ti. tā khiva idaṃ. mā muṇy|aṇe attāṇaaṃ maṃ ca suaïssasi.⌟

3.140 RĀJĀ: eken' âbhisandhinā pratyarpayeyam. n' ânyathā.

ŚAKUNTALĀ: ⌜keṇa?⌟

RĀJĀ: yad' îdam aham eva yathā|sthānaṃ niveśaye.

ŚAKUNTALĀ: *(sva|gatam)* ⌜kā gadī!⌟

KING: *(laying the bracelet on his chest)* Ah! How soothing its touch.

With this playful ornament, O my beloved, 3.135
which slipped from your adored arm
and remained here,
this wretched person has been comforted,
even thought it is inanimate
—though not by you.

SHAKÚNTALA: I am powerless to hold back any longer! Let me see. I will go to him under this very pretext. *(With this she approaches.)*

KING: *(noticing her, joyfully)* Ah! The mistress of my life returns. After my laments, fate has granted me a favor.

Begged by one who asks but rarely,
his throat parched, a downpour
discharged by new-formed clouds
gushed upon his face.

SHAKÚNTALA: *(facing the king)* Hurry! When I was halfway, I remembered that this fiber bracelet had fallen from my hand and I returned. It was as if my heart was telling me that you had taken it. Therefore give it back, so that you do not betray yourself and me to the hermits.

KING: I'll hand it over on one condition, not otherwise. 3.140

SHAKÚNTALA: What?

KING: That I alone may fasten it in its place.

SHAKÚNTALA: *(to herself)* How can I escape this!

RĀJĀ: imaṃ śilā|paṭṭam eva saṃśrayāvaḥ. *(ubhau parikramy' ôpaviṣṭau.)*

3.145 RĀJĀ: *(Śakuntalā|hastam ādāya sva|gatam)*

Hara|kop'|âgni|dagdhasya
 daiven' âmṛta|varṣiṇā
prarohaḥ sambhṛto bhūyaḥ
 kiṃ svit Kāma|taror ayam?

ŚAKUNTALĀ: *(harṣa|romañcaṃ rūpayantī)* ⌜tuvaraadu ayya|utto!⌟

RĀJĀ: *(sva|gatam)* idānīm asmi viśvasto bhartur ābhāṣaṇena. *(prakāśam)* sundari! n' âtiśliṣṭas sandhir asya mṛṇāla|valayasya. yadi te 'bhiprāya etad anyathā ghaṭayiṣyāmi.

ŚAKUNTALĀ: *(vihasya)* ⌜kāla|kkhevo kusalo. jaṃ te roadi.⌟

3.150 RĀJĀ: *(sa|vyāja|vilambitam; avamucy' âvalambya ca)* sundari, dṛśyatām idam!

ayam hi te śyāma|latā|mano|haraṃ
 viśeṣa|śobh"|ârtham iv' ôjjhit'|âmbaraḥ
mṛṇāla|rūpeṇa navo niśā|karaḥ
 karaṃ samet'|ôbhaya|koṭir āśritaḥ.

ŚAKUNTALĀ: ⌜ṇa dāva ṇaṃ pekkhāmi, pavaṇa|kampiṇā kaṇ-ṇ|uppala|reṇuṇā kalusīkadā me diṭṭhī.⌟

KING: Let's go to this stone slab. *(They both walk and sit down.)*

KING: *(taking Shakúntala's hand, to himself)* 3.145

> Might this be a sprout of the tree of love, burned
> by the fire of Shiva's anger, revived again
> by a chance rain of nectar?

SHAKÚNTALA: *(shows that her hair stands on end with delight)* Be quick, my noble lord!

KING: *(to himself)* Now I am assured by this address used for a husband. *(aloud)* Beautiful lady! The clasp of this lotus-fiber bracelet is not very secure. If you wish, I will fasten it differently.

SHAKÚNTALA: *(laughs)* You are clever at delaying. However you like it.

KING: *(contrives a delay; fastens it, then holds on to her)* Look at this, my beautiful one! 3.150

> For this your arm, ravishing
> like a dark vine,
> appears as if graced
> by the new moon
> in the form of a fiber bracelet,
> who has rejected the sky
> because of your hand's superior beauty,
> and finds himself spliced together
> at both tips.

SHAKÚNTALA: I cannot really see it. I am blinded by pollen from my ear-lotus, shaken by the breeze.

RĀJĀ: *(sa|smitam.)* yadi manyase tad" âham enāṃ vadana|mārutena viśadāṃ kariṣye.

ŚAKUNTALĀ: ⌜aṇukampidā bhaveaṃ. kiṃ uṇa ṇa de vīsasāmi.⌟

3.155 RĀJĀ: mā m" âivam. navo hi parijanaḥ sevyānām ādeśāt paraṃ na vartate.

ŚAKUNTALĀ: ⌜eso yyeva de accuvaāro avīsambha|janao.⌟

RĀJĀ: n' âham evam ramaṇīyam ātmanaḥ sev"|âvakāśaṃ śithilayiṣye. *(mukham unnamayituṃ pravṛttaḥ.)*

ŚAKUNTALĀ: *(kāma|pratiṣedhaṃ rūpayantī viharati.)*

RĀJĀ: aye! paryaśrutāṃ te gataṃ cakṣuḥ. alam asmān praty avinaya|śaṅkayā. unnīyatām ānanam!

3.160 ŚAKUNTALĀ: *(kiṃ cid dṛṣṭvā sthitā.)*

RĀJĀ: *(mukham unnamayy' âṅgulībhyāṃ, sva|gatam)*

cāruṇā sphuriten' âyam
  aparikṣata|komalaḥ
pipāsato mam' ânujñāṃ
  karoty eva priy"|âdharaḥ.

ŚAKUNTALĀ: ⌜paḍiṇṇādaṃ mantharo via ayya|utto saṃvutto.⌟

RĀJĀ: sundari! karṇ'|ôtpala|saṃnikarṣād īkṣaṇa|sādṛśyena mūḍho 'smi. *(mukha|mārutena netraṃ siñcati.)*

KING: *(smiling)* If you permit I will blow upon it to clear it.

SHAKÚNTALA: I would become someone to be pitied. And, anyway, I don't trust you!

KING: Don't say that! For a new servant does not overstep the orders of those whom he serves.

SHAKÚNTALA: It's your excessive servility that arouses my distrust.

KING: I will not let this delightful opportunity to make myself useful slip through my fingers. *(He begins to raise up her face.)*

SHAKÚNTALA: *(Mimes resistance, then stops.)*

KING: Alas! Your eye is filled with tears! Do not fear misconduct from me. Raise your face!

SHAKÚNTALA: *(Casts him a partial glance.)*

KING: *(raising her face with two fingers, to himself)*

> By its attractive trembling,
> my beloved's lip,
>   tender because never bitten,
>   appears to invite me who thirsts for it.

SHAKÚNTALA: My noble lord seems hesitant to fulfill his promise.

KING: My beautiful lady, because your ear-lotus is so close, I was perplexed by its similarity to your eye. *(He blows on her eye.)*

3.165 ŚAKUNTALĀ: ⌜bhodu! païdittha mhi saṃvuttā. lajjāmi uṇa aṇuvaāriṇī pi'|āriṇo ayya|uttassa.⌟

RĀJĀ: kim anyat?

idam apy upakṛtam abale
  surabhi mukhaṃ mayā yad āghrātam
. . . *(sa/smitam)* na tu kamalasya madhu|karaḥ
  saṃtuṣyati gandha|mātreṇa.

ŚAKUNTALĀ: ⌜a|santoseṇa kiṃ karaïssasi?⌟

RĀJĀ: idam! *(iti vyavasitaḥ.)*

3.170 NEPATHYE: ayyā Godamī!

ŚAKUNTALĀ: *(karṇaṃ dattvā, sa/saṃbhramam)* ⌜Porava! esā mama sarīra|vuttānt'|ôvalabhāa tādassa dhamma|kaṇīasī uvatthidā. tā viḍav'|ântarido hohi.⌟

RĀJĀ: *(tathā karoti.)*

tataf praviśati pātra/hastā GAUTAMĪ.

GAUTAMĪ: *(upasṛtya)* ⌜accāhidaṃ. idha devadā|sahāā ciṭṭhasi.⌟

3.175 ŚAKUNTALĀ: ⌜idāṇīṃ yeva Māliṇiṃ avaḍiṇṇāo Piaṃvadā|missāo.⌟

GAUTAMĪ: *(darbh'/ôdakena Śakuntalām abhyukṣya)* vatse, nirābādhā tvaṃ ciraṃ jīva. ⌜avi lahua|santāvāiṃ de aṅgāiṃ?⌟

SHAKÚNTALA: That will do! I feel better now. But I am ashamed that I render no service to my noble lord who shows me such kindness.

KING: What more could I want.

> Even this is a favor, girl,
>   that I have smelled your fragrant face;
> . . . *(smiling)* but the bee is not content
>   just with the scent of the lotus.

SHAKÚNTALA: If not content, what will you do?

KING: This! *(Stops at that moment.)*

OFFSTAGE: Venerable Gáutami!

SHAKÚNTALA: *(listens, alarmed)* Páurava! Father's younger sister-in-*dharma* has come to check on my well-being. Hide among the shrubs!

KING: *(Does so.)*

GÁUTAMI *enters with a bowl in her hand.*

GÁUTAMI: *(approaching)* Scandalous! Here you are with just God to keep you company.

SHAKÚNTALA: Just now Priyam·vada and company have descended to the Málini.

GÁUTAMI: *(sprinkles Shakúntala with* darbha *water)* Child, live long in good health! Your limbs are but lightly inflamed?

ŚAKUNTALĀ: ⌜atthi viseso.⌟

GAUTAMĪ: ⌜vacche pariṇado diaso. tā ehi. uḍaam yeva gacchamha.⌟

ŚAKUNTALĀ: *(apavārya)* ⌜hiaa, maṇo|radha|dullahaṃ jaṇaṃ pāvia kāla|haraṇaṃ karesi, aṇusaa|vighaṭṭidassa kadhaṃ de saṃpadaṃ?⌟ *(padāni gatvā, pratinivṛtya, prakāśam)* ⌜ladā|gharaa! āmantemi tumaṃ puṇo vi paribhoāa!⌟ *(iti niṣkrānte.)*

3.180 RĀJĀ: *(pūrva/sthānam upetya, sa/niḥśvāsam)* aho vighnavatyaf prārthita|siddhayaḥ. mayā hi,

muhur aṅguli|saṃvṛt'|âdhar'|ōṣṭham
pratiṣedh'|âkṣara|viklav'|âbhidhānam
mukham aṃsa|vivarti pakṣmal'|âkṣyāḥ
katham apy unnamitaṃ, na cumbitaṃ tu.

kva nu khalu sāmpratam gacchāmi? atha vā ih' âiva priyā|paribhukte 'timukta|latā|valaye sthāsyāmi. *(sarvato 'valokya.)*

SHAKÚNTALA: I feel better.

GÁUTAMI: Child, the day is at its end. So come! Let us go to the cottage.

SHAKÚNTALA: *(aside)* O my heart, when you attained that person, who is as unattainable as a wish, you strung him along, so how can you now be tormented by remorse? *(walks a few steps, turns around, aloud)* Bower of vines! I bid you farewell until I may enjoy you again! *(With this they exit.)*

KING: *(returns to his former position, sighing)* Ah! The attain- 3.180
ment of desires is beset with difficulties. For

The face of the girl with long eyelashes,
  its lower lip covered by her fingers repeatedly,
  falteringly stammering syllables of denial,
  averted to her shoulder;
I somehow managed to raise it up,
  —but it was not kissed.

Where shall I go now? Rather, I must remain right here in the abandoned vine enclosure enjoyed by my beloved. *(Looking all around.)*

tasyāf puṣpa|mayī śarīra|lulitā
śayyā śilāyām iyam
kānte manmatha|lekha eṣa nalinī|
patre nakhair arpitaḥ
hastād bhraṣṭam idaṃ bis'|ābharaṇam ity
āsādya hīn'|ēkṣaṇān
nirgantuṃ sahasā na vetasa|gṛhād
īśo 'smi śūnyād api.

hā hā dhik! na samyag āceṣṭitaṃ mayā priyām āsādya kāla|haraṇaṃ kurvatā. idānīṃ

3.185 «rahaḥ|pratyāsattiṃ
yadi su|vadanā yāsyati punaḥ
na kālaṃ hāsyāmi
praṇaya|duravāpā hi viṣayāḥ.»
iti kliṣṭaṃ vighnair
gaṇayati ca me mūḍha|hṛdayaṃ
priyāyāf pratyakṣaṃ
kim api ca tathā kātaram idam.

NEPATHYE: rājan! rājan!

sāyaṃtane savana|karmaṇi sampravṛtte
vedīṃ hut'|âśanavatīṃ paritaf prayastām
chāyāś caranti bahudhā bhayam ādadhānāḥ
saṃdhy"|âbhra|kūṭa|kapiśāf piśit'|âśanānām.

This is her bed of flowers upon the boulder,
  disturbed by her body;
  this is the love letter incised
    on the lovely lily leaf with her nails;
  this is the ornament of lotus filaments
    fallen from her hand—
encountering these,
because they dim my eyes, I am powerless
  to wrest myself away
  from the reed enclosure, thought it be empty.

Alas! I did not do well by tarrying when I had my beloved. Now

"If the fair-faced girl should come 3.185
  to another secret rendezvous
  I will not waste any time;
  Prizes cannot be won as favors!"
So schemes my foolish heart,
  thwarted by complications,
  but when face to face with my beloved
  somehow it is nonetheless hesitant.

OFFSTAGE: King! King!

The evening libation has commenced.
  The shades of flesh-eating demons, tawny
    like the crests of twilight clouds,
  prowl around the altar flaring
    with the sacrificial fire, spreading terror.

RĀJĀ: *(sa/sambhramam.)* bho bhos tapasvino! mā bhaiṣṭa! ayam aham āgato 'smi!

iti niṣkrāntaḥ.

3.190 iti mahā|kavi|Kālidāsa|viracite
Śakuntalā|nāmani nāṭake
tritīyo 'ṅkaḥ.

KING: *(alarmed)* Ye hermits! Fear not, here I come!

Exit.

The end of the third act in the play called "Shakúntala," 3.190
composed by the great poet
Kali·dasa.

ACT FOUR: THE FAREWELL

tataf praviśataḥ kusum'|âvacayaṃ nāṭayantyau tapasvi|kanyake.

ANASŪYĀ: ⌜Piaṃvade! jaï vi gandhavveṇa vivāha|vihiṇā ṇivutta|kallāṇā Saüntalā aṇurūva|bhaṭṭi|bhāiṇī saṃvuttā tahā vi ṇa ṇivuttaṃ me hiaaṃ.⌟

PRIYAṂVADĀ: ⌜kadhaṃ via?⌟

ANASŪYĀ: ⌜ajja so rāā itthi|parisamattīe isīhiṃ visajjido attaṇo ṇaaraṃ pavisia anteure ido|gadaṃ sumarissadi vā ṇa vatti.⌟

4.5 PRIYAṂVADĀ: ⌜ettha vīsatthā hohi. ṇa tādisā āidi|visesā guṇa|virohiṇo honti. itthiaṃ uṇa cintaṇijjaṃ. tādo dāṇiṃ imaṃ vuttantaṃ suṇia ṇa jāṇe kiṃ paḍivajjissadi tti. . .⌟

ANASŪYĀ: ⌜sahi! jadhā maṃ pucchasi tadhā tādassa aṇumadaṃ piaṃ ca.⌟

PRIYAṂVADĀ: ⌜kadhaṃ via aṇumadaṃ piaṃ ca?⌟

ANASŪYĀ: ⌜kiṃ aṇṇaṃ? «guṇavade kaṇṇaā paḍivādaïdavva» tti aaṃ dāva paḍhamo se saṅkappo. taṃ jaï devvaṃ saṃpādedi ṇaṃ appaāseṇa kad'|attho gurv|aṇo.⌟

PRIYAṂVADĀ: ⌜evaṇ|ṇ|edaṃ!⌟ *(puṣpa|bhājanam avalokya)* ⌜sahi avacidāiṃ khu Bali|kamma|payyattāiṃ kusumāiṃ.⌟

4.10 ANASŪYĀ: ⌜sahi! Saüntalāe vi sohagga|devadāo accaṇīāo.⌟

Enter the two hermit-daughters picking flowers.

ANASÚYA: Priyam·vada! Even though Shakúntala has found her happiness in a marriage of secret consent, winning a worthy husband, nevertheless my heart is uneasy.

PRIYAM·VADA: How come?

ANASÚYA: Today, at the end of the sacrifice, the seers have dismissed the king. Returning to the women's apartments in his city, will he remember what happened here or not?

PRIYAM·VADA: You can rest assured about it. Men of such 4.5
distinguished composure do not turn against their virtues. But I am worried about this: When father hears of this affair I do not know what will happen...

ANASÚYA: My dear! If you ask me, father will approve and rejoice.

PRIYAM·VADA: What do you mean, "approve and rejoice?"

ANASÚYA: How could it be otherwise? "My daughter should be entrusted to a worthy suitor,"—such was his original resolve. If fate itself has brought this about, then the patriarch has achieved his purpose without effort.

PRIYAM·VADA: That's right! *(looking at her flower basket)* My dear! We have collected ample flowers for the Bali-offering.

ANASÚYA: My dear! The deities directing Shakúntala's mar- 4.10
ital harmony need to be worshipped, too.

PRIYAMVADĀ: ⌜jujjadi!⌟ *(tad eva karma nāṭayataḥ.)*

NEPATHYE: ayam ahaṃ bhoḥ!

ANASŪYĀ: *(śrutvā)* ⌜sahi! adidhiṇā via ṇivedidaṃ.⌟

PRIYAMVADĀ: ⌜sahi! ṇaṃ uḍaja|saṇṇihidā Saüntalā.⌟

4.15 ANASŪYĀ: ⌜āṃ, ajja uṇa hiaeṇa ṇa saṇṇihidā.⌟

PRIYAMVADĀ: *(sa|tvaraṃ)* ⌜teṇa hi bhodu ettiāiṃ kusumāiṃ.⌟ *(prasthitā.)*

NEPATHYE: āḥ! atithi|paribhāvini!

vicintayantī yam an|anya|mānasā
  yato 'tithiṃ vetsi na mām upasthitam
smariṣyati tvāṃ na sa bodhito 'pi san
  kathāṃ pramattaf prathamaṃ kṛtām iva.

UBHE: *(śrutvā, viṣaṇṇe)* ⌜haddhī! yeva saṃvuttaṃ! kassiṃ pi pū"|ârihe avaraddhā suṇṇa|hiaā pia|sahī.⌟

4.20 ANASŪYĀ: *(avalokya)* ⌜ṇa kkhu jassiṃ tassiṃ sulaha|kovo kkhu eso Duvvāsā mahesī hudāso via acalida|pād'|oddhārāe gadīe gacchiduṃ paütto.⌟

PRIYAMVADĀ: ⌜ko aṇṇo hudavahādo dahiduṃ pahavissadi? Aṇasūe! gaccha pāesu paḍia pasāehi ṇaṃ jāva ahaṃ se aggh'|'|ôdaaṃ uvakappemi.⌟

PRIYAM·VADA: Of course! *(They continue miming the same action.)*

BEHIND THE SCENES: Ho, here I am!

ANASÚYA: *(listening)* My dear! It sounds like a guest announcing himself.

PRIYAM·VADA: My dear! Surely Shakúntala is near the hut.

ANASÚYA: Yes, but today she is not present with her heart. 4.15

PRIYAM·VADA: *(hastily)* Then this quantity of flowers will have to suffice. *(Sets off.)*

BEHIND THE SCENES: Ah! Derider of guests!

He on whom you mused so single-mindedly,
wherefore you did not perceive
me, come as a guest,
he will not remember you even if reminded,
just as a drunkard does not recall
what was just said.

BOTH: *(listening, dejected)* Alas! It has already happened! Our empty-hearted friend has offended someone worthy of respect.

ANASÚYA: *(looking)* Oh no! Not just anyone—it is the great 4.20
seer Durvásas. Quick to lose his temper, he is making off with unfaltering strides like a fire.

PRIYAM·VADA: Who other than fire himself has power to burn? Anasúya! Throw yourself at his feet to calm him while I prepare the welcome-water.

ANASŪYĀ: *(niṣkrāntā.)*

PRIYAMVADĀ: *(pad'|ântare skhalitaṃ nirūpya)* ⌜ammo! āvea|kkhalidāe pabbhaṭṭhaṃ agga|hatthādo puppha|bhāaṇaṃ me. tā puṇo vi avaciṇissaṃ.⌟ *(tathā karoti.)*

(praviśya) ANASŪYĀ: ⌜sahi, sarīra|baddho via kovo kassa so aṇuṇaaṃ geṇhadi? kim ca uṇa s'|âṇukkoso kado.⌟

4.25 PRIYAMVADĀ: ⌜tassiṃ bahuaṃ edaṃ. tado kadhehi kadhaṃ via.⌟

ANASŪYĀ: ⌜jadā ṇivattiduṃ ṇa icchadi tadā viṇṇāvido mae: «bhaavaṃ! paḍhama|bhattiṃ avekkhia ajja tuha ppahāva|viṇṇāda|sāmatthassa duhidā|jaṇassa bhaavadā avarāho marisidavvo tti.»⌟

PRIYAMVADĀ: ⌜tado tado?⌟

ANASŪYĀ: ⌜tado: «ṇa me vaaṇam aṇṇadhā bhaviduṃ arihadi, āharaṇ'|âhiṇṇāṇa|daṃsaṇeṇa me sāvo ṇivattissidi» tti mantaanto yyeva antarihido.⌟

PRIYAMVADĀ: ⌜sakkaṃ dāṇiṃ assasidum. atthi teṇa rā'|êsiṇā sampatthideṇa sa|ṇāma|he'|aṅkidaṃ aṅgulīaṃ sumaraṇīaṃ ti Saüntalāe saaṃ yyeva hatthe piṇaddhaṃ. tassiṃ ca s'|āhīṇe aaṃ uvāo bhavissadi tti.⌟ *(parikrāmataḥ.)*

4.30 ANASŪYĀ: ⌜halā Piaṃvade! pekkha pekkha! vāma|hatth'|ôvaṇihida|vaaṇā ālihidā via sahī bhaṭṭi|gaḍāe cintāe attāṇaaṃ vi esā ṇa vibhāvedi kiṃ uṇa āgantuaṃ?⌟

PRIYAMVADĀ: ⌜halā Aṇasūe! doṇham yyeva amhesu eso sāva|vuttanto ciṭṭhadu. rakkhaṇīā khu païdi|pelavā sahī.⌟

ANASÚYA: *(Exit.)*

PRIYAM·VADA: *(takes a step and stumbles)* Oh no! Stumbling in my haste, the flower basket has slipped through my fingers. I will have to gather them again.* *(Does so.)*

(enter) ANASÚYA: My dear, he is like an incarnation of wrath: Whose apologies will he accept? But he showed some mercy.

PRIYAM·VADA: For him that is quite a lot. Tell me, how did 4.25
it happen?

ANASÚYA: When he did not want to come back I said to him: "Your holiness! Consider her former devotion, forgive now this offense of your daughter whose worthiness you can perceive by your powers."

PRIYAM·VADA: What then?

ANASÚYA: Then, saying, "What I have said cannot but come true; my curse will be lifted by the sight of a token of recognition", he vanished.

PRIYAM·VADA: We can breathe now. There is a ring that the departing royal sage himself put on Shakúntala's hand as a memento. As long as it stays with her this remedy will work. *(Walk about.)*

ANASÚYA: Dear Priyam·vada, look, look! Our friend, her 4.30
face resting on her left hand, looks like a painting. With her thoughts engrossed in her husband, she is not even mindful of herself, how much less of a stranger arriving?

PRIYAM·VADA: Dear Anasúya! This affair of the curse must remain between you and me. We have to protect our tender-hearted friend.

ANASŪYĀ: ko dāṇiṃ uṇh'|ôdaeṇa ṇava|māliaṃ siñcadi.

iti niṣkrānte.

praveśakaḥ.

4.35 *tataf praviśati supt'|ôtthitaḥ Kāśyapa|śiṣyaḥ.*

KĀŚYAPAŚIṢYAḤ: vel"|ôpalakṣaṇ'|ârtham ādiṣṭo 'smi tatra|bhavatā Prabhāsāt pratinivṛtten' ôpādhyāya|Kāśyapena. tat prākāśyaṃ nirgatya tāvad avalokayāmi kim avaśiṣṭaṃ rajanyā iti. *(parikramy' âvalokya)* hanta prabhātam. tathā hi—

karkandhūnām upari tuhinaṃ
rañjayaty agra|sandhyā
dārbhaṃ muñcaty uṭaja|paṭalaṃ
vīta|nido mayūraḥ
vedi|prāntāt khura|vilikhitād
utthitaś c' âiṣa sadyaḥ
paścād uccair bhavati hariṇo
gātram āyacchamānaḥ.

api ca,

pāda|nyāsaṃ kṣiti|dhara|guror
mūrdhni kṛtvā Sumeroḥ
krāntaṃ yena kṣapita|tamasā
madhyamaṃ dhāma Viṣṇoḥ
so 'yaṃ candraf patati gaganād
alpa|śeṣair mayūkhaiḥ—
dūr'|āroho bhavati mahatām
apy apabhraṃśa|niṣṭhaḥ.

ANASÚYA: Who now would sprinkle hot water on a jasmine vine?

Exeunt ambo.

End of the prelude.

Enter a disciple of Káshyapa, arisen from sleep. 4.35

DISCIPLE: His reverence Káshyapa, returned form Prabhása, has sent me to check what time it is. Going out into the open, I will see what remains of the night. *(walks about, looking)* Ah! The dawn breaks. For,

The breaking dawn reddens
  the mist hanging over the jujube trees,
the peacock, shaking off sleep, leaves
  the *darbha* thatch of the cottage,
and this antelope, jumping up with a start
  from the hoof-scratched verge of the altar,
  then stretching its limbs, stands upright.

Moreover,

He who had *cast down his rays : placed his feet*
  upon the peak of Suméru,
    greatest of mountains,
he who, dispelling darkness, reached
    the middle station of Vishnu,
that moon now falls from the sky
    with but few remaining rays—
the towering ascendancy of even the great
    ends with a downfall.

4.40 yat satyaṃ sūryā|candramasau jagato 'sya sampad|vipattyor anityatāṃ darśayata iva. tathā ca

yāty ekato 'sta|śikharaṃ patir oṣadhīnām
  āviṣkṛt'|âruṇa|puraḥsara ekato 'rkaḥ
tejo|dvayasya yugapad vyasan'|ôdayābhyām
  loko niyamyata iv' ātma|daś"|ântareṣu.

api ca asmin kāle

antar|hite śaśini s" âiva kumudvatī me
  dṛṣṭiṃ na nandayati saṃsmaraṇīya|śobhā
iṣṭa|pravāsa|janitāny abalā|janasya
  duḥkhāni nūnam atimātra|durutsahāni.

tataf praviśaty apaṭī|kṣepen' Ânasūyā.

4.45 ANASŪYĀ: ⌜evaṃ vi ṇāma visaya|paraṃmuhassa vi edaṃ ṇa vididaṃ jadhā teṇa raṇṇā Saüntalāe aṇ|ayyadā āaridavva tti.⌟

ŚIṢYAḤ: yāvad upasthitāṃ velāṃ nivedayāmi. *(iti niṣkrāntaḥ.)*

ANASŪYĀ: ⌜paḍibuddhā vi kiṃ karaïssaṃ? ṇa me utthidāe cintidesu pabhāda|vāvāresu hatthā pādā vā pahavanti. sa|kāmo dāṇiṃ kāmo bhodu, jeṇa siṇiddha|hiaā sahī asacca|sandhe jaṇe padaṃ kāridā. *(smṛtvā)* adha vā ṇa tassa rā'|êsiṇo avarāho Duvvāsa|kovo ettha vippakaredi. aṇṇadhā kadhaṃ tādiso rā'|êsī tādisāiṃ vaṇāiṃ mantia

The sun and moon seemingly show to this world that prosperity and misfortune are impermanent,—a truth. For, 4.40

> On one side the moon, lord of the herbs, descends
> to the western horizon-mountain,
> on the other side the sun has appeared,
> heralded by dawn;
> by the simultaneous descent and rise
> of the two luminaries
> the world is bound to the fluctuations of life.

Moreover, at this time,

> When the moon has disappeared,
> the same lily pond no longer gladdens my eyes,
> its beauty remaining only in memory;
> no doubt, the sorrows caused by the absence
> of her beloved are exceedingly hard to bear
> for a powerless woman.

Enter Anasúya with a toss of the curtain.

ANASÚYA: Even the sage averse to pleasures did not know how ignobly the king would behave toward Shakúntala. 4.45

DISCIPLE: I will announce that it is time. *(Exit.)*

ANASÚYA: Though I am awake, what can I do? Now that I am up, my hands and feet lack the strength to carry out the early morning tasks I had planned. May Love be appeased, now that my tenderhearted friend has placed her confidence in a person untrue to his word. *(remembering)* Or, rather, the royal sage is not at fault, the anger of Durvásas is here countermanding him. Otherwise, how ettiassa kālassa leha|mettaaṃ vi ṇa vissajjaïssadi? *(vicintya)* ido aṅguliaṃ se ahiṇṇāṇaṃ visajjema. adha vā dukkha|sīle tavassi|aṇe ko abbhatthīadu. ṇa a sahi|gamaṇeṇa doso tti vavasidaṃ dāṇiṃ pāremha, Pahāsa|ṇivvuttassa tāda|Kassavassa Dussanta|pariṇīdaṃ āvaṇṇa|sattaṃ ko vi Saüntalaṃ ṇivedaïssadi? itthaṃ|gade kiṃ ṇu kkhu amhehiṃ kādavvaṃ?

tataf praviśati Priyaṃvadā.

PRIYAṂVADĀ: ⌜Aṇasūe. Saüntalāe patthāṇa|koduāiṃ karīanti.⌝

4.50 ANASŪYĀ: ⌜sahi. kadhaṃ ṇ·edaṃ?⌝

PRIYAṂVADĀ: ⌜Aṇasūe, suṇu. idāṇiṃ suha|saïda|vibuddhāe Saüntalāe samīvaṃ gada mhi jāva taṃ lajj"|āvaṇada-muhiṃ parissajia tāda|Kassavo saaṃ ahiṇandadi: «diṭ-ṭhiā dhūm'|ôvaruddha|diṭṭhiṇo vi jaṇassa pāvake yyeva āhudī paḍidā. su|sissa|paḍipādidā via bijjā asoaṇijj" âsi me saṃvuttā. tā ajja yyeva isi|pariggihīdaṃ tumaṃ bhaṭṭiṇo saāsaṃ visajjemi tti.»⌝

ANASŪYĀ: ⌜adha keṇa ācakkido tādassa aaṃ Saüntalā|vuttanto?⌝

PRIYAṂVADĀ: ⌜tādassa aggi|saraṇe paviṭṭhassa kila sarīraṃ viṇā chandovadīe vāāe.⌝

could such a royal sage, speaking such words as he did, not send even a letter after such a long time? *(pondering)* We will send him the ring from here to remind him. But whom among the hermits, familiar only with penitence, dare we ask? And, because he will assume: "The fault lies with her friends!" we are powerless. Who can tell father Káshyapa, who has returned from Prabhása, that Shakúntala is wedded to Dushyánta and pregnant. This being the situation, what can we do about it?

Enter Priyam·vada.

PRIYAM·VADA: Anasúya! The ceremonies for Shakúntala's departure are under way.

ANASÚYA: My dear! How come? 4.50

PRIYAM·VADA: Anasúya, listen. Just now I went to Shakúntala, who had awoken from a restful sleep when father Káshyapa embraced her, as she bowed with bashfulness, and congratulated her: "Luckily, though his vision was obscured by smoke, his oblation has fallen into the sacred fire. Like wisdom imparted to a bright pupil, you have not become a cause of grief to me. So this very day I will send you, escorted by seers, to your husband."

ANASÚYA: Well, then, who told father about Shakúntala's affair?

PRIYAM·VADA: A disembodied voice, in Vedic verse, when father had entered the fire-sanctuary.

ANASŪYĀ: *(sa|vismayam)* ⌜kadhaṃ via?⌟

4.55 PRIYAṂVADĀ: ⌜sahi, suṇu.⌟ *(Saṃskṛtam āśritya paṭhati...)*

Duṣyanten' āhitaṃ vīryaṃ
  dadhānāṃ bhūtaye bhuvaḥ
avehi tanayāṃ brahman
  agni|garbhāṃ śamīm iva.

ANASŪYĀ: *(sa|harṣaṃ Priyaṃvadām āśliṣya)* ⌜sahi, piaṃ me, kiṃ tu Saüntalā ṇīadi tti ukkaṇṭhā|sāhāraṇaṃ khu dāṇiṃ paridosaṃ samuvvahāmi.⌟

PRIYAṂVADĀ: ⌜ukkaṇṭhaṃ viṇodaïssāmo. sā dāṇiṃ ṇivvudā bhodu.⌟

ANASŪYĀ: ⌜teṇa hi imassiṃ cūda|sāh"|âvalambie nāriela|samuggae taṇ|ṇimittaṃ yyeva kāl'|antara|kkhamā khittā mae sa|kesara|guṇā. te tumaṃ hattha|saṇṇihide karehi jāva ahaṃ se maa|goroaṇaṃ tittha|mittiaṃ duvvā|kisalaāiṃ maṅgala|samālahaṇ'|atthaṃ viraemi.⌟ *(iti niṣkrāntā.)*

4.60 PRIYAṂVADĀ: *(nāṭyena sumanaso gṛhṇāti.)*

NEPATHYE: ādiśyantāṃ Śārṅgarava|miśrāḥ Śakuntal"|ānayanāya sajjībhavat' êti.

PRIYAṂVADĀ: *(ākarṇya)* ⌜Aṇasūe! tuvara tuvara! ede kkhu Hatthiṇ"|ôra|gāmiṇo isīo sajjī|bhavanti tti.⌟ *(praviśya samālabhana|hastā.)*

ANASŪYĀ: ⌜sahi, ehi, gacchamha.⌟ *(ubhe parikrāmataḥ.)*

ANASÚYA: *(astonished)* What did it say?

PRIYAM·VADA: My dear, listen. *(Recites in Sanskrit. . .)* 4.55

> Know O Brahman, that for the welfare
> of the world your daughter bears
> the virility deposited by Dushyánta,
> like a *shami* tree holding fire within it.

ANASÚYA: *(joyfully embraces Priyam·vada)* My dear, I am so happy, but, realizing that Shakúntala is being led away, I now feel a joy that is the same as yearning.

PRIYAM·VADA: We must dispel our grief. Let her be happy now.

ANASÚYA: Well, then, in the coconut-shell box hanging from the branches of that mango tree I have kept for this very purpose some lotus fibers* suitable for storage. Take them with your hands while I mix yellow antelope orpiment, clay from the sacred ford and *durva* shoots for an auspicious unguent for her. *(With this, she exits.)*

PRIYAM·VADA: *(Mimes picking up flowers.)* 4.60

OFFSTAGE: Instruct Sharnga·rava and his companions: "Prepare to escort Shakúntala!"

PRIYAM·VADA: *(listening)* Anasúya, hurry, hurry! The seers are preparing to depart for Hastína·pura. *(Enters with unguent in her hands.)*

ANASÚYA: My dear! Come, let's go! *(Both walk about.)*

PRIYAMVADĀ: *(vilokya)* ⌜esā khu suyy'|ôdae yyeva visajjidā paḍicchida|ṇīvāra|bhāaṇāiṃ tāvasīhiṃ ahiṇandīamāṇā Saüntalā ciṭṭhadi. tā uvasappamha ṇaṃ.⌟ *(tathā kurutaḥ.)*

(tataf praviśati yathā|nirdiṣṭ'|āsana|sthā Śakuntalā, Gautamī, tāpasyaś ca.)

EKĀ TĀPASĪ: ⌜jāde! bhaṭṭiṇo bahu|māṇa|uttaaṃ mahā|devī|saddaṃ adhigaccha!⌟

ANYĀ: ⌜vacche! vīra|pasaviṇī hohi!⌟

āśiṣo dattvā Gautamī|varjaṃ niṣkrāntāḥ.

SAKHYAU: *(upagamya)* ⌜sahi! sumaj|janaṃ de hodu.⌟

ŚAKUNTALĀ: *(dṛṣṭvā s'|ādaraṃ)* ⌜s'|āadaṃ pia|sahīṇaṃ. ido ṇisīdadha.⌟

UBHE: *(upaviśya)* ⌜halā Saüntale! ujjua|gadā hohi jāva de maṅgala|samāladdhaṃ aṅgaṃ karīadu.⌟

ŚAKUNTALĀ: ⌜uïdam idaṃ vi bahumaṇidavvaṃ. dullahaṃ dāṇim me sahī|maṇḍaṇaṃ bhavissadi.⌟ *(rudaty uttiṣṭhati.)*

UBHE: ⌜sahi! na de icchidavve maṅgala|kāle roïdavvaṃ.⌟ *(aśrūṇi pramṛjya nāṭyena prasādhayataḥ.)*

PRIYAMVADĀ: ⌜āharaṇ'|ârhaṃ rūvaṃ assama|sulahehiṃ pasāhaṇehiṃ vippaārīadi.⌟

tataf praviśata upāyana|hastāv ṛṣi|kumārakau.

PRIYAM·VADA: *(looking)* There is Shakúntala, being sent off as soon as the sun rises, congratulated by nuns holding* bowls of wild rice. So let's go up to her. *(They do so.)*

(Enter Shakúntala, seated as described, together with Gáutami 4.65
and nuns.)

FIRST NUN: Child! Attain the title "great queen" in consequence of your husband's high esteem.

ANOTHER NUN: My dear! Give birth to a hero.

Exit after giving blessings, with the exception of Gáutami.

FRIENDS: *(approaching)* My dear! May you be happy!

SHAKÚNTALA: *(looks respectfully)* Welcome, my dear friends. 4.70
Be seated here.

BOTH: *(sitting down)* Dear Shakúntala! Stand up while the auspicious unguent is applied to your body.

SHAKÚNTALA: Though I am used to it I think highly of this. Seldom, now, will I be adorned by my friends. *(Rises crying.)*

BOTH: My dear! You must not cry at a longed for auspicious occasion. *(Wipe her tears and act adorning her.)*

PRIYAM·VADA: Your beauty, deserving jewelry, is slighted by the ornaments we can easily find in a hermitage.

Enter two young sages with finery in their hands. 4.75

ṚṢI|KUMĀRAKAU: idam alaṅkāraṇam. tāvad alaṅkriyatām atra|bhavatī.

tathā vilokya vismitāḥ.

GAUTAMĪ: ⌜vacca Hārīda. kudo edaṃ?⌟

PRATHAMAḤ: tāta|Kāśyapa|prasādāt.

4.80 GAUTAMĪ: ⌜kiṃ māṇasī siddhī?⌟chnotekiṃ mānasī siddhiḥ?

DVITĪYAḤ: na khalu, śrūyatām! tatra|bhavatā vayam ājñāpitāḥ Śakuntalā|hetor vanas|patibhyaḥ kusumāny āharat' êti. tata idānīm—

kṣaumaṃ kena cid indu|pāṇḍu taruṇā
māṅgalyam āviṣkṛtam
niṣṭhyūtaś caraṇ'|ôpabhoga|sulabho
lākṣā|rasaḥ kena cit
anyebhyo vana|devatā|kara|talair
ā|parva|mūl'|ôtthitaiḥ
dattāny ābharaṇāni naḥ kisalaya|
chāyā|pratispardhibhiḥ.

PRIYAṂVADĀ: *(Śakuntalāṃ vilokya)* ⌜halā! adbhuda|sampattī sūïdā, bhaṭṭiṇo gehe aṇubhavidavvā de rāa|lacchī.⌟

ŚAKUNTALĀ: *(vrīḍāṃ rūpayati.)*

4.85 ANASŪYĀ: ⌜sahi! kallāṇinī dāṇiṃ si. koḍara|saṃbhavā via mahu|arī pukkhara|mahuṃ ahilasasi.⌟

PRIYAṂVADĀ: *(maṇḍayantī)* ⌜aṇupahutta|bhūsaṇo aaṃ jaṇo. citta|kamma|paricaeṇa dāṇiṃ de aṅgesu āharaṇa|nioaṃ karedi.⌟

TWO YOUNG SAGES: Here are ornaments, so adorn her ladyship.

Look on astonished.

GÁUTAMI: Child, Haríta! Where does this come from?

FIRST: From the grace of father Káshyapa.

GÁUTAMI: A mind-born accomplishment? 4.80

SECOND: Not at all, listen! We were ordered by his reverence to gather flowers from the trees for Shakúntala. Now there,

> One tree produced an auspicious linen garment,
> pale like the moon;
> one exuded red lac juice, ready to apply to the feet;
> others offered us ornaments with the hands
> of forest deities stretching out as far as the wrists,
> rivalling the beauty of new shoots.

PRIYAM·VADA: *(looking at Shakúntala)* My dear! This betokens incredibly good fortune, you will enjoy royal fortune in the house of your huband.

SHAKÚNTALA: *(Mimes bashfulness.)*

ANASÚYA: My dear! Now you are beautiful! Like a female bee born in a hollow, you long for lotus-honey. 4.85

PRIYAM·VADA: *(adorning)* I have never worn such finery, so I will place the ornaments on you according to what I have seen in paintings.

ŚAKUNTALĀ: *(sa|smitam)* ⌜jāne vo ṇiunattaṇaṃ.⌟

ubhe nāṭyen' ābharaṇam āmuñcataḥ.

ṚṢI| KUMĀRAḤ: Gautama, ehi. abhiṣekād avatīrṇāya tāta|Kāśyapāya vanas|pati|sevāṃ nivedayāvaḥ.

4.90 DVITĪYA: evaṃ kurvaḥ. *(iti niṣkrāntau.)*

tataf praviśati snān'|ôtthitaḥ Kāśyapaḥ.

KĀŚYAPAḤ: *(niḥśvasya)*

yāsyaty adya Śakuntal" êti hṛdayaṃ
  saṃspṛṣṭam utkaṇṭhayā
kaṇṭhaḥ stambhita|bāṣpa|vṛtti|kaluṣaḥ
  cintā|jaḍaṃ darśanam
vaiklavyaṃ mama tāvad īdṛśam idaṃ
  snehād araṇy'|âukasaḥ
pīḍyante gṛhiṇaḥ kathaṃ na tanayā|
  viśleṣa|duḥkhair navaiḥ.

(parikrāmataḥ) SAKHYAU: ⌜halā Saüntale. avasida|maṇḍaṇ" âsi. paridhehi saṃpadaṃ imaṃ pavittaṃ khoma|ṇimmoaṃ.⌟

4.95 ŚAKUNTALĀ: *(latā|gṛhān nirgatya paridhāya punaf praviśy' ôpaviṣṭā.)*

KĀŚYAPAḤ: *(upasarpati.)*

SHAKÚNTALA: *(smiling)* I know your skill.

Both act the fastening of ornaments.

YOUNG SEER: Gáutama, come! Let us tell father Káshyapa who has gone down for his ablutions about the generosity of the trees.

SECOND: Let us do so. *(With this, they exit.)* 4.90

Enter Káshyapa arisen from his bath.

KÁSHYAPA: *(sighing)*

> "Today departs Shakúntala," realizing this
> my heart is touched by yearning,
> my throat is sore with suppressed tears;
> my vision is dulled by worry.
> If such be the melancholy produced by affection
> even for me, a forest-dwelling hermit,
> then how must not householders be crushed
> by the fresh sorrows of separation
> from their daughters.

(walking about) FRIENDS: Dear Shakúntala! Your adornment is complete. Now put on this linen garment.

SHAKÚNTALA: *(Leaves the bower, puts it on, comes back in and sits down.)* 4.95

KÁSHYAPA: *(Approaches.)*

GAUTAMĪ: ⌜eso de ānanda|vappha|parivāhiṇā cakkhuṇā parissajanto via gurū uvatthido. tā āāraṃ se paḍivajja.⌟

ŚAKUNTALĀ: *(utthāya sa/lajjā.)* ⌜tāda vandāmi.⌟

KĀŚYAPAḤ: vatse,

4.100 Yayāter iva Śarmiṣṭhā
bhartur bahu|matā bhava
putraṃ tvam api samrājaṃ
s" êva Pūrum samāpnuhi.

GAUTAMĪ: ⌜bhaavam! varo kkhu eso, ṇa āsīsā.⌟

KĀŚYAPAḤ: vatse, itaḥ sadyo hutān agnīn pradakṣiṇī|kuruṣva. *(sarve parikrāmanti.)*

amī vediṃ paritaḥ kḷpta|dhiṣṇyāḥ
samidvantaf prānta|saṃstīrṇa|darbhāḥ
apaghnanto duritaṃ havya|gandhaiḥ
vaitānās tvāṃ vahnayaf pālayantu.

ŚAKUNTALĀ: *(pradakṣiṇī/karoti.)*

4.105 KĀŚYAPAḤ: vatse! pratiṣṭhasv' êdānīm. *(sa/dṛṣṭi/kṣepam.)* kva te Śārṅgarava|miśrāḥ?

praviśya samaṃ trayaḥ.

ŚIṢYĀḤ: bhagavann ime vayam.

GÁUTAMI: Here is your father, embracing you, as it were, with eyes filled with tears of joy. Perform your salutation.

SHAKÚNTALA: *(arises, bashfully)* Father, I salute you.

KÁSHYAPA: Child,

Be honored by your husband, 4.100
as Sharmíshtha was by Yayáti.
May you, too, bear a son to be emperor,
as she did to Puru.

GÁUTAMI: Your reverence! That was a boon not a blessing.

KÁSHYAPA: Child, from here quickly circumambulate the fires bearing oblations. *(All walk about.)*

May these fires of the three rites protect you,
fixed in the directions surrounding the altar,
fed with fuel, their verges strewn
with *darbha* grass,
dispelling evil by the scent of offerings.

SHAKÚNTALA: *(Circumambulates in a clockwise direction.)*

KÁSHYAPA: Child! Set out now. *(casting a glance)* Where are 4.105
you, Sharnga·rava and company?

Enter the three together.

DISCIPLES: Your reverence, here we are.

KĀŚYAPAḤ: Śārṅgarava! bhaginyā mārgam ādeśaya.

ŚĀRṄGARAVAḤ: ita ito bhavatī. *(sarve parikrāmanti.)*

4.110 KĀŚYAPAḤ: vatse Śakuntale. vijñapyantāṃ sannihita|devatās tapo|vana|taravaḥ:

pātuṃ na prathamaṃ vyavasyati jalaṃ
yuṣmāsv asikteṣu yā
n' ādatte priya|maṇḍan" âpi bhavatāṃ
snehena yā pallavān
ādye vaḥ kusuma|prabodha|samaye
yasyā bhavaty utsavas
s" êyaṃ yāti Śakuntalā pati|gṛhaṃ
sarvair anujñāyatām.

NEPATHYE:

ramy'|ântaraḥ kamala|kīrṇa|jalais sarobhiḥ
chāyā|drumair niyamit'|ârka|mayūkha|tāpaḥ
bhūyāt kuśe|śaya|rajo|mṛdu|reṇur asyāḥ
śānt'|ânukūla|pavanaś ca śivaś ca panthāḥ.

sarve sa|vismayam ākarṇayanti.

KÁSHYAPA: Sharnga·rava, show your sister the way.

SHARNGA·RAVA: This way, this way, your ladyship. *(All walk about.)*

KÁSHYAPA: Child Shakúntala. Let it be known to the her- 4.110
mitage trees, harboring deities within:

She who was not willing to drink first
if you had not been watered,
she who, though fond of ornaments,
would not pick buds out of affection for you,
for whom the occasion of the first awakening
of your flowers was a festival,
that Shakúntala leaves for her husband's house,
given permission by all of you.

OFFSTAGE:

May her path be pleasantly varied with ponds,
their water strewn with lotuses,
may it have the heat of the sun's rays be warded off
by shady trees,
may it have dust soft as the pollen
of water-floating lilies,
may it have gentle and favorable breezes,
and may it be good.

All listen with amazement.

4.115 ŚĀRṄGARAVAḤ:

anumata|gamanā Śakuntalā
 tarubhir iyaṃ vana|vāsa|bandhubhiḥ
para|bhṛta|rasitaṃ priyaṃ yadā
 prativacanī|kṛtam ebhir ātmanaḥ.

GAUTAMĪ: ⌜jāde. ṇādi|jaṇa|siṇiddhaṃ abbhaṇuṇṇāda|gamaṇ" âsi tavo|vaṇa|devadāhiṃ. tā paṇama bhaavadīe.⌟

ŚAKUNTALĀ: *(tathā kṛtvā; parikramya, jan'|ântikam)* ⌜halā Piaṃvade. ayya|utta|daṃsaṇ'|ôssuāe vi assamaṃ pariccaantīe dukkha|dukkheṇa me calaṇā puro|muhā pahavanti.⌟

PRIYAṂVADĀ: ⌜ṇa kevalaṃ tava viraha|payyussuāaḥ sahīo yyeva. jāva tae uvatthida|vioassa tavo|vaṇassa vi avekkhaṃ avatthantaraṃ. tadhā a.⌟

4.120 ⌜ullalaï dabbha|kavalaṃ
 maī parīsanta|ṇaccaṇā morī
osaria|paṇḍu|vattā
 dhuanti aṅgāi va laāo.⌟

ŚAKUNTALĀ: ⌜tāda, ladā|bahiṇiaṃ dāva mādhaviṃ āmantaïssaṃ.⌟

KĀŚYAPAḤ: avaimi te 'syāṃ saudarya|sneham. imāṃ tāṃ dakṣiṇen' āmantrayatāṃ bhavatī.

ŚAKUNTALĀ: *(latām upety' āliṅgya ca sa|sneha|gadgadam.)* ⌜māhavi. paccāliṅga maṃ sāhā|maehiṃ bāhūhiṃ. ajja|pahudi dūra|vattiṇī de bhavissaṃ.⌟

SHARNGA·RAVA: 4.115

Shakúntala is permitted to depart by the trees,
her kinsfolk during her stay in the forest,
since they replied to you with the sweet call
of a cuckoo.

GÁUTAMI: Child! The hermitage deities have given you leave, as affectionately as kinfolk. Bow to the Godesses.

SHAKÚNTALA: *(does so; walks about, to her friends)* Dear Priyam·vada! Though I am eager to see the noble lord, as I leave the hermitage my feet move forward with great anguish.

PRIYAM·VADA: It is not only your friends who are sad about separation from you. As your departure approaches so the penance grove, too, is seen to be in a sad state. For—

The doe lets go its mouthful of *darbha* grass, 4.120
the peacock is weary of dancing,
the vines, dropping yellow leaves,
seem to have trembling limbs.

SHAKÚNTALA: Father, I will bid farewell to my tendril-sister, the *mádhavi*-vine.

KÁSHYAPA: I know your sisterly affection toward it. Greet it here to your right.

SHAKÚNTALA: *(approaches the vine and embraces it, stammering affectionately) Mádhavi!* Embrace me with your branch-arms. From today onward I will be far from you.

KĀŚYAPAḤ: vatse. iyam idānīṃ cintanīyā me. paśya—

4.125 saṅkalpitaṃ prathamam eva mayā tav' ârthe
bhartāram ātma|sadṛśaṃ sva|guṇair gatā tvam,
asyās tu samprati varaṃ tvayi vīta|cintaḥ
kāntaṃ samīpa|sahakāram ahaṃ kariṣye.

ŚAKUNTALĀ: *(sakhyāv upetya)* ⌜esā doṇhaṃ pi vo hatthe ṇikkhevo.⌟

SAKHYAU: *(s'|âsram)* ⌜aaṃ jaṇo dāṇiṃ kassa sandiṭṭho.⌟ *(rudataḥ.)*

KĀŚYAPAḤ: Anasūye, alaṃ ruditvā. nanu bhavatībhyām Śakuntalā sthāpayitavyā. *(parikrāmanti.)*

ŚAKUNTALĀ: *(vilokya)* ⌜tāda. esā uḍaja|payyanta|cāriṇī gabbha|mantharā maa|vahū jadā āsaṇṇa|pasaviṇī bhave tadā me kaṃ pi piaṃ ṇivedaïttaaṃ visajjaïssaha.⌟

4.130 KĀŚYAPAḤ: vatse. n' êdaṃ vismariṣyate.

ŚAKUNTALĀ: *(gati|bhaṅgaṃ rūpayati.)*

SAKHYAU: ⌜ko ṇu kkhu eso māda|kkanto via puṇo vasaṇassa antaṃ geṇhadi?⌟

KĀŚYAPAḤ: vatse!

yasya tvayā vraṇa|virohaṇam iṅgudīnāṃ
tailaṃ nyaṣicyata mukhe kuśa|sūci|viddhe
śyāmāka|muṣṭi|parivardhitako jahāti
so 'yaṃ na putraka|kṛtaf padavīṃ mṛgas te.

KÁSHYAPA: Child! She is my worry now. Look—

What I first had intended for you, 4.125
a husband like yourself, you have attained
by your own merits.
Now that my worry about you is over,
I will make her a husband
out of this nearby mango tree.

SHAKÚNTALA: *(approaches her friends)* I entrust her into your hands.

FRIENDS: *(tearfully)* To whom are we entrusted? *(They cry.)*

KÁSHYAPA: Anasúya, stop crying. Should you not be supporting Shakúntala? *(They walk on.)*

SHAKÚNTALA: *(looking)* Father! When this doe, roaming at the edge of the hut, slow with child, is about to give birth, please send me someone to announce the happy news.*

KÁSHYAPA: Child, this will not be forgotten. 4.130

SHAKÚNTALA: *(Mimes that her movement has been interrupted.)*

FRIENDS: Who can this be, who comes right up to her, as it were, who takes hold of the end of her garment?

KÁSHYAPA: Child,

The deer into whose mouth,
pierced by *kusha*-grass spikes,
you sprinkled wound-healing *íngudi* oil,
who was raised with handfuls
of *shyámaka*-grains and adopted as a son,
he will not leave your footsteps.

4.135 ŚAKUNTALĀ: *(dṛṣṭvā)* ⌜vaccha! kiṃ maṃ saha|vāsa|pariccāiṇiṃ kedava|siṇehaṃ aṇṇesasi? acira|pasūd'|ôvaradāe jaṇaṇīe viṇā vaḍḍhido 'si. idāṇiṃ pi mae virahidaṃ tumaṃ tādo cintaïssadi. tā paḍiṇiattasu.⌟ *(rudatī prasthitā.)*

KĀŚYAPAḤ: vatse!

utpakṣmaṇor nayanayor uparuddha|vṛttiṃ
bāṣpaṃ kuru sthirataraṃ vihit'|ânubandham
asminn alakṣita|nat'|ônnata|bhūmi|bhāge
mārge padāni khalu te viṣamī|bhavanti.

ŚĀRṄGARAVAḤ: «ā udak'|ântāt snigdho 'nugamyata iti» smaryatām. tad idaṃ saras|tīram. atra saṃdiśya tataf pratigantum arhasi.

KĀŚYAPAḤ: tena h' îmāṃ kṣīra|vṛkṣa|cchāyām āśrayāmaḥ.

4.140 *upaviśya sarve tathā kṛtvā tiṣṭhanti.*

KĀŚYAPAḤ: *(apavārya)* kiṃ nu khalu tatra|bhavato Duṣyantasya yukta|rūpam asmābhiḥ saṃdeśyam? *(cintayati.)*

ANASŪYĀ: ⌜sahi! ṇa so assame cintaṇijjo atthi jo tae virahaantīe ṇa ussuīkado ajja. pekkha dāva.⌟

⌜padamiṇī|patt'|antariaṃ
vāhariaṃ ṇ' âṇuvāharadi jāaṃ
muha|uvvūḍha|muṇālaḥ
tayi diṭṭhiṃ dei cakk'|āo.⌟

SHAKÚNTALA: *(looking)* Child, why do you follow me, who abandons her companions, whose affection is false. You were raised without your mother, who passed away soon after your birth; now, abandoned by me as well, father will look after you. So turn back. *(Sets off, weeping.)* 4.135

KÁSHYAPA: Child!

> Restrain the flow of your tears about to break loose,
> which hinders the function of your eyes
> with their upturned eyelashes.
> Your steps are uncertain on this path,
> where depressions and elevations cannot be seen.

SHARNGA·RAVA: Scriptures teach that a loved one should be accompanied up to the edge of water. This, then, is the bank of the lake. Please instruct us here and turn back.

KÁSHYAPA: Let us resort to the shade of this fig tree.

All sit down and remain so. 4.140

KÁSHYAPA: *(aside)* Now, what would be an appropriate message from us to his honor Dushyánta? *(Reflects.)*

ANASÚYA: My dear! There is no one imaginable in the hermitage who has not been made despondent by your departure. Look, here,

> The *chakra·vaka* bird,
> called by his wife hidden among the lotus leaves,
> does not reply, scattering fibers from his mouth,
> he glances at you.

ŚAKUNTALĀ: *(vilokya)* ⌜sahi. saccaṃ yeva ṇalinī|patt'|antaridaṃ piaṃ saha|araṃ avekkhantī āduraṃ cakka|vāī ārasadi: "dukkaraṃ khu ahaṃ karemi."⌟

4.145 PRIYAṂVADĀ:

⌜ajja vi viṇā pieṇaṃ
  gamaadi rāiṃ visūraṇā|dīhaṃ
hanta garuaṃ pi dukkhaṃ
  āsā|bandho sahavedi.⌟

KĀŚYAPAḤ: Śārṅgarava iti tvayā mad|vacanāt sa rājā Śakuntalāṃ puras|kṛtya vaktavyaḥ.

ŚĀRṄGARAVAḤ: ājñāpayatu bhagavān.

KĀŚYAPAḤ:

4.150 asmān sādhu vicintya saṃyama|dhanān
  uccaiḥ kulaṃ c' ātmanas
tvayy asyāḥ katham apy abāndhava|kṛtāṃ
  sneha|pravṛttiṃ ca tām
sāmānya|pratipatti|pūrvakam iyaṃ
  dāreṣu dṛśyā tvayā
bhāgy'|âdhīnam ataf paraṃ na khalu tat
  strī|bandhubhir yācyate.

ŚĀRṄGARAVAḤ: gṛhītaḥ saṃdeśaḥ.

KĀŚYAPAḤ: *(Śakuntalāṃ prati)* vatse. tvam idānīm anuśāsanīyā. paśya. van'|âukaso 'pi loka|jñā vayam.

ŚĀRṄGARĀVAḤ: na khalu dhīmatāṃ kaś cid aviṣayo nāma.

SHAKÚNTALA: *(looking)* Dear! It is true. The female *chakra·vaki* bird, not seeing her mate hidden by lotus leaves nearby, cries out piteously: "How I suffer!"

PRIYAM·VADA: 4.145

Today again she will pass the night,
long with suffering, without her beloved.
The bond of hope sustains
even deep sorrow.

KÁSHYAPA: Sharnga·rava, you must speak to the king in my name about Shakúntala as follows.

SHARNGA·RAVA: Command, your reverence.

KÁSHYAPA:

Having well considered 4.150
us who are rich in self-control,
and the noble family of yourself,
her spontaneous flow of affection toward you,
unaided by the intervention of kinsfolk,
she ought to be regarded among your wives
with equal honor;
more than that depends on fate,
indeed a woman's relatives do not beg for it.

SHARNGA·RAVA: I have memorized the message.

KÁSHYAPA: *(to Shakúntala)* Child! You must now be instructed. Look, we are forest-dwellers yet know the ways of the world.

SHARNGA·RAVA: Nothing is really beyond the ken of the wise.

KĀŚYAPAḤ: vatse. sā tvam itaf pati|kulam avāpya:

4.155 śuśrūṣasva gurūn kuru priya|sakhī|
vṛttiṃ sapatnī|jane
bhartur viprakṛt" âpi roṣaṇatayā
mā sma pratīpaṃ gamaḥ
bhūyiṣṭhaṃ bhava dakṣiṇā parijane
bhāgyeṣv anutsekinī
yānty evaṃ gṛhiṇī|padaṃ yuvatayo
vāmāḥ kulasy' âdhayaḥ.

kiṃ vā Gautamī bravīti?

GAUTAMĪ: ⌜ittiaṃ khu yyeva edaṃ vahu|aṇe uvadeso.⌟ *(Śakuntalāṃ prati)* ⌜jāde, evaṃ khu avadhārehi.⌟

KĀŚYAPAḤ: vatse. ehi pariṣvajasva mām.

ŚAKUNTALĀ: ⌜tāda. kim ido yyeva pia|sahio ṇiattanti?⌟

4.160 KĀŚYAPAḤ: vatse ime api pradeye. tan na yuktam anayos tatr' āgantum. tvayā saha Gautamī yāsyati.

ŚAKUNTALĀ: *(utthāya pitaram āliṅgya)* ⌜kadhaṃ dāṇiṃ tādeṇa virahidā kari|sattha|paribaṭṭhā kareṇuā via pāṇā dhāraïssaṃ.⌟ *(iti roditi.)*

KĀŚYAPAḤ: kim evaṃ kātar" âsi.

KÁSHYAPA: Child! When you have reached your husband's family from here:

Obey your elders, be a fair friend 4.155
to your fellow wives;
though slighted by your husband do not
reciprocate with anger;
always be polite to servants, do not be arrogant
in your prosperity;
in this way young girls become the matron
of the family;
those who act contrary are the misfortune
of the family.

What does Gáutami say?

GÁUTAMI: That is all that needs to be taught to a bride. *(To Shakúntala)* Child, remember it well.

KÁSHYAPA: Child, come embrace me.

SHAKÚNTALA: Father, must my friends turn back right here?

KÁSHYAPA: Child, they too are to be given in marriage. 4.160
Therefore it is not proper for them to go there. Gáutami will go with you.

SHAKÚNTALA: *(gets up and embraces her father)* How, separated from my father, like a female elephant strayed from the herd, will I support my vital breath? *(She cries.)*

KÁSHYAPA: Why are you so cowardly?

abhijanavato bhartuḥ ślāghye sthitā gṛhiṇī|pade
vibhava|gurubhiḥ kṛtyair asya pratikṣaṇam ākulā
tanayam acirāt prāc" îv' ârkaṃ prasūya ca pāranaṃ
mama viraha|jāṃ na tvaṃ vatse śucaṃ gaṇayiṣyasi.

api c' êdam avadhāraya:

4.165 yadā śarīrasya śarīriṇaś ca
pṛthaktvam ekāntata eva bhāvī
āhārya|yogena vibhajyamānaf
pareṇa ko nāma bhaved viṣādī?

(Śakuntalā pituf pādayof patati.)

KĀŚYAPAḤ: yad icchasi tat te 'stu.

ŚAKUNTALĀ: *(sakhyāv upagamya)* ⌜halā! edha duve yyeva maṃ samaṃ parīsaadhaṃ!⌟

SAKHYAU: *(tathā kṛtvā)* ⌜sahi. so rāā jaï paccahiṇṇāṇa|mantharo bhave tadā se imaṃ tadīa|ṇāma|he'|aṅkidaṃ aṅgulīyaaṃ daṃsehi.⌟ *(ity aṅgulīyakaṃ dattaḥ.)*

4.170 ŚAKUNTALĀ: *(s'|āśaṅkam)* ⌜ā sandeseṇa aṇukampida mhi.⌟

SAKHYAU: ⌜mā bhāāhi. siṇeho vāmaṃ āsaṅkadi.⌟

Assuming the celebrated status of matron
to a husband of worthy family,
involved every minute in his affairs,
important because of his status,
soon giving birth to a son who will fulfill you
just as the east gives birth to the sun,
you will count for nothing the grief
of separation from me.

And remember this:

When the absolute separation 4.165
of the soul and the body is inevitable,
who would be upset about the
surgical removal of a tumor?

(Shakúntala falls at the feet of her father.)

KÁSHYAPA: What you desire, that you shall have.

SHAKÚNTALA: *(approaches her two companions)* Friends! Embrace me both at once.

FRIENDS: *(do so)* My dear! If that king is slow to remember, then show him this ring marked with his name. *(With this, they give her the ring.)*

SHAKÚNTALA: *(worried)* I am pitied right until I am sent off. 4.170

FRIENDS: Do not worry. Affection is apprehensive of the untoward.

ŚĀRṄGARAVAḤ: *(ūrdhvam avalokya)* yug'|ântaram adhirūḍhaḥ savitā. tat tvaratāṃ bhavatī. *(utthāya)* ita ito bhavatī.

sarve parikrāmanti.

ŚAKUNTALĀ: *(bhūyaf pitaram āśliṣya sa|gadgadaṃ)* ⌜tāda, kadā ṇu kkhu bhūas tavo|vaṇaṃ pekkhissaṃ?⌟

4.175 KĀŚYAPAḤ: vatse! śrūyatām

bhūtvā cirāya catur|anta|mahī|sapatnī
dauṣyantim apratirathaṃ tanayaṃ prasūya
tasmin niveśita|dhureṇa sah' âiva bhartrā
śānte kariṣyasi padaṃ punar āśrame 'smin.

GAUTAMĪ: ⌜jāde. parihīadi gamaṇa|velā. tā nivaṭṭehi pitaraṃ *(Kāśyapaṃ prati)* adha vā cireṇa esā pidaram ṇa ṇivaṭṭaïssadi. tā ṇivaṭṭadu bhavaṃ.⌟

KĀŚYAPAḤ: vatse, uparudhyate me tapo|'nuṣṭhānam. pratinivartitum icchāmi.

ŚAKUNTALĀ: *(punaf pitaram āśliṣya)* ⌜tādo ṇirukkaṇṭho bhavissadi, ahaṃ dāṇiṃ ukkaṇṭhā|bhāiṇī saṃvuttā.⌟

4.180 KĀŚYAPAḤ: ayi! kiṃ māṃ jaḍī|karoṣi?

SHARNGA·RAVA: *(looking up)* The sun has climbed into another sector of the sky. So make haste, your ladyship. *(arises)* This way, this way, your ladyship.

All walk about.

SHAKÚNTALA: *(embraces her father once more, sobbing)* Father, when will I see the penance grove again?

KÁSHYAPA: Child, listen, 4.175

When you have been the fellow wife of the earth
bounded by the cardinal points,
when you have given birth to Dushyánta's son,
whom none can withstand in battle,
when he has taken up the yoke,
with your husband alone you shall
set foot in this tranquil hermitage.

GÁUTAMI: Daughter, the time for your departure is slipping away. So send your father back. *(to Káshyapa)* But no, she will not send her father back after ever so long a time. Therefore please turn back, your reverence.

KÁSHYAPA: Child, my observance of penitence is interrupted. I wish to return.

SHAKÚNTALA: *(embraces her father again)* Father will be freed from sorrow, but I am now taking on sorrow.

KÁSHYAPA: Ah! Why are you stupefying me? 4.180

śamam eṣyati mama vatse
  katham iva śokas tvayā racita|pūrvam
uṭaja|dvāra|virūḍhaṃ
  nīvāra|Baliṃ vilokayataḥ.

vatse, gaccha śivās te panthānaḥ santu!

iti niṣkrāntā Śakuntalā anuyāyibhiḥ saha.

SAKHYAU: *(ciraṃ vilokya)* ⌜haddhī! antaridā Saüntalā vaṇa|rāīhiṃ.⌟

4.185 KĀŚYAPAḤ: Anasūye, gatā vāṃ saha|dharma|cāriṇī. nigṛhyatāṃ śok'|āvegaḥ. anugacchataṃ māṃ prasthitam.

UBHE: ⌜tāda. Saüntalā|viraïdaṃ suṇṇaṃ via tavo|vaṇaṃ pavisāmo.⌟

KĀŚYAPAḤ: sneha|vṛttir iva darśanīyā. *(sa|vimarśam parikramya.)* hanta bhoḥ! Śakuntalāṃ visṛjya labdham idānīṃ svāsthyam. kutaḥ.

artho hi kanyā parakīya eva
  tām adya sampreṣya parigrahītuḥ
jāto mam' âyaṃ viśad'|ântar|ātmā
  cirasya nikṣepam iv' ârpayitvā.

iti niṣkrāntāḥ sarve.

4.190 iti mahā|kavi|Kālidāsa|viracite
Śakuntalā|nāmani nāṭake
caturtho 'ṅkaḥ.

Child, how will my grief be assuaged,
when I see the Bali-offering of wild rice,
just now planted by you,
sprouting at the cottage door?

Child, go, may your paths be happy!

Exit Shakúntala with her followers.

FRIENDS: *(looking for a long while)* Alas! Shakúntala is hidden by the rows of trees.

KÁSHYAPA: Anasúya, your companion in *dharma* is gone. 4.185
Control your grief. Follow me as I set off.

BOTH: Father, we enter a penance grove which seems empty without Shakúntala.

KÁSHYAPA: Love makes things seem like that. *(walks about, reflecting)* Well, now! Now that Shakúntala is seen off, I am at ease. Why?

A daughter is really another's possession.
Now that she is sent to her husband,
my inner self has become tranquil,
as if by returning a deposit after a long time.

All withdraw.

The end of the fourth act 4.190
in the play called "Shakúntala,"
composed by the great poet
Kali·dasa.

ACT FIVE: THE TRAGEDY

tataf praviśati kañcukī.

KAÑCUKĪ: *(ātmānaṃ vilokya)* aho bata kīdṛśīm vayo|'va-sthāṃ prāpto 'smi.

«ācāra ity» adhikṛtena mayā gṛhītā
yā vetra|yaṣṭir avarodha|gṛheṣu rājñaḥ
kāle s" âiva parihīna|niyoga|śakteḥ
gantuṃ mam' êyam avalambana|vastu jātā.

yāvad abhyantara|gatayā devāy' ânuṣṭheyaṃ akāla|kṣep'|ârhaṃ nivedayāmi. *(dve pade gatvā)* kiṃ punas tat? *(saṃsmṛtya)* āṃ, Kaṇva|śiṣyās tapo|dhanā devaṃ draṣṭum icchanti. bhoś citram idam,

5.5 kṣaṇāt prabodham āyāti
laṅghyate tamasā punaḥ
nirvāsyataf pradīpasya
śikh" êva jarato matiḥ.

parikramya.

ĀKĀŚE: Maudgalya! dharma|kāryam anatipātyaṃ devasya nivedayitum icchāmi. kiṃ bravīṣi? «nanv idānīm eva dharm'|āsanād utthitaf punar avarudhyate deva iti.» nanv īdṛśo loka|tantr'|âdhikāraḥ. paśya,

Enter the chamberlain.

CHAMBERLAIN: *(looking at himself)* Dear me, how old I have become.

The cane staff of office I accepted
when I was put in charge
of the royal ladies' apartments, thinking:
"It is a customary formality," that very staff,
with the passing of time,
has become a means of support for me
as I fail to muster the strength to walk.

I must inform His Majesty, who is within, of matters that brook no delay. *(takes two steps)* But what was it again? *(tries to remember)* Ah, yes. Disciples of Kanva, ascetics, wish to see His Majesty. Ah, how strange,

The intellect of an aged man 5.5
awakens suddenly,
then is once more overwhelmed
by darkness, just like the flame of a lamp
about to burn out.

Walks about.

OFFSTAGE: Maudgálya! I wish to inform His Majesty of a religious duty that cannot be postponed. What do you say? "But then His Majesty, who has just arisen from the seat of judgment, will be disturbed again." But such is the office of governing the world. Look,

bhānuḥ sakṛd yukta|turaṅga eva
  rātriṃ|divaṃ gandha|vahaf prayāti
avekṣya dāhyaṃ na śamo 'sti vahneḥ
  ṣaṣṭh'|âṃśa|vṛtter api dharma eṣaḥ.

kiṃ bravīṣi? «tena hi saṅgīta|śālā|saṅgataṃ maṇḍapaṃ gaccha!» anuṣṭhīyatāṃ niyogaḥ, yāvat tatra gacchāmi. *(parikramy' âvalokya ca)* eṣa devaḥ,

5.10 Manuf prajāḥ svā iva tantrayitvā
  niṣevate śrānta|manā viviktam
yūthāni sañcārya ravi|prataptaḥ
  śītaṃ divā sthānam iva dvip'|êndraḥ.

tataf praviśaty āsana|sthaf parimita|parivāraḥ rājā vidūṣakaś ca.

VIDŪṢAKAḤ: *(karṇaṃ dattvā)* ⌜bho ṇaṃ saṅgīda|sāliā? teṇa avadhāṇaṃ dehi, tāla|gadīe visuddhāe kkhu vīṇāe sara|sañjoā suṇīanti. jāṇe! tattha|bhodī Haṃsavadiā vaṇṇa|paricaaṃ karedi tti.⌟

RĀJĀ: *(ākarṇya)* Mādhavya, tūṣṇīṃ bhava yāvad ākarṇayāmi.

KAÑCUKĪ: aye! vyāsakta|citto devaḥ. avasaraṃ tāvat pratipālayāmi. *(vilokayan sthitaḥ.)*

The sun has yoked his horses once and for all,
wind blows day and night, behold:
there is no respite
for the burning of fire,
and such too is the duty of him
who receives the sixth part as tax.

What do you say? "Then go to the pavilion beside the music hall." Carry on with your duty while I go there. *(walks about and looks around)* Here is His Majesty,

Who governs his subjects 5.10
like the law-giver Manu,
retreating into solitude, mentally exhausted,
just like a bull elephant, scorched by the sun,
who resorts to a cool place after he has led
the herds to graze by day.

Enter the king and the buffoon, seated, surrounded by a retinue.

BUFFOON: *(listening)* Oho! Is this not the music hall? Pay attention, I hear notes played on the *vina* keeping perfect time. I know! It must be her ladyship Hamsa·pádika practicing her musical phrases.

KING: *(trying to listen)* Madhávya, shut up so I can listen.

CHAMBERLAIN: Alas! His Majesty is engrossed. I will await an opportune moment. *(Remains watching.)*

5.15 NEPATHYE: *(gīyate:)*

⌜ahiṇava|mahu|loha|bhāvio
  taha paricumbia cūa|mañjariṃ
kamala|vasaï|metta|ṇivvuo
  mahu|ara vīsario si ṇaṃ kahaṃ?⌟

RĀJĀ: aho rāga|parivāhiṇī gītiḥ.

VIDŪṢAKAḤ: ⌜kiṃ dāva se gīdiāe avi gahido bhaavadā akkhar|attho?⌟

RĀJĀ: *(smitaṃ kṛtvā)* vayasya, sakṛt|kṛta|praṇayo 'yaṃ janaḥ, tad asyāḥ kṛte Kulaprabhām antareṇa samupālambhaṃ upagato 'smi. tan mad|vacanād ucyatāṃ Haṃsapadikā: «nipuṇam upālabdhāḥ sma» iti.

5.20 VIDŪṢAKO: ⌜jaṃ bhavaṃ āṇavedi.⌟ *(utthāya)* ⌜bho vaassa! gahido tae parakīehiṃ hatthehiṃ sihaṇḍae accha|bhallo! avīda|rāssa via ṇatthi me mokkho.⌟

RĀJĀ: vayasya, gaccha! nāgarika|vṛttyā saṃjñāpay' âinām.

VIDŪṢAKAḤ: ⌜kā gadī!⌟ *(iti niṣkrāntaḥ.)*

RĀJĀ: *(sva|gatam)* kiṃ nu khalu gītam ākarṇy' êdam evaṃ|vidh'|ârtham iṣṭa|jana|virahād ṛte 'pi balavad utkaṇṭhito 'smi? atha vā,

OFFSTAGE: *(a song is sung:)* 5.15

> After you kissed the mango blossoms,
>   the way you did,
> lusting for fresh honey;
>   how have you forgotten it, O bee,
>   contented to just linger on the lotus?

KING: Ah! A song suffused with passionate melody.

BUFFOON: What? You mean you could understand the point of the lyrics?

KING: *(smiling)* My friend! I was once in love with her, and so she rebukes me about lady Kula·prabha. Please say to Hamsa·pádika in my name: "I am skillfully rebuked."

BUFFOON: As His Majesty commands. *(stands up)* My friend! 5.20
You are using another's hands to grab a bear by its tuft. I am doomed to find no release,—just as one who has not mastered his cravings.

KING: My friend, go! Address her in a gentlemanly manner.

BUFFOON: What a mess! *(Exit.)*

KING: *(to himself)* Now, why, I wonder, on hearing a song of this kind, am I filled with a deep yearning, even though I am not separated from a loved one? Or, rather,

ramyāṇi vīkṣya madhurāṃś ca niśamya śabdān
paryutsukībhavati yat sukhito 'pi jantuḥ
tac cetasā smarati nūnam abodha|pūrvaṃ
bhāva|sthirāṇi janan'|ântara|sauhṛdāni.

5.25 KAÑCUKĪ: *(upasṛtya, praṇipatya)* jayatu jayatu deva! ete khalu Hima|girer upatyak"|âraṇyakāḥ Kāśyapa|saṃdeśam ādāya sa|strīkās tapasvinaḥ saṃvṛttāḥ. śrutvā prabhaviṣṇuf pramāṇam.

RĀJĀ: kiṃ Kāśyapa|saṃdeśa|hāriṇaḥ sa|strīkās tapasvinaḥ?

KAÑCUKĪ: atha kim?

RĀJĀ: tena hi mad|vacanād vijñāpyatām upādhyāyaḥ Somarātaḥ: «amūn āśrama|vāsinaḥ śrautena vidhinā sat|kṛtya svayam eva praveśayitum arhas' îti.» aham apy enān tapasvi|darśan'|ôcite deśe pratipālayāmi.

KAÑCUKĪ: yad ājñāpayati devaḥ. *(iti niṣkrāntaḥ.)*

5.30 RĀJĀ: *(utthāya)* Vasumati, agni|śaraṇam ādeśaya.

PRATIHĀRĪ: ⌜ido ido devo.⌟ *(Parikrāmanti.)*

RĀJĀ: *(adhikāra|khedaṃ nirūpayitvā)* sarvaf prārthitam adhigamya sukhī saṃpadyate, rājñāṃ tu carit'|ârthatā duḥkh'|ôttar" âiva. kutaḥ?

When even a happy being is filled with longing,
on seeing pleasing sights or hearing sweet words,
then, surely, his mind recalls, unconsciously,
deeply felt friendships of former births.

CHAMBERLAIN: *(approaches, prostrates)* Be victorious, be vic- 5.25
torious, Your Majesty! Ascetics dwelling in the forests of the Himálaya's foothills are approaching, accompanied by womenfolk. They bring a message from Káshyapa. Hearing this, you are the authority to make a decision.

KING: Ascetics with women bearing a message from Káshyapa?

CHAMBERLAIN: What now?

KING: Request the preceptor Soma·rata, in my name: "Please welcome these hermit-dwellers according to the rite sanctioned by the scriptures and introduce them to me yourself." I, for my part, will receive them in a place befitting an audience with ascetics.

CHAMBERLAIN: As His Majesty commands. *(Exit.)*

KING: *(arises)* Vásumati! Lead the way to the fire-sanctuary. 5.30

PORTRESS: This way, this way, Your Majesty. *(They walk about.)*

KING: *(shows the weariness of his office)* Everyone who has won his desire becomes happy. But, for kings, even the attainment of the desired object is followed by pain. How so?

autsukya|mātram avasādayati pratiṣṭhā
kliśnāti labdha|paripālana|vṛttir eva
n' âtiśram'|âpanayanāya yathā śramāya
rājyaṃ sva|hasta|dhṛta|daṇḍam iv' ātapa|tram.

(nepathye) VAITĀLIKAḤ: vijayatāṃ devaḥ.

5.35 sva|sukha|nirabhilāṣaḥ khidyase loka|hetoḥ
pratidinam atha vā te sṛṣṭir evaṃ|vidh" âiva
anubhavati hi mūrdhnā pādapas tīvram uṣṇam
śamayati paritāpaṃ chāyayā saṃśritānām.

api ca,

niyamayasi vimārga|prasthitān ātta|daṇḍaḥ,
praśamayasi vivādaṃ, kalpase rakṣaṇāya
a|tanuṣu vibhaveṣu jñātayaḥ santu nāma
tvayi tu parisamāptaṃ bandhu|kṛtyaṃ prajānām.

RĀJĀ: *(ākarṇya)* ete klānta|manasaf punar navī|bhūtāḥ smaḥ. *(parikramya.)*

PRATĪHĀRĪ: ⌈eso ahiṇava|sammajjaṇa|ramaṇīo saṇṇihida|kavila|dheṇū aggi|saraṇ'|ālindo. tā ārohadu devo!⌋

Ascendancy satisfies merely the longing for it,
protecting the won only brings pain.
Sovereignty does not so much alleviate fatigue
as it produces it, like a parasol held up
by its handle
with one's own hand.

(offstage) HERALD: Victory to His Majesty!

Day by day you toil for the welfare of the world, 5.35
indifferent to your own ease
—yet such is your birth.
For the tree endures with its crown fierce heat
and cools those
sheltering in its shade.

Moreover,

Taking up your magistrate's rod
you discipline those who have strayed
onto a wrong path;
you settle disputes; you afford protection.
When wealth is abundant,
relatives may be at hand;
but on you ultimately falls the kinsman's duty
toward your subjects.

KING: *(listening)* My wearied mind is refreshed. *(Walks about.)*

PORTRESS: Here is the terrace of the fire-sanctuary, pleasingly scoured clean, with its tawny cow nearby. Ascend, Your Majesty!

RĀJĀ: *(ārohaṇaṃ nāṭayitvā, parijan'|âṃs'|âvalambī tiṣṭhati. sa|vitarkam)* Vasumati. kim uddiśya tatra|bhavatā Kāśyapena mat|sakāśam ṛṣayaf prahitāḥ syuḥ?

kiṃ tāvad vratinām upoḍha|tapasāṃ
 vighnais tapo dūṣitam?
dharm'|âraṇya|gateṣu kena cid uta
 prāṇiṣv asac|ceṣṭitam?
āho svit prasavo mam' âpacaritair
 viṣṭambhito vīrudhām?
ity ārūḍha|bahu|pratarkam apari-
 cched'|ākulaṃ me manaḥ.

PRATĪHĀRĪ: ⌜devassa bhuaṇa|parīsaṅga|nivvude catur|assame kudo edaṃ? kim tu suarid'|âhiṇandiṇo isīo devaṃ sabhājaïdum āgadatti takkemi.⌟

(tataf praviśanti Gautamī|sahitāḥ Śakuntalāṃ puraskṛtya munayaḥ. puraś c' âiṣāṃ purohita|kañcukinau.)

KAÑCUKĪ: ita ito bhavantaḥ.

(sarve parikrāmanti.)

KING: *(mimes climbing up, stops supported by the shoulder of an attendant, deliberating)* Vásumati. With what intention can his reverence Káshyapa have dispatched seers to me? 5.40

Might it be that the penance
of those following observances
who have amassed penitence is impeded?
Or is someone harming the animals
in the sacred forest?
Or is perhaps the flowering of the vines stunted
through my misdeeds?
My mind, filled with many conjectures,
is confounded by a lack of discernment.

PORTRESS: How could this be, while the four estates of life are free from fear, thanks to His Majesty's embrace of the earth? I imagine that the sages have come to laud His Majesty, rejoicing in his good deeds.

(Then enter the sages with Gáutami, preceded by Shakúntala. Before them go the priest and the chamberlain.)

CHAMBERLAIN: This way, this way, reverends.

(All walk about.) 5.45

ŚĀRṄGARAVAḤ:

mahā|bhāgaḥ satyaṃ nara|patir abhinna|sthitir asau
na kaś cid varṇānām apatham apakṛṣṭo 'pi bhajate
tath" âpi idaṃ śaśvat|paricita|viviktena manasā
jan'|ākīrṇaṃ manye huta|vaha|parītaṃ gṛham iva.

ŚĀRADVATAḤ: sthāne bhavataf pura|praveśād itthaṃ|bhūtaḥ saṃvegaḥ, aham api,

abhyaktam iva snātaḥ,
śucir aśucim iva, prabuddha iva suptam
baddham iva svaira|gatir
janam avaśaḥ saṅginam avaimi.

5.50 ŚAKUNTALĀ: *(durnimittaṃ sūcayantī, sa|khedam)* ⌜ammo! kiṃ pi vām'|êtaraṃ me ṇaaṇaṃ vipphuradi?⌟

GAUTAMĪ: ⌜paḍihadaṃ amaṅgalam! suhāiṃ de bhaṭṭi|kula|devadāo vidarantu!⌟ *(parikrāmati.)*

PUROHITAḤ: *(rājānaṃ nirdiśya)* bhoh! tapasvinaḥ! asāv atra|bhavān varṇ'|āśramāṇāṃ rakṣitā prāg eva mukt'|āsanaf pratipālayati. paśyat' âinam.

SHARNGA·RAVA:

True, the magnanimous king
  does not violate order;
no one among the social classes,
  no matter how lowly,
  pursues wrong ways;
Nevertheless, with my mind ever accustomed
    to solitude
  I consider this house,
  crowded with people, as if it were on fire.

SHARAD·VATA: Justly you feel such disquiet as we enter the citadel. I, too,

As a free man,
perceive these people attached to pleasure
  as one who has bathed does one smeared,
  as one who is pure does the impure,
  as one who is awake does the sleeping,
  as one who goes at will does the bound.

SHAKÚNTALA: *(acting an ominous portent, distressed)* Oh dear! Why now should my right eye throb? 5.50

GÁUTAMI: May misfortune be warded off! May your husband's familial deities grant you happiness! *(They walk about.)*

PRIEST: *(indicating the king)* Ye ascetics! Here is His Majesty, protector of the classes and stages of life, awaiting you arisen from his seat. Behold him!

ṚṢAYAḤ: mahā|brāhmaṇa! kāmam etad abhinandanīyam, tath" âpi vayam atra madhya|sthāḥ. kutaḥ?

bhavanti namrās taravaf phal'|ôdgamaiḥ
  nav'|âmbubhir dūra|vilambino ghanāḥ
anuddhatāḥ sat|puruṣāḥ samṛddhibhiḥ
  sva|bhāva ev' âiṣa par'|ôpakāriṇām.

5.55 PRATĪHĀRĪ: ⌜deva! pasaṇṇa|muha|rāā dīsanti sattha|kayyā isīo.⌟

RĀJĀ: *(Śakuntalāṃ dṛṣṭvā)* ath' âtrabhavatī—

kā svid avaguṇṭhanavatī
  n' âtiparisphuṭa|śarīra|lāvaṇyā
madhye tapo|dhanānāṃ
  kisalayam iva pāṇḍu|patrāṇām?

PRATĪHĀRĪ: ⌜deva kudūhaladāe vimhida mhi. ṇa me takko pasīdadi.⌟

PARIJANAḤ: ⌜bhaṭṭā, daṃsaṇīā kkhu se ākidī lakkhīadi.⌟

5.60 RĀJĀ: anirvarṇanīyaṃ para|kalatram!

ŚAKUNTALĀ: *(ātma/gatam, hastam urasi dattvā)* ⌜hiaa! kim evaṃ vevasi? ayya|uttassa bhāva|tthidiṃ sumaria dhīram dāva hohi.⌟

PUROHITAḤ: *(puro gatvā)* deva! ete vidhivad arcitās tapasvinaḥ. kaś cid eṣām upādhyāya|saṃdeśah. taṃ devaḥ śrotum arhati.

RĀJĀ: *(s'/ādaram)* avahito 'smi.

ṚṢAYAḤ: *(upasṛtya, hastān udyamya)* vijayasva rājan!

SEERS: Great Brahmin! Granted, this is praiseworthy, nevertheless we remain indifferent. How so?

> Trees are bent low when they bear fruit,
> clouds hang low when loaded with fresh water,
> good men are not made conceited by wealth,
> this is simply the nature of those who help others.

PORTRESS: Your Majesty! The seers appear to have serene 5.55
countenances, inspiring confidence.

KING: *(seeing Shakúntala)* Then this lady—

> Who might be this veiled lady,
>   the beauty of her body not quite revealed,
> in the midst of those rich in penitence,
>   like a fresh bud among pale leaves?

PORTRESS: Your Majesty! I am filled with curiosity. I have no idea.

RETINUE: Lord, her form is beautiful to behold.

KING: Another's wife must not be looked at! 5.60

SHAKÚNTALA: *(to herself, placing her hand on her chest)* My heart, why do you flutter so? Remember my noble lord's constancy and then be calm.

PRIEST: *(going ahead)* Your Majesty! Here are the ascetics, honored according to custom. They have a message from their teacher. Please hear it.

KING: *(respectfully)* I am attentive.

SEERS: *(approaching, stretching out their hands)* Be victorious, O king!

5.65 RĀJĀ: sarvān abhivādaye vaḥ.

ṚṢAYAḤ: svasti bhavate!

RĀJĀ: api nirvighnaṃ tapaḥ?

ṚṢAYAḤ:

kuto dharma|kriyā|vighnaḥ
satāṃ rakṣitari tvayi
tamas tapati gharm'|âṃśau
katham āvir|bhaviṣyati?

5.70 RĀJĀ: arthavān me khalu rāja|śabdaḥ. atha bhagavāl̃ lok'|ânugrahāya kuśalī Kāśyapaḥ?

ŚĀRṄGARAVAḤ: svādhīna|kuśalāḥ siddhimantaḥ. sa bhavantam anāmaya|praśna|pūrvakam idam āha.

RĀJĀ: kim ājñāpayati bhagavān?

ŚĀRṄGARAVAḤ: *(Śakuntalām uddiśya)* «yan mithaḥ|samavāyād imāṃ madīyāṃ duhitaram upayeme, tan mayā prīta|manasā yuvayor anujñātam. kutaḥ?

tvam arhatāṃ prāgra|haraḥ smṛto hi naḥ
Śakuntalā mūrtimat" îva sat|kriyā,
samānayaṃs tulya|guṇaṃ vadhū|varam
cirasya vācyaṃ na gataḥ Prajāpatiḥ.

5.75 tad idānīm āpanna|sattvā pratigṛhyatām saha|dharma|caraṇāy' êti.»

KING: *(bowing)* I salute you all.

SEERS: Good fortune to you!

KING: Is your penance unimpeded?

SEERS:

> How could there be any hindrance to the holy rites
> of the good while you are their protector?
> While the hot-rayed sun shines
> how could darkness appear?

KING: My title "king" has become meaningful. Is his reverence Káshyapa hale to bless the world with his grace?

SHARNGA·RAVA: The perfect ones have power over their own welfare. After inquiring about your health, he says this to your honor.

KING: What does his reverence command?

SHARNGA·RAVA: *(indicates Shakúntala)* "Since you married this daughter of mine by mutual agreement, I am content and give you both my consent. Why?

> I consider you the foremost of the worthy,
> Shakúntala is the embodiment of virtue,
> as it were,
> uniting a bride and groom of equal merit,
> the creator has at last
> done something commendable.

Now accept her, who is with child, to fulfill your joint obligations."

GAUTAMĪ: ⌜bhadda|muha! vattukāmā thida mhi, ṇa a me vaaṇ'|âvaāso atthi. kadhaṃ ti?⌟

⌜ṇ' âvekkhio guru|aṇo
  imāĕ ṇa a ettha pucchiā bandhū
ekk|ekkameṇa varie
  kim bhaṇṇaü ekkam|ekkamhi?⌟

ŚAKUNTALĀ: *(apavārya, s'|ôtkaṇṭham)* ⌜kiṃ ṇu kkhu ajja|utta bhaṇissadi?⌟

RĀJĀ: *(śaṅk"|ākulam ākarṇya.)* ayi! kim idam upanyastam?

5.80 ŚAKUNTALĀ: *(sva|gatam, s'|āśaṅkam.)* ⌜huṃ! pāvao se vaaṇ'|ôvakkhevo.⌟

ŚĀRṄGARAVAḤ: kathaṃ nāma? atra|bhavanta eva sutarāṃ loka|yātrā|niṣṇātāḥ.

satīm api jñāti|kul'|âika|saṃśrayāṃ
  jano 'nyathā bhartṛmatīṃ viśaṅkate
ataḥ samīpe pariṇetur iṣyate
  tad|a|priy" âpi pramadā sva|bandhubhiḥ.

RĀJĀ: kim atra|bhavatī mayā pariṇīta|pūrvā?

ŚAKUNTALĀ: *(sa|viṣādam, ātma|gatam)* ⌜hiaa, saṃbhāvidā khu de āsaṅkā!⌟

5.85 ŚĀRṄGARAVAḤ: rājan! kiṃ kṛta|kārya|dveṣād dharmaṃ prati vimukhatā rājñaḥ?

GÁUTAMI: Kind sir! I am eager to speak, but it is not my place to speak. Why?

> She did not consult her elders,
> you did not ask her kinsfolk.
> Since you chose one another,
> what will you now say to each other?

SHAKÚNTALA: *(aside, longingly)* What will my noble lord say now?

KING: *(listening, assailed by doubt)* Ah! What are you insinuating?

SHAKÚNTALA: *(to herself, doubting)* Oh! His misgivings about 5.80
her words are fire.

SHARNGA·RAVA: What is this? Your Majesty is well versed in the ways of the world.

> Though she is virtuous,
> people suspect a married woman
> who stays only with her own relatives
> to be otherwise.
> Therefore, her own relatives send her
> to the man who married her,
> even if he loves her not.

KING: Have I married her?

SHAKÚNTALA: *(dejected, to herself)* My heart, your doubt proves itself to be well founded.

SHARNGA·RAVA: O King! Is this a king's aversion to duty 5.85
because he reviles a deed he has done?

RĀJĀ: kuto 'yam a|sat|kalpanā|prasaṅgaḥ?

ŚĀRṄGARAVAḤ: mūrchanty amī vikārāf prāyeṇ' âiśvarya|mattesu.

RĀJĀ: viśeṣeṇ' âdhikṣipto 'smi!

GAUTAMĪ: ⌜jāde! mā muhuttaaṃ lajja. avaṇaïssaṃ dāva de avaguṇṭhaṇaṃ. tado bhaṭṭā tumaṃ ahijāṇissadi tti.⌟ *(yath"| ôktaṃ karoti.)*

5.90 RĀJĀ: *(Śakuntalāṃ nirvarṇayan, sa|vismayam ātma|gatam)*

idam upanatam evaṃ rūpam a|kliṣṭa|kānti
prathama|parigṛhītaṃ syān na v" êty adhyavasyan
bhramara iva vibhāte kundam antas|tuṣāraṃ
na ca khalu paribhoktuṃ n' âpi śaknomi hātum.

(iti vicārayan sthitaḥ.)

PARIJANAḤ: *(jan'|ântikam.)* ⌜aho dhamm'|âvekkhidā bhaṭṭiṇo! īdisaṃ ṇāma suh'|ôvanadaṃ itthī|radaṇaṃ pekkhia, ko aṇṇo viāredi?⌟

ŚĀRṄGARAVAḤ: rājan? kim evaṃ joṣam āsyate?

5.95 RĀJĀ: bhos tapasvin! cintayann api na khalu svī|karaṇam atra|bhavatyāḥ smarāmi. tat katham anabhivyakta|sattva|lakṣaṇāṃ ātmānaṃ kṣetriṇam an|āśaṃsamānaf pratipatsye?

ŚAKUNTALĀ: *(apavārya)* ⌜haddhī! kadhaṃ pariṇae yyeva sandeho? bhaggā dāṇim me dūr'|ārohiṇī āsā!⌟

KING: What is this susceptibility to false fabrications?

SHARNGA·RAVA: Such changes for the worse commonly stupefy men drunk with power.

KING: I am gravely insulted!

GÁUTAMI: My daughter! For a moment, do not be bashful. I will remove your veil. Then the lord will recognize you. *(Does so.)*

KING: *(observing Shakúntala, astonished, to himself)* 5.90

Trying to decide whether this figure
of flawless beauty, thus offered to me,
was in the past married or not,
I find myself unable to accept or relinquish,
just as a bee at dawn does
a jasmine blossom with dew within.

(Remains pondering.)

RETINUE: *(among themselves)* Oh! How the lord must respect his duty! Who else would waver, seeing such a jewel of a woman come by with such ease?

SHARNGA·RAVA: O King? Why do you remain so silent?

KING: Sir ascetic! Though I reflect, I cannot recall marrying 5.95
her ladyship. Then how could I take in a woman faintly showing signs of pregnancy, doubting myself to be her husband?

SHAKÚNTALA: *(aside)* Alas! How can he doubt even the marriage? Broken is my hope that had climbed so high.

ŚĀRṄGARAVAḤ: mā tāvat.

kṛt'|âbhimarśām avamanyamānaḥ
  sutāṃ tvayā nāma munir vimānyaḥ
juṣṭaṃ pratigrāhayatā svam arthaṃ
  pātrī|kṛto dasyur iv' âsi yena.

ŚĀRADVATAḤ: Śārṅgarava! virama tvam idānīm! Śakuntale! vaktavyam uktam asmābhiḥ. so 'yam atra|bhavān idam āha. tad dīyatām asmai pratyayaḥ.

5.100 ŚAKUNTALĀ: *(sva|gatam, sa|khedaṃ niḥśvasya)* ⌜idaṃ avatthantaraṃ gade tādise muhutta|rāge kiṃ vā sumarāvideṇa saṃpadaṃ teṇa? adha vā attā dāṇiṃ me sodhaṇīo tthi vivadissaṃ edaṃ.⌟ *(prakāśam)* ⌜ayya|utta!⌟ *(ity|ardh'|ôkte sva|gatam)* ⌜adha vā saṃsaïdo dāṇiṃ me samudāāro.⌟ *(prakāśam)* ⌜Porava! juttaṃ ṇāma purā assama|pade sabbhāv'|uttāṇa|hiaaṃ imaṃ jaṇaṃ samaa|puravaṃ padāria īdisehiṃ akkharehiṃ paccācakkhiduṃ?⌟

RĀJĀ: *(karṇau spṛṣṭvā)* śāntaṃ pāpam!

vyapadeśam āvilayituṃ
  kim īhase māṃ ca pātayitum
kūlaṃ|kaṣ" êva sindhuḥ
  prasannam oghaṃ taṭa|ruhaṃ ca.

ŚAKUNTALĀ: ⌜jaï param'|atthado para|pariggahaṇa|saṅkiṇā tae evaṃ uttaṃ, tā ahiṇṇāṇeṇa guruṇā tuha sandehaṃ avaṇaïssaṃ.⌟

SHARNGA·RAVA: This will not do!

Are you to insult the sage whom you disrespected
by seducing his daughter;
He who welcomed you
to accept what was his,
and treated you, who were like a robber,
as a worthy recipient?

SHARAD·VATA: Sharnga·rava! You stop now! Shakúntala! We have said what we had to say. This is what His Majesty says. Give him proof.

SHAKÚNTALA: *(to herself; sighing, distressed)* What is the use 5.100
now of reminding one who has undergone such a change, one whose love was so short-lived? Nevertheless, my name must be cleared, so I will dispute it. *(aloud)* My noble lord! *(to herself in midsentence)* But no, this address is now contested. *(aloud)* Páurava! Is it right to reject with such words this person whose heart is by nature open, whom you seduced in the hermitage grounds making promises?

KING: *(holding his ears)* Stop this evil!

Why do you attempt to befoul your name
and cause my downfall,
just as a river, surging against its bank
does to its pure stream and tree on its verge.

SHAKÚNTALA: If you speak like this because you truly fear that I am another's wife, then I will dispel your doubt with this weighty token of recognition.

RĀJĀ: udāram!

5.105 ŚAKUNTALĀ: *(mudrā|sthānaṃ parāmṛśya)* ⌜haddhī! aṅgulīa| suṇṇā me aṅgulī.⌟ *(tāpasīṃ paśyati.)*

GAUTAMĪ: ⌜ṇa kkhu de Sakk'|âvadāre Sacī|titth'|ôdaaṃ avagāhamāṇāe pabbhaṭṭho aṅgulīao?⌟

RĀJĀ: *(sa|smitam)* idaṃ tad yautukaṃ pratyutpannaṃ strīṇām iti yad ucyate.

ŚAKUNTALĀ: ⌜ettha dāva vihiṇā daṃśidaṃ pahuttaṇāṃ. avaraṃ de kadhaïssaṃ.⌟

RĀJĀ: śrotavyam idānīṃ saṃvṛttam.

5.110 ŚAKUNTALĀ: ⌜ṇa kkhu tatth|ekka|diase ṇo|māliā|maṇḍavae ṇaliṇī|patta|bhāaṇa|gadaṃ udaaṃ tava hattha|saṇṇihidaṃ āsi?⌟

RĀJĀ: śṛṇumas tāvat.

ŚAKUNTALĀ: ⌜tak|khaṇaṃ ca mama so kidaa|puttao hariṇao uvatthido, «tado tae aam dāva paḍhamaṃ pivadu» tti aṇukampiṇā uvacchandido, ṇa uṇa de avariïdassa hatthabbhāso uvagado. pacchā tassim yeva udae mae gahide paṇaa|pakāsa|puvvaṃ pahasido si. bhaṇidaṃ ca tae: «savvo sa|gandhe vīsasidi duve vi ettha āraṇṇaa tti.»⌟

RĀJĀ: *(vihasan)* ebhir ātma|kārya|nirvartinīnām yoṣitām an|ṛta|vāṅ|madhubhir ākṛṣyante viṣayiṇaḥ.

KING: How noble!

SHAKÚNTALA: *(feels the place of the signet ring)* Oh no! The ring is not on my finger. *(Looks to the female ascetic.)* 5.105

GÁUTAMI: Might not the ring have slipped off when you submerged yourself into the waters of Shachi-ford at the place of Indra's Descent?

KING: *(smiling)* This must be what is called the ready wit that is the dowry of women.

SHAKÚNTALA: Here fate has shown its lordship. I will tell you something else.

KING: Now we come to something that must be heard.

SHAKÚNTALA: One day, in the jasmine bower, did you not have water in a lily-leaf bowl held in your hand? 5.110

KING: Let's hear it, then.

SHAKÚNTALA: At that moment the young antelope whom I had adopted as my son appeared. Then you coaxed him kindly, saying: "Well, let him drink first." But, unfamiliar with you, he did not take it from your hand. Then, when he took that same water from me, you laughed after you showed affection. And you said: "Everyone trusts someone who bears the same scent. Both of you are foresters."

KING: *(laughing)* With such honey of false words, women, scheming to meet their own ends, ensnare pleasure-seekers.

GAUTAMĪ: ⌜mahā|bhāa! ṇ' ârihasi ittikaṃ mantaïdum. tavo|vaṇa|saṃvaḍḍhido kkhu aaṃ jaṇo aṇabhiṇṇo kedavassa.⌟

5.115 RĀJĀ: tāpasa|vṛddhe!

strīṇām aśikṣita|paṭutvam amānuṣīṣu
  saṃdṛśyate kim uta yāf pratibodhavatyaḥ,
prāg antarikṣa|gamanāt svam apatya|jātam
  anya|dvijaif para|bhṛtaḥ kila poṣayanti.

ŚAKUNTALĀ: *(sa|roṣam)* ⌜attaṇo hia'|âṇumāṇeṇa savvaṃ pekkhasi! ko aṇṇo dhamma|kañcua|pavesiṇo taṇa|chaṇṇa|kūv'|ôvamassa tav' âṇukārī bhavissadi?⌟

RĀJĀ: *(sva|gatam.)* vana|vāsād avibhramaf punar atra|bhavatyāḥ kopo lakṣyate. tathā hi,

na tiryag avaloki cakṣur atilohitaṃ kevalaṃ
  vaco 'pi paruṣ'|âkṣaraṃ na ca padeṣu saṃsajjate
him'|ârta iva vepate sakala eṣa bimb'|âdharaḥ
  svabhāva|vinate bhruvau yugapad eva bhedaṃ gate.

5.120 *(prakāśam)* bhadre, Duṣyanta|caritam prajāsu prathitaṃ, tath" âp' îdaṃ na lakṣaye.

GÁUTAMI: Your Majesty! You must not speak thus. Raised in the penance grove, she does not know deceit.

KING: Old nun!* 5.115

Untaught cunning is evident among females
    not human,
  how much more so among those
    that are intelligent.
Before flying away into the sky,
  female cuckoos ensure
  their offspring is reared by other birds.

SHAKÚNTALA: *(angrily)* You perceive everything according to the workings of your own heart! Can there be anybody else like you, girding himself in the armor of righteousness, resembling a well concealed by grass?

KING: *(to himself)* On the other hand, the lady's unfeigned anger appears to be that of one raised in the forest. For,

Her eye casts no side glances,
    but just glares very red,
  her voice is harsh and does not slur its words,
  her whole *bimba*-red lower lip shivers
    as if pained by the cold,
  her naturally curved brows
    have at once knitted together.

(aloud) Good woman, Dushyánta's behavior is well known 5.120
to his subjects, yet I note no such thing.

ŚAKUNTALĀ:

⌜tumhe yyeva pamāṇaṃ
  jāṇadha dhamma|tthidiṃ ca loassa
lajjā|viṇijjidāo
  jāṇanti khu kiṃ ṇṇu mahilāo?⌟

⌜suṣṭhu dāva! sacchand'|āriṇī kad" amhi jā ahaṃ imassa Puru|vaṃsa|paccaeṇa hiaa|sattha|dhārassa muha|mahuṇo hatth'|abbhāsaṃ uvagadā.⌟ *(iti mukham āvṛtya roditi.)*

BHĀGURIḤ: ittham apratihataṃ cāpalaṃ dahati. ataḥ khalu,

5.125 parīkṣya sarvaṃ kartavyaṃ
  viśeṣāt saṃvidaḥ kriyāḥ
ajñāta|hṛdayeṣv evaṃ
  vairī|bhavati sauhṛdam.

RĀJĀ: ayi bhoḥ! kim atra|bhavatī|pratyayād ev' âsmān atibalena kṣiṇvanti bhavantaḥ?

ŚĀRṄGARAVAḤ: śrutaṃ bhavadbhir adhar'|ôttaram.

ā janmanaḥ śāṭhyam aśikṣito yas
  tasy' âpramāṇam vacanam janasya!
par'|âbhisaṃdhānam adhīyate yair
  «vidy" êti» te santu kil' āpta|vācaḥ!

RĀJĀ: hanta bhoḥ, satya|vādin! abhyupagataṃ tāvad asmābhir, evam|vidhā vayam. kiṃ punar imām abhisaṃdhāya labhyate?

SHAKÚNTALA:

> You alone are the authority
> and you know the ways of the world,
> what possibly can timid women know?

So be it! I have been made a wanton woman, I who, trusting in the lineage of Puru, have fallen into the hands of a man with a honeyed mouth but a blade in his heart. *(Averts her face and weeps.)*

BHÁGURI: This is how an unrestrained rash deed burns. That is why,

> One should enter into alliances, above all, 5.125
> after checking everything carefully.
> This is how among those
> whose hearts are unknown,
> affection turns to hatred.

KING: Ah! sir! Why with just the testimony of her ladyship do you grieveously cast a slur upon me.

SHARNGA·RAVA: Your Majesty has got it upside down.

> The words of a person
> who since birth has not known deceit
> have no authority!
> Those who have made a study
> of cheating others,
> calling it "politics,"
> they are reliable authorities!

KING: Alas, speaker of the truth! We admit to being political. But what would be gained from deceiving her?

ŚĀRADVATAḤ: vinipātaḥ.

RĀJĀ: taṃ n' âhaṃ prārthaye.

ŚĀRADVATAḤ: bho rājan! kim uttar'|ôttarair? anuṣṭhita|guru|saṃdeśāḥ smaḥ. saṃprati nirgacchāmahe vayam.

tad eṣā bhavataf patnī
  tyaja v" âināṃ gṛhāṇa vā
upayantur hi dāreṣu
  prabhutā sarvato|mukhī.

Gautami, gaccha gacch' âgrataḥ! *(iti prasthitāḥ.)*

ŚAKUNTALĀ: *(sa|dainyam)* ⌜huṃ! imiṇā dāva kedaveṇa vippaladdha mhi. tumhe vi maṃ pariccaïduṃ icchadha. tā kā gadī?⌟ *(iti Gautamīm anugacchati.)*

GÁUTAMI: *(sthitvā)* ⌜vaccha Saṅgarava! aṇugacchady esā karuṇa|parideviṇī Saüntalā. paccādesa|kaluse bhaṭṭāre kiṃ vā puttiā me karedu?⌟

ŚĀRṄGARAVAḤ: *(purodhasā saṃjñitaf pratinivṛttya)* āḥ! puro|bhāge! kim idaṃ svātantryam avalambyate? *(Śakuntalā bhītā vepate.)*

ŚĀRṄGARAVAḤ: śṛṇotu bhavatī!

yadi yathā vadati kṣiti|pas tathā
  tvam asi kiṃ pitṛ|śoka|dayā tvayā
atha tu vetsi śuci vratam ātmanaḥ
  pati|gṛhe tava dāsyam api kṣamam.

SHARÁDVATA: Ruin! 5.130

KING: That is not what I seek.

SHARÁDVATA: King! What's the point of this dispute? We have carried out our preceptors command. Now we depart.

> So she is your wife, take her or leave her.
> For a husband's power over his wives
> is all-encompassing.

Gáutami, go, go ahead! *(They set off.)*

SHAKÚNTALA: *(pitifully)* Oh no! I really have been deceived 5.135
by this cheat. You, too, are about to abandon me. What is the way out? *(With this, she follows Gáutami.)*

GÁUTAMI: *(stops)* Child, Sharnga·rava. Shakúntala, lamenting piteously, is following us. When her husband is so vile as to reject her, what can my daughter do?

SHARNGA·RAVA: *(turns around, beckoned by the priest)* Ah! You forward woman! Are you being willful? *(Shakúntala trembles with fear.)*

SHARNGA·RAVA: Listen!

> If you are as the king says,
> then what have we to do with you,
> who brings grief to your father?
> But if you know your conduct to be pure,
> then even slavery in your husband's house
> is bearable.

5.140 tiṣṭha! sādhayāmo vayam.

RĀJĀ: bhos tapasvin! kim atra|bhavatīṃ vipralabhase?

kumudāny eva śaś'|âṅkaḥ
savitā bodhayati paṅka|jāny eva
vaśināṃ hi para|parigraha|
saṃśleṣa|parāṅ|mukhī vṛttiḥ.

ŚĀRṄGARAVAḤ: rājan! atha pūrva|parigraho 'ny'|āsaṅgād vismṛto bhavet, tadā katham adharma|bhīro?

RĀJĀ: bhavantam eva guru|lāghavaṃ prakṣyāmi.

5.145 mūḍhaḥ syām aham eṣā vā
vaden mithy" êti saṃśaye—
dāra|tyāgī bhavāmy āho
para|strī|sparśa|pāṃsulaḥ.

PURODHĀḤ: *(vicārya)* yadi tāvad evaṃ kriyate...

RĀJĀ: ...anuśāstu māṃ bhavān.

PURODHĀḤ: atra|bhavatī tavad ā prasavād mad|gṛhe tiṣṭhatu. bhūtam idam ucyate: tvaṃ sādhubhir ādiṣṭaf prathamam cakra|vartinaṃ janayiṣyas' îti. sa cen muni|dauhitras tal|lakṣaṇ'|ôpapanno bhaviṣyati tataf pratinandya śuddh'|ântam enāṃ praveśayiṣyas' îti. viparyaye pitur asyāḥ samīpa|gamanam upasthitam eva.

Stay! We are leaving. 5.140

KING: Ascetic! Why do you deceive the lady?

> The moon awakens only night-lilies,
> the sun only lotuses.
> The character of the self-restrained recoils
> from embracing the wife of another.

SHARNGA·RAVA: King! What if your previous conquest has been forgotten because you are preoccupied with another woman, then what, O shunner of dishonor?

KING: Let me ask his honor what is more plausible here.

> Doubting whether I might be oblivious 5.145
> or whether she might speak falsely—
> shall I become a wife-reviler
> or a defiler of another's wife?

PRIEST: *(considering)* What if we were to do this...

KING: ... Please advise me.

PRIEST: Let her ladyship stay in my house until she has given birth. I say this advisedly: You were told by the wise that your firstborn will be an emperor. If the son of the sage's daughter is endowed with the appropriate marks, then congratulate her and welcome her into the female apartments. Otherwise, you should send her back to her father.

RĀJĀ: yathā gurubhyo rocate.

5.150 PURODHĀḤ: vatse, anugaccha mām!

ŚAKUNTALĀ: *(rudatī)* ⌜bhaavadi Vasu|he! dehi me viaraṃ!⌟ *(iti niṣkrāntā saha sakalaif purodhasā ca.)*

RĀJĀ: *(śāpa|vyavahita|smṛtiḥ Śakuntalām eva cintayati.)*

NEPATHYE: āścaryam āścaryam!

RĀJĀ: *(karṇaṃ dattvā)* kiṃ nu khalu syāt?

5.155 PUROHITAḤ: *(praviśya)* deva! adbhutaṃ khalu saṃvṛttam.

RĀJĀ: kim iva?

PURODHĀḤ: parivṛtteṣu Kaṇva|śiṣyeṣu,

sā nindantī svāni bhāgyāni bālā
bāh'|ûtkṣepaṃ kranditum ca pravṛttā. . .

RĀJĀ: kiṃ ca?

KING: As my preceptor wishes.

PRIEST: Child! Follow me.

SHAKÚNTALA: *(crying)* Goddess Earth, give me an opening.

(She goes out with the priest and all others.)

KING: *(His memory blocked by the curse, he thinks about Shakúntala.)*

OFFSTAGE: A miracle, a miracle!

KING: *(listening)* What can be happening now?

PRIEST: *(entering)* Your Majesty! A miracle has occurred.

KING: What kind of miracle?

PRIEST: When Kanva's disciples had departed,

When the girl, lamenting her lot,
began to weep,
tossing up her arms. . .

KING: What then?

PURODHĀḤ:

strī|saṃsthānaṃ c' âpsaras|tīrtham ārād
ākṣipy' âiva jyotir enāṃ tiro 'bhūt.

(sarve vismitāḥ.)

RĀJĀ: bhagavan, prāg api sa asmābhir arthaf pratyādiṣṭa eva. kiṃ vṛthā tarkeṇ' ânviṣṭeṇa viśramāmi?

PURODHĀḤ: vijayasva! *(iti niṣkrāntaḥ.)*

RĀJĀ: *(sa/smitam)* Vasumati! paryākulo 'smi. śayana|bhūmim ādeśaya.

PRATĪHĀRĪ: *(s'/ādaraṃ)* ⌜ido ido devo.⌟ *(parikrāmanti.)*

RĀJĀ: *(ātma/gatam)*

kāmaṃ pratyādiṣṭāṃ
  smarāmi na parigrahaṃ munes tanayām
balavat tu dūyamānaṃ
  pratyāyayat' îva māṃ hṛdayam.

iti niṣkrāntāḥ sarve.

iti mahā|kavi|Kālidāsa|viracite
Śakuntalā|nāmani nāṭake
pañcamo 'ṅkaḥ.

PRIEST:

> A light in female shape fell upon her
> near Nymph-ford and whisked her away.

(All are amazed.)

KING: Your reverence, I have already settled this matter. Why should I weary myself with vain conjectures?

PRIEST: Be victorious. *(Exit.)*

KING: *(smiling)* Vásumati! I am troubled. Lead the way to the bedchamber.

CHAMBERLAIN: *(respectfully)* This way, Your Majesty, this way. *(They walk about.)*

KING: *(to himself)*

> Though I cannot recall marrying
> the sage's daughter I rejected,
> but my sorely pained heart seems to want me to.

All go out.

Thus ends the fifth act
in the play called "Shakúntala,"
composed by the great poet Kali·dasa.

ACT SIX: THE LONGING

(tataḥ praviśati nāgarika|śyālaḥ paścād|baddhaṃ puruṣam ādāya rakṣiṇau ca.)

RAKṢIṆAU: *(puruṣaṃ tāḍayitvā)* ⌜ale kumbhilaā! kadhehi kahiṃ tae eśe mahā|maṇi|patthal|ukkiṇṇa|ṇām|akkhale lāakī'|aṅgulīae śamāśadite?⌟

PURUṢAḤ: *(bhayaṃ nāṭayitvā)* ⌜paśīdantu paśīdantu bhādua|miśśā! hage kkhu īdiśaśśa kammaṇo ṇa kalle!⌟

PRATHAMAḤ: ⌜kiṃ ṇu kkhu śohaṇe bamhaṇe tti kalia laññā paḍiggahe diṇṇe?⌟

6.5 PURUṢAḤ: ⌜āṇadha daṇiṃ! hage Śakkāvadāla|vāśike dhīvale. . .⌟

DVITĪYAḤ: ⌜pāḍac|calā! kiṃ khu de amhehiṃ jādī puścidā?⌟

ŚYĀLAḤ: ⌜Sūaa! kadhedu savvaṃ aṇukkameṇa. mā ṇaṃ antarā paḍibandhiṭṭha.⌟

RAKṢIṆAU: ⌜jaṃ āutte āṇavedi. . . bhaṇa, bhaṇa!⌟

PURUṢAḤ: ⌜śe hage jāla|baḍiś'|ādīhiṃ maśca|bandhaṇ'|ôvāehiṃ kuḍumba|bhalaṇaṃ kalemi.⌟

6.10 ŚYĀLAḤ: *(prahasya)* ⌜visuddho dāṇiṃ de ājīo!⌟

PURUṢAḤ: ⌜bhaṭṭā!⌟

⌜śahajaṃ kila jaṃ pi ṇindidaṃ
   ṇa hi taṃ kamma vivajjaṇīaaṃ
paśu|mālaka|kamma|ḍāluṇe
   aṇukampā|midu eva śottie.⌟

(Enter the city's captain of the police with a man whose hands are bound behind his back and two guards.)

GUARDS: *(beating the man)* Hey, you bandit! Confess where you got the king's signet ring, set with a valuable stone, incised with his name?

MAN: *(acting fear)* Have mercy, have mercy, my esteemed brothers! I'm not capable of such a thing.

FIRST GUARD: Perhaps the king gave it to you as a present, thinking that you are a saintly brahmin?

MAN: Hear me out now! I'm a fisherman living at "Indra's 6.5
Descent"...

SECOND GUARD: You thief! Did we ask you about your caste?

POLICE CAPTAIN: Súchaka! Let him recount everything in order. Stop interrupting him.

GUARDS: As the brother-in-law commands... Confess, confess!*

MAN: I support my family with fishing tackle such as nets and hooks.

BROTHER-IN-LAW: *(laughing)* A saintly profession! 6.10

MAN: Lord!

It is said that whatever one's hereditary trade,
even if it be despised,
it must not be abandoned.
A learned brahmin, gentle with compassion,
can cruelly sacrifice animals.

ŚYĀLAḤ: ⌜tado tado!⌟

PURUṢAḤ: ⌜adh'|ekka|diaśe khaṇḍaśo lohida|maśce mae kappide. jāva taśśa udal'|abbhantale edaṃ ladaṇa|bhāśulaṃ aṅgulīyaaṃ pekkhāmi. paścā idha ṇaṃ vikkaāa daṃśanaante gahide bhāva|miśśehiṃ. ittike dāva edaśśa āgame; adhuṇā māledha kuṭṭedha vā!⌟

6.15 ŚYĀLAḤ: *(aṅgulīyakam āghrāya)* ⌜Jāṇaa! macch|odara|saṇṭhidaṃ ti ṇatthi saṃdeho. tadhā aaṃ se vīsa|gandho. āgamo dāṇiṃ edassa vimarisidavvo: tā edha rā|ulaṃ yeva gacchamha.⌟

RAKṢIṆAU: ⌜gaśca, ṇāḍha gaṇṭhi|bhedaa!⌟ *(sarve parikrāmanti.)*

ŚYĀLAḤ: ⌜Sūaa! idha maṃ goula|duvāre appamattā paḍivāledha jāva imaṃ jadh|āgamaṃ aṅgulīaaṃ bhaṭṭiṇo uvaṇīa tadīya|sāsaṇaṃ paḍicchia ṇikkamāmi.⌟

UBHAU: ⌜paviśadu āutte śāmi|paśādāa!⌟ *(śyālo niṣkrāntaḥ.)*

PRATHAMAḤ: ⌜Jāṇaā, cilāadi āutte.⌟

6.20 DVITĪYAḤ: ⌜ṇaṃ avaśal'|ôvaśappaṇīā lāāṇo.⌟

PRATHAMAḤ: ⌜vaaśā, phulanti mama hatthā imaśśa vaśaṇiṇo piṇaddhuṃ.⌟ *(puruṣaṃ nirdiśati.)*

PURUṢAḤ: ⌜ṇ' ālihadi bhādu|bhāduke akāla|mālake bhaviduṃ.⌟

DVITĪYAḤ: *(vilokya)* ⌜. . . eśe amhāṇaṃ īśale patte geṇhia lāa|śāśaṇaṃ.⌟ *(puruṣaṃ prati)* ⌜śaülāṇaṃ muhaṃ pekkhaśi adhavā giddha|śiālāṇaṃ balī bhaviśaśśi.⌟

BROTHER-IN-LAW: Ok, ok!

MAN: Now, one day I was chopping up a *róhita* carp, when I saw in its guts this ring gleaming with a jewel. Afterwards, as I was showing it around here for sale, you gents arrested me. That is how I got it; now kill me or beat me!

BROTHER-IN-LAW: *(smelling the ring)* Jánaka! There can be 6.15
no doubt, it has been in the guts of a fish. This is why it reeks of raw flesh. Its origin must now be investigated: let us go to the royal court.

GUARDS: Move along, lord pick-pocket! *(All walk about.)*

BROTHER-IN-LAW: Súchaka! You two be vigilant and wait for me here at the main gate until I inform his majesty of the provenance of the ring, receive his orders, and return.

BOTH: May the sister's husband be favorably received by his majesty! *(Exit the brother-in-law.)*

FIRST: Jánaka, the sister's husband is taking his time.

SECOND: You must take into account that you have to wait 6.20
for the right moment to approach a king.

FIRST: Buddy, my hands are itching to throttle this wretch. *(Points to the man.)*

MAN: It is not right for someone addressed with the good name "brother" to bring an untimely death.

SECOND: *(looking)* . . . here comes our master with the king's orders. *(to the man)* You'll either see the faces of your family* or become an offering to vultures and jackals.

(praviśya) ŚYĀLAḤ: ⌜sigghaṃ sigghaṃ edaṃ. . .⌟ *(ity ardh'|ôkte)*

PURUṢAḤ: ⌜hā hade mhi!⌟ *(iti viṣadaṃ nāṭayati.)*

ŚYĀLAḤ: ⌜muñcedha re muñcedha jāl'|ôvajīviṇaṃ! uvavaṇṇo se kila aṅgulīaassa āgamo. amha|sāmiṇā yeva me kadhidaṃ.⌟

PRATHAMAḤ: ⌜jaṃ āṇavedi āütte! Jama|vaśadiṃ gamia. . . khaṇḍaṃ ca via paḍiṇiutte⌟ *(puruṣaṃ muñcati)*

PURUṢAḤ: *(śyālaṃ praṇamya)* ⌜bhaṭṭā! tava kelake me jīvide!⌟

ŚYĀLAḤ: ⌜utthehi! esa bhaṭṭiṇā aṅgulīaa|mulla|sammido pāridosio vi de dāvido.⌟

PURUṢAḤ: *(sa|harṣaṃ pragṛhya)* ⌜aṇugahide mhi.⌟

PRATHAMAḤ: ⌜tadhā ṇāma aṇugahide jaṃ śūlādo avadālia hatthi|kkhandhe paḍiṭṭhāvide.⌟

DVITĪYAḤ: ⌜āuttā! pālidosio kadhedi mah"|âliha|ladaṇeṇa teṇa aṅgulīaeṇa bhaṭṭiṇo paḍhama|bahu|madeṇa hodavvaṃ.⌟

ŚYĀLAḤ: ⌜ṇa ca tassiṃ mah"|âriha|radaṇaṃ ti bahu|māṇaṃ bhaṭṭiṇo takkemi.⌟

UBHE: ⌜kiṃ khu?⌟

ŚYĀLAḤ: ⌜takkemi tassa daṃsaṇeṇa ko vi ahilasido jaṇo bhaṭṭiṇā sumārido tti, jado taṃ pekkhia muhuttaṃ païdi|gambhīro payyussuamaṇo saṃvutto.⌟

(enter the) BROTHER-IN-LAW: Quickly, quickly, he. . . *(in mid-sentence)*

MAN: Oh! I'm dead! *(Mimes despair.)* 6.25

BROTHER-IN-LAW: Free him! Hey! Free the fisherman! His account of the ring's origin checks out. Our master has told me so himself.

FIRST: As the brother-in-law orders! Entering the house of Death he has slipped out again through a crack. *(He releases the man.)*

MAN: *(bowing to the brother-in-law)* Master! My life is yours.

BROTHER-IN-LAW: Get up! This reward, equal in value to the ring, is to be given to you.

MAN: *(accepting it joyfully)* I am favored. 6.30

FIRST: Favored to the extent of being taken down from impalement and set upon an elephant's back.

SECOND: Sister's husband! The reward reveals that the king must greatly value this ring with its precious stone.

BROTHER-IN-LAW: I do not think that his majesty valued it because of its precious stone.

BOTH: Why then?

BROTHER-IN-LAW: I hazard a guess that its sight reminded 6.35
his majesty of some cherished person, because upon seeing it he, normally so composed, showed for a moment a yearning.

DVITĪYAKAḤ: ⌜sādhu mantidaṃ ṇāma āutteṇa.⌟

PRATHAMAḤ: ⌜ṇaṃ bhaṇāmi imaśśa kade maścaliā|śattuṇo tti!⌟ *(iti puruṣam s'|āsūyaṃ paśyati.)*

PURUṢAḤ: ⌜bhaṭṭā! ido addham tumhāṇaṃ śumaṇo|mullaṃ bhodu⌟.

UBHAU: ⌜ittike jujjadi.⌟

6.40 ŚYĀLAḤ: ⌜dhīvara, mahattarako hi sampadaṃ pia|vaassako si me saṃvutto. kādambarī|sakkhiaṃ ca amhāṇaṃ paḍhama|sohidaṃ icchīadi. tā ehi suṇḍia|sālaṃ gacchamha.⌟

iti niṣkrāntāḥ.

praveśakaḥ.

SECOND: The sister's son has ably assisted him.

FIRST: I would say this fish-foe has benefitted! *(He looks at the man with malice.)*

MAN: Master! Let half of it be your flower-money.

BOTH: The decent thing to do.

BROTHER-IN-LAW: Fisherman, now you have become my 6.40
best friend. Our new friendship calls for endorsement by wine, so let's go to the tavern.

All go out.

End of the prelude.

(tataf praviśaty ākāśa|yātaken' Âkṣamālā.)

AKṢAMĀLĀ: ⌜ṇivattidaṃ mae payyāya|ṇivaṭṭanīam accharā| tittha|saṇṇijjhaṃ. tā jāva imassa rā'|êsiṇo udantaṃ paccakhī|karemi. Menaā|sambandheṇa sarīra|bhūdā me Saüntalā, tāe a etaṇ|ṇimittaṃ yeva sadiṭṭha|purav' amhi.⌟ *(parikramya puraḥ samantād avalokya ca)* ⌜kiṃ ṇu kkhu ūsavaṃ|diṇe vi ṇirūsav'|ārambhaṃ via rāa|ulaṃ dīsadi. adhavā atthi me vibhavo paṇidhāṇeṇa savvaṃ jāṇidum. kiṃ tu sahīe ādaro āṇidavvo. bhodu. imāṇāṃ dāva ujjāṇa|vāliṇīṇāṃ tirakkariṇī|pacchaṇṇā pāsa|parivattiṇī bhavia uvālahisse.⌟ *(tathā karoti.)*

6.45 *(tataf praviśati cūt'|âṅkuram avalokayantī ceṭī tasyāś ca pṛṣṭhato 'parā.)*

PRATHAMĀ:

⌜āamba|haria|veṇṭaa
  jo ūsasio 'si surahi|māsassa
diṭṭhŏ a cūa|cchāraa
  chaṇa|maṅgalaaṃ va pekkāmi.⌟

DVITĪYĀ: *(upasṛtya)* ⌜halā Parahudike! kiṇ·ṇ·edaṃ eāiṇī mantesi.⌟

PRATHAMĀ: ⌜sahi, cūḍa|ladiaṃ pekkhia ummattā parahudiā bhodi.⌟

6.50 DVITĪYĀ: *(sa|harṣaṃ)* ⌜kadhaṃ uvatthido mahu|māso?⌟

PRATHAMĀ: ⌜Mahu|arie, tav' êdāṇīṃ kālo eso mada|vibbham'|ôggīdāṇāṃ.⌟

(Enter Aksha·mala in an aerial vehicle.)

AKSHA·MALA: I have seen to my routine duties at the nymph's bathing-place. Now let me see for myself how fares the royal sage. Because of my friendship with Ménaka I have come to cherish Shakúntala, and she herself has sent me on this errand. *(walks forward, looking around)* How can it be that the royal court seems unprepared for festivity on a festival day? To tell the truth, I have the power to know anything by meditative concentration, but I must honor my friend's wishes. Very well, concealed by my spell of invisibility, I will find out by standing beside these two gardeners. *(Does so.)*

(Enter a servant girl examining a mango shoot, and behind her another.) 6.45

FIRST GARDENER:

> O spray of mango blossoms, seeing you,
> the exhalation of the spring month,
> with your green stalk tawny,
> It seems to me that I see a seasonal blessing.*

SECOND GARDENER: *(approaching)* Dear Para·bhrítika, what is it you are saying to yourself?

FIRST GARDENER: Friend, a cuckoo becomes intoxicated when she sees a mango tendril.*

SECOND GARDENER: *(joyfully)* Has spring arrived? 6.50

FIRST GARDENER: Madhu·kárika, now is the time for your songs intense with passion.

DVITĪYĀ: ⌜sahi, avalambassa jāva agga|pāda|paḍiṭṭhiviā bhavia Kāma|devassa accaṇaṃ karemi.⌟

PRATHAMĀ: ⌜jaï mamā vi addham accaṇaa|phalassa.⌟

DVITĪYĀ: ⌜halā! abhaṇide vi edam bhodi, jado ekkam yeva ṇo duhā|ṭhidam sarīram.⌟ *(sakhy|avalambitaṃ kṛtvā cūta|bhaṅgaṃ nāṭayati)* ⌜ammahe! appaḍibuddho vi cūda|pasavo eso bandhaṇa|bhaṅga|surahī vādi.⌟ *(kapotakaṃ kṛtvā)* ⌜ṇamo bhaavade maara|ddhajāa!⌟

⌜arihasi me cū'|aṅkura!
  diṇṇo Kāmassa gahia|dhaṇuassa
saṇṭhavia|juvaï|lakkho
  'pacchākkhalio saro houṃ!⌟

(cūt'|âṅkuraṃ kṣipati.)

(praviśya ruṣitaḥ kañcukī.)

KAÑCUKĪ: mā tāvad an|ātma|jñe! deven' âpramukhata eva pratiṣiddhe vasant'|ôtsave tvam atra mañjarī|bhaṅgaṃ ārabhase.

UBHE: *(bhīte)* ⌜pasīdadu ayyo! agahid'|atthā khu amhe.⌟

KAÑCUKĪ: hum! na khalu śrutaṃ yuvābhyāṃ yad yathā vāsantais tarubhir api devasya śāsanaṃ pramāṇīkṛtaṃ tad|āśrayibhiś ca? tathā hi—

SECOND GARDENER: My dear, hold me while I stand on tiptoe and worship the God of love.

FIRST GARDENER: If I get half of the fruit of the worship.

SECOND GARDENER: My dear! That goes without saying, for we are one in two bodies. *(mimes plucking a mango blossom supported by her friend)* Oho! Even though the mango blossom is as yet unopened it is fragrant as I break its stalk. *(making the pigeon gesture)* Hail to the crocodile-bannered God of love!

> O mango shoot! I offer you to the God of love, 6.55
> who has seized his bow,
> May you become an infallible arrow
> targetting young women!

(Throws the sprout.)

(Enter the enraged chamberlain.)

CHAMBERLAIN: Stop it, you foolish girl! When the spring festival has been expressly banned by his majesty, you start plucking blossoms.

BOTH: *(frightened)* Forgive us, lord! We heard nothing of this.

CHAMBERLAIN: Hmph! How can you not have heard his 6.60 majesty's command, which even the trees of spring and those living in them have obeyed? For–

cūtānāṃ cira|nirgat" âpi kalikā
badhnāti na svaṃ rajaḥ,
samnaddhaṃ yad api sthitaṃ kuravakaṃ
tat korak'|âvasthayā,
kaṇṭheṣu skhalitaṃ gate 'pi śiśire
puṃs|kokilānāṃ rutam
śaṅke saṃharati Smaro 'pi cakitas
tūṇ'|ârdha|kṛṣṭaṃ śaram.

AKṢAMĀLĀ: ⌜ṇa ettha saṃdeho! mahā|ppahāvo rā'|êsī.⌟

PRATHAMĀ: ⌜ayya, kadi diasā amhāṇaṃ Mittā|vasuṇā raṭṭhieṇa bhaṭṭiṇo pāda|mūlādo pesidāṇam, idha ā kīla|hare paḍikammaṃ appidaṃ. ado ṇa kadā vi suda|puravo eso amhehiṃ vuttanto.⌟

KAÑCUKĪ: bhavatu, na punar evaṃ vartitavyam.

6.65 UBHE: ⌜ayya, kodūhallaṃ ṇo. jaṃ imiṇā jaṇeṇa sodavvam tā kadhedu ayyo kiṃ ṇimittaṃ bhaṭṭiṇā vasanta|komidī paḍisiddhā tti?⌟

AKṢAMĀLĀ: ⌜ūsava|ppiā rāāṇo. ettha guruṇā kāraṇena hodavvam.⌟

KAÑCUKĪ: bahulī|bhūtam etat, tat kiṃ na kathyate? asti bhavatyoḥ karṇa|pathaṃ āyātaṃ Śakuntalā|pratyādeśa|kaulīnam?

UBHE: ⌜ayya! sudaṃ raṭṭhia|muhādo jāva aṅgulīaa|daṃsaṇam.⌟

The mango blossom, though mature,
  will not put forth its pollen,
The amaranth, though poised, will not bud,
The cooing of the male *koil* falters in its throat
  even though the winter has passed.
I fear that even the God of love, startled, puts down
  his arrow, half-drawn from his quiver.

AKSHA·MALA: There can be no doubt about it! Mighty is the royal sage.

FIRST GARDENER: Lord, the royal brother-in-law Mitra·vasu dispatched us for a few days from his majesty's presence to decorate the belvedere over there. That is why we had no news whatsoever of this matter.

CHAMBERLAIN: Very well, but do not do it again.

BOTH: Lord, we are curious. If we may know, please tell us 6.65
why his majesty has banned the vernal full-moon festival.

AKSHA·MALA: Kings are fond of festivities. There must be some weighty reason here.

CHAMBERLAIN: It is well known, so why should I not tell you? Has the scandal of Shakúntala's rejection reached your ears?

BOTH: Lord! We have heard of it from the king's brother-in-law, up to the disclosure of the ring.

KAÑCUKĪ: tena hi sv|alpaṃ kathayitavyam. yadā khalu sv'|âṅgulīyaka|darśanād anusmṛtaṃ devena «satyam ūḍha|pūrvā mayā rahasi tatra|bhavatī Śakuntalā mohāt pratyādiṣṭ" êti!» tadā|prabhṛty eva paścāt|tāpa|parigato devaḥ. kutaḥ?

6.70 ramyaṃ dveṣṭi, yathā|sukhaṃ prakṛtibhir
na pratyahaṃ sevyate,
śayy"|ôpānta|vivartanair vigamayaty
unnidra eva kṣapāḥ
dākṣiṇyena dadāti vācam ucitām
antaḥ|purebhyo yadā
gotreṣu skhalitaṃ tadā bhavati ca
vrīḍā|vilakṣaś ciram.

AKṢAMĀLĀ: ⌜piaṃ me!⌟

KAÑCUKĪ: prabhavato vaimanasyād utsava|pratiṣedha iti.

UBHE: ⌜jujjadi.⌟

NEPATHYE: ⌜edu edu bhavaṃ.⌟

6.75 KAÑCUKĪ: *(karṇaṃ dattvā)* ayam ita ev' âbhivartate devaḥ! sva|karm' ânuṣṭhīyatām. *(iti niṣkrānte ceṭike.)*

(tataḥ praviṣṭaḥ paścāt|tāpa|sadṛśa|veṣo rājā vidūṣakaḥ pratīhārī ca.)

KAÑCUKĪ: *(rājānam avalokya)* aho sarvāsv avasthāsu ramaṇīyatvam ev' ākṛti|viśeṣāṇām. samutsuko 'pi Śākuntalāṃ prati priya|darśano devaḥ. ya eṣa—

CHAMBERLAIN: Then there is little left to tell. When his majesty saw the ring he regained his memory: "It is really true, I did marry mistress Shakúntala in secret and reject her in a fit of delusion!" And since then he has been filled with remorse. How?

> He despises enjoyments, 6.70
> His subjects no longer approach him every day as they wish.
> He passes his nights fitfully tossing back and forth
>   on the end of the bed.
> When out of courtesy he makes
>   polite conversation
>   with the ladies of the inner chambers, he falters
>   in their names, and is ashamed for a long time.

AKSHA·MALA: I like the sound of this!

CHAMBERLAIN: The festival is cancelled because of his majesty's dejection.

BOTH: That makes sense.

OFFSTAGE: Come, come sir.

CHAMBERLAIN: *(listening)* His majesty is heading this way. 6.75
See to your duties! *(Exit the servant girls.)*

(Enter the king wearing a costume suitable to remorse, the buffoon, and the portress.)

CHAMBERLAIN: *(looking at the king)* Ah! The exceptionally beautiful are sublime in any condition. Though he pines for Shakúntala, his majesty is fair to behold. He who–

pratyādiṣṭa|viśeṣa|maṇḍana|vidhir
 vāma|prakoṣṭhe ślathaṃ
bibhrat kāñcanam ekam eva valayaṃ
 śvās'|ôparakt'|âdharaḥ
cintā|jāgaraṇa|pratānta|nayanas
 tejo|guṇād ātmanaḥ
saṃskār'|ôllikhito mahā|maṇir iva
 kṣīṇo 'pi n' ālakṣyate.

AKṢAMĀLĀ: ⌜ṭhāṇe kkhu paccādesa|vimāṇidā vi Saüntalā jaṃ imassa kade kila tammadi.⌟

6.80 RĀJĀ: *(dhyāna|mandaṃ parikramya)*

prathamaṃ sāraṅg'|âkṣyā
 priyayā pratibodhyamānam api suptam
anuśaya|duḥkhāy' êdaṃ
 hata|hṛdayaṃ samprati vibuddham.

AKṢAMĀLĀ: ⌜īdisāiṃ se tavassiṇīe bhāga|dheāiṃ.⌟

VIDŪṢAKAḤ: *(apavārya)* ⌜laṅghido eso bhūo Saüntalā|vādeṇa. ṇa āṇe kadhaṃ cikicchidavvo bhavissadi.⌟

KAÑCUKĪ: *(upagamya)* jayatu jayatu devaḥ. mahā|rāja! tāvad rājñaf pratyavekṣitāf pramadā|vana|bhūmayaḥ yathā|kāmam adhyāstāṃ vinoda|sthānāni devaḥ.

6.85 RĀJĀ: *(pratihārīṃ prati)* Vasumati, mad|vacanād amātya|Piśunaṃ brūhi. «cira|prabodhān na sambhāvitam asmābhir adya dharm'|āsanam adhyāsitum. yat pratyavekṣitaṃ āryeṇa paura|kāryam tat pattrakam āropya dīyatām iti!»

PRATĪHĀRĪ: ⌜jaṃ devo āṇavedi.⌟ *(iti niṣkrāntā.)*

Rejects ostentatious ornamentation,
Wears a loose, single golden bracelet
 on his left forearm,
His lower lip is reddened by sighing,
His eyes are languid with wakeful worries.
Because of his inherent brilliance
 he does not appear wasted, like a great jewel
 polished by abrasion.

AKSHA·MALA: Justifiably Shakúntala pines on his behalf, though he shamed her with rejection.

KING: *(walks around slowly, lost in thought)* 6.80

This wretched heart at first was asleep,
Though my doe-eyed beloved tried to wake it.
Now it has awakened to the grief of remorse.

AKSHA·MALA: The poor girl's fate is much the same.

BUFFOON: *(aside)* He's suffering another bout of the "Shakúntala"-disease. I don't know how he can be cured.

CHAMBERLAIN: *(approaching)* Victory, victory to his majesty! Great king! The royal parklands have been inspected so that you may visit them at your leisure.

KING: *(to the portress)* Vásumati, tell minister Píshuna in my 6.85
name that because of prolonged sleeplessness it is not possible for me to occupy the throne of justice today. Let his honor send me a written report on whatever civil cases he investigates today.

PORTRESS: As his majesty commands. *(Exit.)*

RĀJĀ: Pārvatāyana! tvam api sva|niyogam a|śūnyaṃ kuru.

KAÑCUKĪ: tathā! *(iti niṣkrāntaḥ.)*

VIDŪṢAKAḤ: ⌜kadaṃ bhavadā ṇimakkhiaṃ. sampadam sisira|vicchede ramaṇīe imassiṃ pamada|vaṇe suhaṃ viharissāmo.⌟

6.90 RĀJĀ: vayasya, yad ucyate «randhr'|ôpanipātino 'narthā iti» tad avyabhicāri. paśya—

upahita|smṛtir aṅguli|mudrayā
   priyatamām animitta|nirākṛtām
anuśayād anurodimi c' ôtsukaḥ
   surabhi|māsa|sukhaṃ samupasthitam.

VIDŪṢAKAḤ: ⌜ciṭṭha jāva. imaṃ daṇḍaaṃ cūda|mammadhae pāḍae.⌟

RĀJĀ: *(sa|smitam)* bhavatu. dṛṣṭaṃ brahma|varcasam. sakhe, atr' ôpaviṣṭaf priyāyāḥ kiṃ cid anukāriṇīṣu latāsu dṛṣṭim vilobhayāmi.

VIDŪṢAKAḤ: ⌜ṇaṃ khu bhavadā Medhāviṇī livi|karī sandiṭṭhā: «māhavī|maṇḍave imaṃ khaṇaṃ paḍivālaïssaṃ. tahiṃ me citta|phalae sa|hattha|lihidaṃ tattha|bhodīe Saüntalāe paḍikidim āṇehi tti.»⌟

6.95 RĀJĀ: īdṛśaṃ me hṛdaya|saṃsthānam. tat tam ev' ādeśaya mādhavī|maṇḍapam.

VIDŪṢAKAḤ: ⌜edu bhavaṃ.⌟ *(parikramataḥ. Akṣamāl" ânugacchati.)*

KING: Parvatáyana! You too see to your duties.

CHAMBERLAIN: Very well! *(Exit.)*

BUFFOON: You have got rid of the flies. Now that the winter is over we can relax at ease in this pleasant grove.

KING: My friend, the saying, "Mishaps strike at weaknesses" 6.90
is unfailing. Look—

> As I regain my memory through the signet ring
> and longingly lament with regret
> my beloved, baselessly rejected—
> The joy of the fragrant month of spring
> is at hand.

BUFFOON: Just a second. I will smite this staff upon that mango-cupid.

KING: Never mind. I have seen your brahminical potency. My friend, seated here I will beguile my eyes with these vines that somewhat imitate my beloved.

BUFFOON: But surely you have just informed the painter Medhávini: "I will spend some time in the *mádhavi* bower. Bring me the portrait of lady Shakúntala that I painted on a drawing board with my own hand."

KING: Such is the condition of my heart.* Lead the way to 6.95
the *mádhavi* bower.

BUFFOON: Come, Your Majesty. *(They walk about. Aksha·mala follows.)*

VIDŪṢAKAḤ: *(vilokya)* ⌜eso maṇi|silā|paṭṭaka|saṇādho māhavī|maṇḍavao vivittadāe ṇīsaddaṃ sāgadeṇa via paḍicchadi pia|vaassaṃ. uvavisamha. nisīdadu bhavaṃ.⌟ *(ubhau praviśy' ôpaviṣṭau.)*

AKṢAMĀLĀ: *(latām āśritya sthitā.)*

RĀJĀ: *(smaraṇam abhinīya)* sakhe Mādhavya, sarvam idaṃ smarāmi. Śakuntalāyāf prathama|darśana|vṛttānte yat kathitavān asmi bhavate. sa bhavān pratyādeśa|divase mat|samīpa|gato n' āsīt. prathamam api na tvayā kadā cit saṅkathāsu tatra|bhavatyāḥ kīrtitaṃ nāma. na khalv aham iva mithaḥ|saṃvidaṃ smṛto 'si.

6.100 VIDŪṢAKAḤ: ⌜ṇa visumarāmi. kiṃ tu savvaṃ kadhidaṃ tae yyeva vuttaṃ. parihāsa|viappo eso ṇa bhūd'|attho tti. rahassa|bheda|bhīruṇā mae vi mip|piṇḍa|maṇḍa|buddhiṇā tadhā yeva gahidaṃ. avi a bhavidavvadā balavadī.⌟

AKṢAMĀLĀ: ⌜evaṃ ṇ' êdaṃ.⌟

RĀJĀ: *(dhyātvā)* sakhe, paritrāyasva mām, paritrāyasva mām.

VIDŪṢAKAḤ: ⌜kiṃ ṇ' êdaṃ īdisaṃ uvaṇadaṃ? kadā uṇa sap|purisā soa|baddha|dhiyyā honti? ṇaṃ pavādeṇa vi girīo nippakampā.⌟

RĀJĀ: vayasya. nirākaraṇa|viplavāyāf priyāyāḥ samavasthām anusmṛtya balavad asvastho 'smi. sā mayā—

BUFFOON: *(looking)* This *mádhavi* bower, furnished with a jewelled stone bench, greets my dear friend with a soundless welcome. Let us enter. Take a seat, sir. *(Both enter and sit down.)*

AKSHA·MALA: *(Stands by a vine.)*

KING: *(acts remembrance)* Madhávya my friend. I remember it all. What I said to you the first time I saw Shakúntala.* On the day I rejected her you were not by my side. Even before, you never brought up her name in conversation. Surely you, like me, did not remember what we said to each other.

BUFFOON: I did not forget, on the contrary, you told me everything that happened. You said it was a kind of joke, not a fact. I, dimwitted like a clod of mud, afraid of divulging the secret, took it at face value. Also, fate is powerful. 6.100

AKSHA·MALA: That is true.

KING: *(daydreaming)* My friend, help me, help me.

BUFFOON: How have things got this far? How could the fortitude of good men be affected by grief? Surely mountains remain unshaken even by a storm wind.

KING: My friend. When I remember my beloved reduced to helpless panic, I am violently sick. She—

6.105 itaf pratyādiṣṭā
svaljanam anugantum vyavasitā
sthitā tiṣṭh' êty uccair
vadati guru|śiṣye guru|same
punar dṛṣṭiṃ bāṣpa-
prasara|kaluṣām arpitavatī
mayi krūre yat tat
sa|viṣam iva śalyaṃ dahati mām.

AKṢAMĀLĀ: ⌈ammahe īdisī kaṭṭh'|âvatthā. imassa santāveṇa ahaṃ rame.⌋

VIDŪṢAKAḤ: ⌈atthi deva takko. keṇa tattha|bhodī ākāsa|gāminā avahita tti.⌋

RĀJĀ: ka iva devatābhyo 'nyaḥ sambhāvyate. Menakā kila sakhyās te janma|pratiṣṭh" êti śrutavān asmi. tat|sakhībhis tām eva hṛtāṃ hṛdayam āśaṅkate.

AKṢAMĀLĀ: ⌈ammo! moho kkhu eso vimhaaṇīo ṇa uṇa paḍiboho.⌋

6.110 VIDŪṢAKAḤ: ⌈jaï evaṃ tā atthi kkhu samāgamo vi kāleṇa tattha|bhavadīe.⌋

RĀJĀ: katham iva?

VIDŪṢAKAḤ: ⌈ṇa kkhu mādā|pidaro bhaṭṭi|virahidaṃ duhidaraṃ ciraṃ pekkhiduṃ pārenti.⌋

RĀJĀ: vayasya.

svapno nu māyā nu mati|bhramo nu
kliṣṭaṃ nu tāvat phalam eva puṇyam?
asannivṛttyai tad atītam eṣa
mano|rathānām a|taṭa|prapātaḥ.

Driven out by me, 6.105
When she wanted to follow her own people
Commanded aloud: "Stay!"
  by her father's pupil,
  who was like her father,
  casting one more glance dimmed
    by flowing tears
  at cruel me—
All this stings me like a poisoned dart.

AKSHA·MALA: Ah! What agony. I delight in his pain.

BUFFOON: There is, You Majesty, this conjecture. Her ladyship must have been carried off by some sky-goer.

KING: Who other than a deity would be capable of this? I was told that Ménaka was the mother of your friend. My heart believes her to have been taken by her friends.

AKSHA·MALA: Oho! His confusion was surprising, but not his awakening to reason.

BUFFOON: If that is so then there will eventually be a reunion 6.110
with her ladyship.

KING: How so?

BUFFOON: Her mother and father will not long endure to see her separated from her husband.

KING: My friend.

Was it a dream? An illusion? A fallacy?
A hard-won reward of virtue?
Departed beyond recall
It is become this boundless precipice
  for my desires.*

6.115 VIDŪṢAKAḤ: ⌜mā evaṃ bhaṇa! ṇaṃ khu aṅgulīaaṃ yeva ṇidarisaṇaṃ. evaṃ yeva avassaṃ|bhāviṇo acintaṇīyā samāgamā honti.⌟

RĀJĀ: *(aṅgulīyakaṃ vilokya)* aye! idaṃ tad a|sulabha|sthāna|bhraṃśi śocanīyam.

tava sucaritam aṅgulīya nūnaṃ
 pratanu mam' êva vibhajyate phalena.
aruṇa|nakha|manoharāsu tasyāś
 cyutam asi labdha|padaṃ yad aṅgulīṣu.

AKṢAMĀLĀ: *(ātma|gatam)* ⌜sakhi, dūre vaṭṭasi. eāiṇī dāva kaṇṇa|suhaṃ aṇubhavāmi.⌟

VIDŪṢAKAḤ: ⌜bho vaassa! idaṃ aṅgulīaaṃ keṇa uggādeṇa tattha|bhodīe hattha|saṃsaggaṃ pāvidaṃ?⌟

6.120 RĀJĀ: śrūyatām! yadā tapo|vanāt sva|nagara|gamanāya prasthitaṃ māṃ priyā sa|bāṣpam idam āha: «kiyac|cireṇ' ārya|putro 'smākaṃ saṃsmariṣyat' îti.»

VIDŪṢAKAḤ: ⌜tado tado?⌟

RĀJĀ: paścād imāṃ nāma|mudrāṃ tad|aṅgulau niveśayatā mayā pratyabhihitām:

ek'|âikam atra divase divase madīyaṃ
 nām'|âkṣaraṃ gaṇaya gacchasi yāvad antam
tāvat priye mad|avarodha|gṛha|praveśī
 netā janas tava samīpam upaiṣyat' îti.

BUFFOON: Don't speak like that. Surely the ring itself is 6.115
proof. This is how fated, extraordinary reunions take place.

KING: *(looking at the ring)* Ah! This is the pitiable thing that fell from that inaccessible place.

> Your virtuous deeds, O ring,
> Indeed are triflingly rewarded,
> Like mine.
> You have fallen from her fingers,
> enchanting with reddened nails,
> where you had gained a place.

AKSHA·MALA: *(to herself)* My friend, you are far away. Alone, therefore, I revel in this pleasure for the ears.

BUFFOON: My friend! How did you endeavour to get this ring on to her ladyship's hand?

KING: Listen! As I set out from the penance grove to my 6.120
own city my beloved said this to me with tears in her eyes: "How long will my lord remember me?"

BUFFOON: Then? Then?

KING: Then I placed this signet ring on her finger and told her:

> One by one, day be day,
> Count a syllable of my name.
> When you reach the end, my beloved,
> Someone will come to guide you
> to bring you to my women's quarters.

. . . tac ca mohād dāruṇam anuṣṭhitam.

6.125 AKṢAMĀLĀ: ⌜ramaṇīo de vihiṇā daṃsido maggo.⌟

VIDŪṢAKAḤ: ⌜adha kadhaṃ dāsīe puttassa rohida|macchassa balisaṃ via edam aṅulīaam muhe paviṭṭhaṃ?⌟

RĀJĀ: Śacī|tīrtha|salilaṃ kila vandamānāyās te sakhyā Gaṅgā|srotasi paribhraṣṭam. bhavatu. upālapsye tāvad etat—

kathaṃ nu taṃ bandhura|komal'|âṅgulim
  karam vihāyāsi nimagnam ambhasi?
    athavā,
acetanaṃ nāma guṇān na lakṣayen
  may" âiva kasmād avadhīritā priyā?

AKṢAMĀLĀ: ⌜puvv'|âvvara|virodhī eso vuttānto vāṭṭadi.⌟

6.130 RĀJĀ: a|kāraṇa|parityaktā kad" ânupreksaṇīyā bhaviṣyati?

(tataf praviśati phalaka|hastā lipi|kārī.)

LIPI|KĀRĪ: *(samantād avalokya)* ⌜eso kkhu bhaṭṭā. jāva ṇaṃ uvasappāmi.⌟ *(upasṛtya)* ⌜jaadu, jaadu bhaṭṭā! iaṃ citta|gadā bhaṭṭiṇī.⌟ *(citra|phalakaṃ darśayati.)*

VIDŪṢAKAḤ: *(vilokya)* ⌜he he bho! sabhāva|mahurā āidī khu. sāhu vaassa sāhu. kiṃ bahuṇā? sānt'|âṇupavesa|saṅkāe ālavaṇa|kudūhalaṃ maṃ jaṇaadi.⌟

. . . and committed that horror in delusion.

AKSHA·MALA: Fate showed you a pleasing way. 6.125

BUFFOON: Then how did this ring get into the mouth of that wretched carp as if it were a hook?

KING: Your friend lost it in current of the Ganges as she paid homage to the water of Shachi-ford. Now let me rebuke it—

How could you forsake that hand
with its tender fingers arched
and sink into the water?
But no,
An insentient thing cannot discern virtues,
Yet how did I spurn my beloved?

AKSHA·MALA: The beginning and end of this story are at odds.

KING: When will I see her again, whom I gratuitously 6.130
spurned?

(Enter the artist with a painting board in her hand.)

ARTIST: *(looking around)* Here is His majesty, I will approach him. *(approaching)* Victory, victory, Your majesty! I bring the portrait of her ladyship. *(Shows the painting board.)*

BUFFOON: *(looking)* Hey hey hey! Really quite a natural beauty. Well done, my friend, well done. Why say more? Believing that her soul has entered it, I feel an urge to converse with it.

AKṢAMĀLĀ: ⌜aho, vaassassa vattikā|rehāe ṇiuṇadā! jāṇe sahī aggado me ciṭṭhadi.⌟

6.135 RĀJĀ: *(niḥśvasya)*

sākṣāt priyām upagatām apahāya pūrvaṃ
 citr'|ârpitām aham imāṃ bahu manyamānaḥ.
sroto|vahāṃ pathi nikāma|jalām atītya
 jāto 'smi re praṇayavān mṛga|tṛṣṇikāyām.

AKṢAMĀLĀ: ⌜aaṃ yeva savvaṃ paḍivaṇṇo jamhi vattukāmā.⌟

VIDŪṢAKAḤ: *(nirvarṇya)* ⌜bho, tiṇho attha|bhodīo dīsanti. savvāo daṃsaṇīāo. kadamā ettha dīsadi Saüntalā?⌟

AKṢAMĀLĀ: ⌜moha|dakkho tavassī. avassaṃ ṇa me paccakhā sahī.⌟

RĀJĀ: tvaṃ tāvat katamāṃ tarkayasi?

6.140 VIDŪṢAKAḤ: *(ciraṃ vilokya)* ⌜takkemi jā esā avasea|siṇiddha| pallavaṃ asoa|ladiaṃ saṃsidā siḍhila|kesa|bandh'|ôvva-manta|kusumeṇa baddha|sea|binduṇā vaaṇaeṇa visesa| ṇamida|sāhāiṃ bāhu|ladāhiṃ ūsasida|ṇīviṇā vasaṇena īsi parīsantā via ālihidā esā attha|bhodī Saüntalā. idarāo sahīo.⌟

RĀJĀ: nipuṇo bhavān. asty atra me bhāva|cihnam.

svinn'|âṅgulī|niveśo
 rekhā|prānteṣu dṛśyate malinaḥ
aśru ca kapola|patitaṃ
 lakṣyam idaṃ vartik"|ôcchvāsāt.

AKSHA·MALA: Oh! What skill in his companion's brushwork! I perceive my friend standing before me.

KING: *(sighing)* 6.135

At first I rejected my beloved
when she stood before me.
Sketched in a portrait, I show her respect.
Ignoring the river in my path,
overflowing with water,
I have come to yearn, alas, for a mirage.

AKSHA·MALA: He has just acknowledged all that I wanted to say.

BUFFOON: *(inspecting)* Three ladies can be seen. All of them are beautiful. Which one is Shakúntala?

AKSHA·MALA: The poor man is skilled at self-deception, my friend is not actually here.

KING: Which one do you think it is?

BUFFOON: *(gazing for a long time)* I guess this one who seems 6.140
fatigued, sketched as leaning against the vine on the *ashóka* tree, droplets of perspiration forming on her face shedding flowers from her loosened hair-tie, the vines that are her arms letting their branches droop low, the girdle of her garment untied, must be the lady Shakúntala. The others are her companions.

KING: You are clever. There is the telltale sign of my love.*

A smudge of moist fingerprints
can be seen on the outlines,
And a tear, fallen from my cheek
can be spotted by the splaying of the brush.

Medhāvini, ardha|likhitam etad vinoda|sthānam. gaccha. vartikāṃ tāvad ānaya.

LIPI|KĀRĪ: ⌜ayya mādhavva! avalambha citta|phalaaṃ jāva gacchāmi.⌟ *(iti vidūṣakāya dattvā niṣkrāntā.)*

6.145 VIDŪṢAKAḤ: ⌜kiṃ avaraṃ ettha ahilihidavvaṃ?⌟

AKṢA|MĀLĀ: ⌜asaṃsaaṃ jo jo sahīe me ahiruido padeso taṃ taṃ ālihidukāmo bhavissado tti takkemi.⌟

RĀJĀ: Mādhavya, śrūyatām.

kāryā saikata|līna|haṃsa|mithunā
  sroto|vahā Mālinī
pād'|ânte nibhṛtaṃ niṣaṇṇa|camare
  Gaurī|guroḥ pāvane
śākh"|âlambita|valkalasya ca taror
  nirmātum icchāmy adhaḥ
śṛṅge kṛṣṇa|mṛgasya vāma|nayanaṃ
  kaṇḍūyamānāṃ mṛgīm.

VIDŪṢAKAḤ: *(ātma|gatam)* ⌜tadhā takkemi pūridaṃ aṇeṇa citta|phalaaṃ kucc'|âlaehiṃ tāvasāṇaṃ ti.⌟

6.150 RĀJĀ: Mādhavya, anyac ca. Śakuntalāyāḥ prasādhanam abhiprītam atra vismṛtam asmābhiḥ.

VIDŪṢAKAḤ: ⌜kiṃ via?⌟

AKṢAMĀLĀ: ⌜vaṇa|vāsassa tassā a soamallassa jaṃ aṇusadisaṃ bhavissadi tti.⌟

Medhávini! The pleasure grove is half-finished. Go, fetch the brush.

ARTIST: Noble Madhávya! Hold the drawing board until I return. *(Gives it to the buffoon and goes out.)*

BUFFOON: What else needs to be painted here? 6.145

AKSHA·MALA: I think, without a doubt, he wants to paint all the places that my dear friend was fond of.

KING: Madhávya, listen.

> I must draw the river Málini
>   its sandy banks lined by pairs of wild geese,
> The valley of the holy foothills of Himálaya,
>   father of Gauri, where rest yaks,
>   And beneath the tree from which hang
>   bark-garments
> I want to sketch a doe rubbing her left eye
>   on the stag's horn.

BUFFOON: *(to himself)* In addition I think he will fill the painting with the bushy beards of ascetics.

KING: Madhávya, another thing. I forgot an ornament Shakúntala was fond of. 6.150

BUFFOON: What was it like?

AKSHA·MALA: Something befitting a forest-dweller and her tenderness.

RĀJĀ:

kṛtaṃ na karṇ'|ârpita|bandhanaṃ sakhe
  śirīṣam ā|gaṇḍa|vilambi|kesaram.
na vā śarac|candra|marīci|komalaṃ
  mṛṇāla|sūtraṃ racitaṃ stan'|ântare.

VIDŪṢAKAḤ: ⌜kiṃ ṇu attha|bhodī ratta|kuvalaa|sohiṇā agga|hattheṇa muhaṃ ovāria cakida|cakidā via ṭhidā.⌟ *(dṛṣṭvā)* ⌜he he bho! eso dāsīe putto kusuma|pāḍaccaro mahu|aro attha|bhodīe vaaṇa|kam alaṃ ahilasadi.⌟

6.155 RĀJĀ: nanu nivāryatām eṣa dhṛṣṭaḥ!

VIDŪṢAKAḤ: ⌜bhavaṃ yeva aviṇīd'|âṇusāsī vāraṇe pahavadi.⌟

RĀJĀ: yujyate. «ayi bhoḥ! kusuma|latā|priy'|âtithe, kim itaf paripatana|khedam anubhavasi?»

eṣā kusuma|niṣaṇṇā
  tṛṣit" âpi satī bhavantam anuraktā
pratipālayati madhu|karī
  na khalu madhu vinā tvayā pibati.

AKṢAMĀLĀ: ⌜ahijādaṃ khu vārido.⌟

6.160 VIDŪṢAKAḤ: ⌜paḍisiddha|vāmā esā jādī.⌟

RĀJĀ: evaṃ bhoḥ! «na me śāsane tiṣṭhasi. śrūyatāṃ tarhi saṃprati.»

KING:

My friend, I have not drawn the *shirísha* flower,
with its stalk fixed to her ear,
and its filaments hanging down to her cheek,
Nor the necklace of lotus fibres,
mild like the rays of the autumn moon
draped between her breasts.*

BUFFOON: Now why does the lady seem startled, shielding her face with her fingers, as beautiful as red lilies? *(looking)* Hey hey hey! This son of a slave, this flower-raider, this bee, is hungry for her ladyship's lotus face.

KING: Go on, chase this impertinent vandal away! 6.155

BUFFOON: Only you, the chastiser of the wicked, are capable of warding him off.

KING: That's right. "Ho! You are a welcome guest to every flowering vine. Why are you tiring yourself flitting around here?"

There waits your loving she-bee
nestling in a flower.
Although she is thirsty
She will not drink nectar without you.

AKSHA·MALA: What a graceful dismissal.

BUFFOON: His kind can become stubborn when chased away. 6.160

KING: You are right! "You will not abide by my command, so hear me now."

akliṣṭa|bāla|taru|pallava|lobhanīyaṃ
  pītaṃ mayā sa|dayam eva rat'|ôtsaveṣu
bimb'|âdharaṃ daśasi ced bhramara priyāyās
  tvāṃ kārayāmi kamal'|ôdara|bandhana|stham!

VIDŪṢAKAḤ: ⌜evaṃ tikkha|daṇḍassa kadhaṃ de ṇa bhāissadi?⌟ *(prahasya, ātma|gatam)* ⌜eso unmattao kkhu! ahaṃ pi īdisassa saṃsaggeṇa īdisa|vaṇṇo via saṃvutto.⌟

AKṢAMĀLĀ: ⌜mam' âvi attaṇo aṇantaram gaṇehi jā ahaṃ dāṇiṃ paḍibuddhā.⌟

6.165 RĀJĀ: priye! sthito 'yam etāvati?

AKṢAMĀLĀ: ⌜aho! dhīre vi jaṇe raso padaṃ karedi.⌟

VIDŪṢAKAḤ: ⌜bho, cittaṃ khu edaṃ.⌟

RĀJĀ: *(sa|viṣādam)* vayasya, kim idam anuṣṭhitaṃ pauro|bhāgyam?

darśana|sukham anubhavataḥ
  sākṣād iva tanmayena hṛdayena
smṛti|kāriṇā tvayā me
  punar api citrīkṛtā kāntā.
(roditi.)

6.170 AKṢAMĀLĀ: ⌜vaassa, sumaridaṃ tae paccādesa|vimāṇaṇaṃ Saüntalāe sahīe diṭṭhaṃ khu paccakhaṃ amhehiṃ.⌟

LIPI|KĀRĪ: *(praviśya)* ⌜bhaṭṭā, devīe Kula|ppahāe parijaṇeṇa antarā avacchiṇṇo de vattiā|karaṇḍao.⌟

If you, O bee, bite my beloved's lower lip
red like a *bimba* fruit,
as appealing as a virgin bud on a young tree,
that I tenderly drunk in a celebration of passion,
I will imprison you in a lotus!

BUFFOON: With such harsh punishment how could he not be terrified of you? *(laughing, aside)* He really is stark raving mad! I too have become tainted by his company.

AKSHA·MALA: Count also me who is now awakened.

KING: My beloved! Is he still there? 6.165

AKSHA·MALA: Ah! Love can overwhelm even a resolute man.

BUFFOON: It is a picture.

KING: *(sadly)* My friend, why show me such malice?

While I was enjoying the bliss of seeing her,
my heart absorbed,
seemingly before me
you, reawakening my memory,
once more made her into a painting.
(Weeps.)

AKSHA·MALA: My friend, I have indeed seen with my own 6.170
eyes that you remember the disrespect you showed by rejecting Shakúntala.

ARTIST: *(entering)* Lord, your paintbox has fallen into the hands of the entourage of Queen Kula·prabha.

RĀJĀ: bhavatu, vayam apy akṣamāḥ samprati vartikā|karmaṇi.

AKṢAMĀLĀ: ⌜bahu|maṇṇā se Kula|ppahā. adha vā ṇa edaṃ kiṃ ci. vipañcie kkhu asannidhāṇe eka|tantū vi agghadi.⌟

RĀJĀ: vayasya, paśya. katham aviśrāma|duḥkham anubhavāmaḥ?

6.175 prajāgarāt khalī|bhūtas
tasyāḥ svapne samāgamaḥ
bāṣpo 'pi na dadāty enāṃ
draṣṭuṃ citra|gatām api.

LIPI| KĀRĪ: ⌜bhaṭṭā, idaṃ pi dāṇiṃ citta|paḍikidaṃ Piṅgaliā|missīo avahaṭhṭhidaṃ yadanti.⌟

VIDŪṢAKAḤ: ⌜bhiṇṇā dāṇiṃ se āsā!⌟

RĀJĀ: hum! *(stan'|ântare hastaṃ nikṣipati.)*

NEPATHYE: ⌜jaadu jaadu bhaṭṭiṇī!⌟

6.180 VIDŪṢAKAḤ: *(karṇaṃ dattvā)* ⌜avedha bho! Medhāviṇiṃ maïṃ via anusarantī uvatthidā ante|ura|vvagghī Piṅgalikā.⌟

RĀJĀ: vayasya, imāṃ rakṣa priyā|pratikṛtim.

VIDŪṢAKAḤ: ⌜«attāṇaaṃ ti» bhaṇāhi!⌟

KING: Very well, I am now anyway not in the frame of mind for painting.

AKSHA·MALA: He holds Kula·prabha in high regard. But it means nothing. If a *vipañchi* lute is not at hand, then a single stringed lute is prized.

KING: My friend, look. Why do I suffer pain with no respite?

> Wakefulness foils reunion with her in a dream; 6.175
> tears will not let me see her in a painting.

ARTIST: Lord, Píngalika and her friends are on their way to manhandle the portrait.

BUFFOON: Now his hope is dashed!

KING: Ah! *(Places his hand on his chest.)*

OFFSTAGE: Victory, victory mistress!

BUFFOON: *(listening)* Oh dear! Píngalika, the tigress of the 6.180
women's quarters, is upon us, tracking Medhávini like a deer.

KING: My friend, protect this portrait of my beloved.

BUFFOON: You mean to say I should protect yourself.

AKṢAMĀLĀ: ⌜sahi, esā paḍikidī vi de paḍivakkhassa alaṅghaṇīā karīadi.⌟

VIDŪṢAKAḤ: *(phalakam ādāya)* ⌜eso ṇaṃ tahiṃ govemi jattha pārāvadim vajjia avaro ṇa pekkhadi.⌟ *(druta|padam niṣkrāntaḥ.)*

6.185 PRATĪHĀRĪ: *(praviśya patra|hastā)* ⌜jaadu jaadu devo!⌟

RĀJĀ: Vasumati! na khalu devy āgatā?

PRATĪHĀRĪ: ⌜bhaṭṭā, patta|hatthaṃ maṃ pekkhia paḍiṇivuttā.⌟

RĀJĀ: kāla|jñā kāry'|ôparodhaṃ me pariharati.

PRATĪHĀRĪ: ⌜deva, amacco viṇṇavedi. attha|jādassa gaṇanā|bahuladāe ekkaṃ yeva pora|kayyaṃ avekkhidaṃ, taṃ devo soḍhuṃ arihadi.⌟

6.190 RĀJĀ: Medhāvini, vācyatām!

LIPI|KĀRĪ: ⌜jaṃ bhaṭṭā āṇavedi.⌟ *(pattrakaṃ prasārya vācayati)* «viditam astu deva|pādānāṃ yathā Dhana|vṛddha iti yath"|ârtha|nāmā vaṇig vārī|path'|ôpajīvī nau|vyasane vipannaḥ. sa c' ân|apatyaḥ. tasya koṭi|śata|saṃkhyātaṃ vasu. tad idānīṃ rāj'|ârtham āpadyate. śrutvā rājā pramāṇam iti.»

RĀJĀ: *(ā|kampitaḥ)* kaṣṭā khalv an|apatyatā. Vasumati! mahā|dhanatvād bahu|patnīkena tatra|bhavatā bhavitavyam. vicāryatāṃ yadi kadā cid āpanna|sattvā k" âpi tasya bhāryā syāt.

AKSHA·MALA: My friend, even this portrait is removed from you, a foe.

BUFFOON: *(taking the board)* I will hide it where none but turtle-doves will see it. *(Exit with a quick step.)*

PORTRESS: *(entering with a letter)* Victory, victory to Your 6.185
majesty!

KING: Vásumati! Has the queen not come?

PORTRESS: Lord, she turned back when she saw me bearing a missive.

KING: She is mindful of timing and avoids interfering with my business.

PORTRESS: Lord, the minister reports that because of the large volume of affairs he investigated only one citizen's case. Your majesty should look at it.

KING: Medhávini, read it! 6.190

SCRIBE: As your majesty commands. *(opens the document and reads)* "Let it be known to his majesty that the aptly named merchant Dhana·vriddha* who trafficked by sea has perished in a shipwreck. He is without issue. His wealth amounts to thousands of millions. This now falls to the royal estate. Hearing this, may the king make a ruling."

KING: *(shaken)* It is a misery to have no children. Vásumati! Because he was wealthy he must have had many wives. Enquire whether one of his wives may be pregnant.

PRATĪHĀRĪ: ⌜deva, idāṇiṃ yeva Kesava|seṭṭhiṇo duhidā ṇivutta|puṃsavaṇā jāā suṇīadi.⌟

RĀJĀ: nanu garbhaf pitryaṃ riktham arhati. gaccha. evam ārya|Piśunaṃ brūhi.

6.195 PRATĪHĀRĪ: ⌜jaṃ deva āṇavedi!⌟ *(prasthitā.)*

RĀJĀ: ehy ehi tāvat.

PRATĪHĀRĪ: *(nivṛtya)* ⌜iamhi.⌟

RĀJĀ: api ca tatra|bhavān vaktavyaḥ. kim anena saṃtatir asti n' âst' îti.

yena yena viyujyante
   prajāḥ snigdhena bandhunā
sa sa pāpād ṛte tāsāṃ
   Duḥṣyanta iti ghoṣyatām.

6.200 PRATĪHĀRĪ: ⌜idaṃ ṇāma itthaṃ ghosidavvaṃ.⌟ *(niṣkramya punaf praviṣya ca)* ⌜deva, kāle ghuṭṭhaṃ iva ahiṇandidaṃ deva|sāsaṇaṃ mahā|aṇeṇa.⌟

RĀJĀ: *(dīrgham nihśvasya)* evaṃ santati|cheda|niravalambānāṃ mūla|puruṣāṇām avasāne sampadaf param upatiṣṭhante. mam' âpy ante Pūru|vaṃśa|śriya eṣa eva vṛttāntaḥ.

PRATĪHĀRĪ: ⌜paḍihadaṃ āsaṅkidam!⌟

RĀJĀ: dhiṅ māṃ upasthita|śreyo 'vamāninam!

AKṢAMĀLĀ: ⌜asaṃsaaṃ sahiṃ yeva hiae kadua ṇindido ṇeṇa attā.⌟

PORTRESS: Lord, just now we have learnt that his wife, the daughter of the guildsman Késhava, has performed the pregancy rite to ensure the birth of a son.

KING: Well then the unborn child is entitled to the father's inheritance. Go, tell the honorable Píshuna so.

PORTRESS: As his majesty commands! *(Departs.)* 6.195

KING: Come back for a second.

PORTRESS: *(returning)* Here I am.

KING: Tell his honor this too. What does it matter whether he has children or not?

> Proclaim that whatever dear kinsman
> my subjects lose,
> Dushyánta will take his place,
> if they are free from sin.

PORTRESS: So it will indeed be proclaimed. *(exits and re-* 6.200
enters) Your majesty, the people rejoiced in your proclamation as they do in timely thunder.*

KING: *(sighing deeply)* This is how, when the last male of the family, unsupported through the severing of the lineage, passes away, wealth passes to another. When I die this too will befall the glory of the Puru line.

PORTRESS: May this prospect not come to pass!

KING: Shame on me for reviling the good that providence brought to me!

AKSHA·MALA: No doubt he is blaming himself because of my friend.

6.205 RĀJĀ:

saṃropite 'py ātmani dharma|patnī
  tyaktā mayā nāma kula|pratiṣṭhā
kalpiṣyamāṇā mahate phalāya
  vasuṃ|dharā kāla iv' ôpta|bījā.

LIPI| KĀRĪ: *(jan'|ântikam)* ⌜imaṃ pattakaṃ pesaanteṇa kiṃ sumāridaṃ amacceṇa jaṃ pekkhia dāva bhaṭṭiṇo jal'|âvaseo saṃvutto?⌟ *(vicintya)* ⌜adhavā ṇa so abuddhi|puravaṃ pavaṭṭadi.⌟

RĀJĀ: aho Duḥṣyantasya saṃśayam ārūḍhāf piṇḍa|bhājaḥ.

asmāt paraṃ bata yathā|śruta|sambhṛtāni
  ko naḥ kule nivapanāni kariṣyat' îti
nūnaṃ prasūti|vikalena mayā pramuktaṃ
  dhaut'|âśru|śeṣam udakaṃ pitaraf pibanti.

6.210 AKṢAMĀLĀ: ⌜sadisaṃ khu de vavadhāṇam! vaattho pahū avarāsu devīsu aṇurūva|putta|jammaṇā puvva|purisāṇāṃ ariṇo bhavissadi tti.⌟ *(sva|gatam)* ⌜ṇa me vaaṇaṃ paḍigeṇhadi! adhavā aṇurūvaṃ yeva osaham ādaṅkaṃ ṇivāredi.⌟

RĀJĀ: *(śok'|āvega|nāṭitakena)*

ā|mūla|śuddha|santati
  kulam etat Pauravaṃ prajā|vandhye
mayy astam|itam an|ārye
  deśa iva Sarasvatī|srotaḥ. *(saṃmohaṃ gataḥ.)*

KING: 6.205

I have abandoned my lawful wife,
the foundation of my family,
though my self was embedded in her—
She who will bear a great fruit,
just as does the earth
in which a seed is sown in the right season.

SCRIBE: *(aside)* What did the minister have in mind when he sent this missive, that, once he saw it, would dampen his majesty's spirits? *(reflecting)* But no, he would not act without forethought.*

KING: Ah! Dushyánta has imperiled his ancestors.

After me, alas, who in our family can prepare
the offerings prescribed by the sacred law?
Surely my ancestors are drinking for water
the clear tears I shed,
I who am incomplete without offspring.

AKSHA·MALA: A characteristic oversight! A lord in the prime 6.210
of his life will settle his debt to the ancestors through the birth of a worthy son by another queen. *(to herself)* He cannot hear my words! Or rather, only the right medicine can cure the disease.

KING: *(miming grief)*

This Páurava lineage, pure from its beginning
comes to a close since I, unworthy,
have no offspring
Just as the River Sarásvati seeps away
in an unworthy desert. *(Faints.)*

PARIJANAḤ: *(sa|sambhramam avalokya)* ⌜samassasadu samassasadu bhaṭṭā!⌟

AKṢAMĀLĀ: ⌜idāṇīṃ yeva ṇaṃ ṇivvudaṃ karemi. adhavā mahadīhiṃ uṇa devadāhim edaṃ daṃsidaṃ. ṇa sakko mae aṇ|aṇuṇṇādāe hattha|saṃsaggaṃ ṇeduṃ. bhodu. jaṇṇa|bhā|osuāo devāo yyeva tadhā karaïssanti. jadhā eso rā'|êsī tāe saha|dhamma|cāriṇīe samāgamissadi.⌟ *(nabho 'valokya, sa|harṣam)* ⌜karaïssanti kadhaṃ yeva tahi pekkhāmi! jāva imiṇā vuttanteṇa pia|sahiṃ samassāsemi⌟ *(udbhrāntakena niṣkrāntā.)*

6.215 NEPATHYE: ⌜abbamhaṇṇaṃ abbamhaṇṇaṃ bhoḥ! abbamhaṇṇaṃ!⌟

RĀJĀ: *(śanaiḥ pratyāśvasya, karṇaṃ dattvā)* aye! Mādhavyasy' êv' ārta|nādaḥ.

LIPI|KĀRĪ: ⌜tavassī Piṅgaliā|mīsāṇaṃ muhe paḍido bhavissadi.⌟

RĀJĀ: Vasumati, gaccha mad|vacanād a|niṣiddha|parijanāṃ devīm upālabhasva.

PRATĪHĀRĪ: tathā *(iti niṣkrāntā.)*

6.220 RĀJĀ: param'|ârtha|bhīta iva bhinna|svaro brāhmaṇaḥ. kaḥ ko 'tra bhoḥ.

(praviśya) KAÑCUKĪ: ājñāpayatu devaḥ!

RETINUE: *(looking on with alarm)* Wake up lord, wake up!

AKSHA·MALA: I will end his pain here and now. But no, the High Gods have decreed this. Without permission I may not lend a hand. Let it be. The gods, eager for their share of sacrifice, will arrange the royal sage's reunion with his wife. *(looking at the sky, joyfully)* I will watch how they manage it. So let me comfort my dear friend with this news. *(Flies upwards.)*

BEHIND THE SCENE: Sacrilege, sacrilege, help! Sacrilege! 6.215

KING: *(regaining consciousness, listening)* Ah! It seems to be Madhávya's call of distress.

ARTIST: The poor fellow must have fallen into the jaws of Mistress Píngalika.

KING: Vásumati, go and admonish the queen in my name for not restraining her retinue.

PORTRESS: As you wish. *(Exit.)*

KING: The brahmin's voice falters as if he were really afraid. 6.220
Who is in attendance?

(enter the) CHAMBERLAIN: Command, you majesty!

RĀJĀ: kim eṣa Mādhavyo māṇavakaḥ krandati?

KAÑCUKĪ: deva, yāvad avalokayāmi. *(niṣkramya saṃbhramāt punaf praviṣṭaḥ.)*

RĀJĀ: Pārvatāyana! na khalu kiṃ|cid ātyayikam?

6.225 KAÑCUKĪ: deva, n' âivam.

RĀJĀ: tat kuto 'yaṃ vepathuḥ? kiṃ tu

prāg eva jarasā kampaḥ
  sa|viśeṣaṃ tu sāmpratam
āviṣkaroti sarv'|âṅgam
  aśvattham iva mārutah.

KAÑCUKĪ: tat paritrāyatāṃ suhṛdaṃ mahā|rājaḥ.

RĀJĀ: kasmāt paritrātavyaḥ?

6.230 KAÑCUKĪ: mahataḥ kṛcchrāt!

RĀJĀ: aye! a|nirbhinn'|ârtham ucyatām!

KAÑCUKĪ: deva, yo 'sāv abhraṃ|liho nāma prāsādaḥ. . .

RĀJĀ: kiṃ tatra?

KING: Why is that boy Madhávya wailing?

CHAMBERLAIN: Your Majesty, I will go and see. *(Exit and return with alarm.)*

KING: Parvatáyana! Surely it is not a matter of life-and-death?

CHAMBERLAIN: No, your majesty. 6.225

KING: Then what is he afraid of? But,

> The tremor which before was brought on
> by your old age, now your whole body
> displays it exceedingly,
> like an *ashváttha* tree in the wind.

CHAMBERLAIN: So protect your friend, great king.

KING: Protect him from what?

CHAMBERLAIN: From great hardship! 6.230

KING: Ah! Say something that makes sense!

CHAMBERLAIN: Your majesty, that palace called the "cloud-licker"...

KING: What's going on there?

KAÑCUKĪ:

6.235 tasy' âgra|bhūmer gṛha|nīla|kaṇṭhair
anekaׅ|viśranti|vilaṅghya|śṛṅgam
sakhā prakāś'|êtara|mūrtinā te
sattvena ken' âpi nigṛhya nītaḥ.

RĀJĀ: *(sahas" ôtthāya)* mā tāvat! mam' âpi sattvair abhibhūyante gṛhāḥ. athavā bahu|pratyavāyaṃ nṛpatvam.

ahany ahany ātmana eva tāvaj
jñātuṃ pramādaskhalitaṃ na śakyam
prajāsu kaḥ kena pathā prayāt' îty
aśeṣataḥ kasya nu śaktir asti?

NEPATHYE: ⌜dhāva bho!⌟

RĀJĀ: *(gati|bhedena parikrāman)* sakhe, na bhetavyam, na bhetavyam.

6.240 *(nepathye)* VIDŪṢAKAḤ: ⌜kadhaṃ dāṇiṃ ṇa bhāissaṃ? eso maṃ ko vi pacchā|moḍida|siro|dharam ikkhuṃ via thira|bhaṅgaṃ yava karidum icchadi!⌟

RĀJĀ: *(sa|dṛṣṭi|kṣepam)* dhanur dhanus tāvat!

(praviśya śārṅga| hastā Yavanī) ⌜jaadu jaadu bhaṭṭā! edam sar'|āsaṇaṃ hatth'|āvāpa|sahitam.⌟

RĀJĀ: *(sa|śaraṃ dhanur ādatte.)*

CHAMBERLAIN:

From the spire on its highest point, 6.235
reached by tame peacocks after taking many breaks
your friend has been abducted
by some kind of an invisible fiend.

KING: *(jumping up)* It cannot be! Even my home is invaded by fiends. Kingship is beset with many reversals.

From day to day it is not even possible to know
one's own unmindful lapses.
Who has the power to know in full
who among his subjects takes which path?

OFFSTAGE: Please run!

KING: *(changing his pace)* My friend, have no fear, have no fear.

(offstage) BUFFOON: How could I not be afraid? Someone is 6.240
strangling my neck from behind and is trying to crush me like sugar-cane!

KING: *(casting a glance)* My bow, my bow!

(The Ionian woman enters bow-in-hand.) Victory, victory, Lord! Here is your bow and the wrist-guard.

KING: *(Takes up his bow and arrows.)*

NEPATHYE:

6.245 eṣa tvām abhinava|kaṇṭha|śoṇit'|ârthī
śārdūlaf paśum iva hanmi veṣṭamānam
ārtānāṃ bhayam apanetum ātta|dhanvā
Duḥṣyantas tava śaraṇaṃ bhavatv idānīm.

RĀJĀ: *(sa/roṣam)* kathaṃ mām evam uddiśati? tiṣṭha tiṣṭha kula|pāṃsana! ayam idānīṃ na bhavasi. *(cāpam ādāya)* Pārvatāyana! sopāna|mārgam ādeśaya.

KANCUKĪ: ita ito deva. *(sarve satvaram upasarpanti.)*

RĀJĀ: *(samantād vilokya)* śūnyaṃ khalv idam.

(nepathye) VIDŪṢAKAḤ: ⌜ahidhāva bho! ahaṃ bhavantaṃ pekkhāmi. eso bhavaṃ maṃ ṇa pekkhadi. majjāra|gahido via unduro ṇirāso|mhi jīvide saṃvutto.⌟

6.250 RĀJĀ: bhoḥ! tiraskariṇī|garvita madīyam astraṃ tvām paśyati. sthito bhava! mā ca vayasya|samparkād viśvāso 'bhūt. eṣa tvad|arthaṃ tam iṣuṃ saṃdadhe,

yo haniṣyati vadhyaṃ tvāṃ
rakṣyaṃ rakṣiṣyati dvijam
haṃso hi kṣīram ādatte
tan|miśrā varjayaty apaḥ.

(astraṃ saṃdhatte.)

OFFSTAGE:

> I, eager for the fresh blood from your neck, 6.245
> will kill you as I hold you fast like a tiger does its prey.
> Let Dushyánta, taking up his bow
> to allay the fear of the distressed be your protection now.

KING: *(angrily)* Is he mocking me? Stay where you are, stay where you are, you disgrace to your family! Now you will not prevail. *(taking his bow)* Parvatáyana! show me to the stairs.

CHAMBERLAIN: This way, this way, your majesty. *(All come rushing.)*

KING: *(looking all around)* But it is empty.

(behind the curtain) BUFFOON: Hurry! I can see you. You cannot see me. I have lost all hope of life, like a mouse caught by a cat.

KING: O you proud of your invisibility, my arrow will see 6.250
you. Stand still! Take no comfort from your contact with my friend. For you I draw this arrow,

> Which will slay you who deserve death and
> will protect the brahmin worthy of protection,
> for a swan will take the milk
> but discard the water mixed with it.

(Aims the arrow.)

(praviśya saṃbhrānto vidūṣakam utsṛjya Mātalir vidūṣakaś ca.)

MĀTALIḤ: āyuṣman!

6.255 kṛtā śaravyā Hariṇā tav' âsurāḥ
śar'|āsanaṃ teṣu vikṛṣyatām idam
prasāda|saumyāni satāṃ suhṛj|jane
patanti cakṣūṃṣi na dāruṇāḥ śarāḥ.

RĀJĀ: *(astram upasaṃharan)* aye Mātaliḥ! sv|āgataṃ Deva|rāja|sārathaye!

(praviśya) VIDŪṢAKA: *(nikaṭam etya)* ⌜bho! ahaṃ ṇeṇa pasu|māreṇa mārido maṇamhi!⌟

MĀTALIḤ: *(sa|smitam)* āyuṣman, śrūyatāṃ yad asmi Hariṇā bhavat|sakāśaṃ preṣitaḥ.

RĀJĀ: avahito 'smi.

6.260 MĀTALIḤ: asti Kāla|nemi|prasūtir Durjayo nāma dānava|gaṇaḥ.

RĀJĀ: śruta|pūrvo mayā Nāradāt.

MĀTALIḤ:

sakhyus te sa kila Śatakrator avadhyas
tasya tvaṃ raṇa|śirasi smṛto nihantā
ucchettuṃ prabhavati yan na sapta|saptis
tan naiśaṃ timiram apākaroti candraḥ.

(Enter the agitated Mátali releasing the buffoon, and the buffoon.)

MÁTALI: Your Majesty!

> Indra has made the demons to be your targets, 6.255
> draw your bow against them.
> Good men's eyes, mild with favor,
> fall upon a friend, not cruel arrows.

KING: *(withdrawing his arrow)* Oh! Mátali! Welcome to the charioteer of the King of the Gods.

BUFFOON: *(entering, coming close)* Hey! This monster nearly killed me!

MÁTALI: *(smiling)* Your honor, hear why Indra dispatched me to you.

KING: I am attentive.

MÁTALI: There is a demon lord called Dúrjaya, the spawn of Kala·nemi. 6.260

KING: I have already heard of this from Nárada.

MÁTALI:

> It is said that your friend Indra cannot kill him.
> It is said that you can be his slayer in the forefront
> of the battle.
> The darkness of the night that the sun is powerless
> to dispel
> the moon can drive away.

tad bhavān gṛhīta|cāpa ev' êdānīm Aindraṃ ratham adhiruhya vijayāya pratiṣṭhatām.

6.265 RĀJĀ: anugṛhītam anayā Maghavataḥ sambhāvanayā. atha bhavadbhir Mādhavyaṃ prati kim evaṃ prayuktam?

MĀTALIḤ: *(sa|smitaṃ vidūṣakam avalokya)* tad api kathyate. kuto 'pi kiṃ|nimittān manas|tāpād āyuṣmān mayā viklavo dṛṣṭaḥ. paścāt kopayitum āyuṣmantaṃ tathā kṛtavān asmi. kutaḥ?

jvalati calit'|êndhano 'gnir
  viprakṛtaf pannagaf phaṇaṃ kurute
prāyaḥ svaṃ mahimānaṃ
  kṣobhāt pratipadyate jantuḥ.

RĀJĀ: *(jan'|ântikam)* vayasya Mādhavya! an|atikramaṇīyā Divaḥ|pater ājñā. tad atra parigat'|ârthaṃ kṛtvā mad|vacanād amātya|Piśunaṃ brūyāḥ:

tvan|matiḥ kevalā tāvat
  paripālayatu prajāḥ
adhijyam idam anyasmin
  karmaṇi vyāpṛtaṃ dhanuḥ.

6.270 VIDŪṢAKAḤ: ⌜jaṃ bhavaṃ āṇavedi.⌟ *(iti niṣkrāntaḥ.)*

MĀTALIḤ: ita āyuṣmān.

iti parikramya niṣkrāntāḥ sarve.

ṣaṣṭho 'ṅkaḥ.

So take now your bow, mount Indra's chariot, and go forth to victory.

KING: I am favored by Indra's esteem. But why did you manhandle Madhávya in that way? 6.265

MÁTALI: *(looking at the buffoon with a smile)* Let me tell you. I perceived that Your majesty was, for some reason, depressed with regret. Thereafter I acted to awaken Your majesty's wrath. Why?

A fire blazes up when its fuel is stirred,
a serpent expands its hood when it is threatened,
a man usually regains his own spirit
when he is roused.

KING: *(aside)* My friend Madhávya! The decree of the Lord of heaven cannot be flouted. So inform minister Píshuna of what has transpired here and tell him in my name:

May your acuity alone
for now protect the subjects.
This strung bow is now employed
in another matter.

BUFFOON: As his majesty commands. *(Exit.)* 6.270

MÁTALI: This way, your honor.

All walk about and exit.

Thus ends the sixth act.

ACT SEVEN: THE ABSOLUTION

(tataḥ praviśati Nākalāsikā.)

NĀKALĀSIKĀ: ⌜āṇattaṃ hi guruṇā Ṇāraeṇa jahā edesu yyeva diasesu macca|loado uttiṇṇeṇa rāesiṇā Dussanteṇa bhaavado Purandarassa pi'|āriṇā dāṇava|vaha|ṇimittaṃ gantavvaṃ. jāva abbhaccia imaṃ hy āpucchīamāṇo ṇikkhivadi tāva yyeva mae vibuha|paccakkhaṃ maṅgala|ṇimittam kiṃ pi pekkhaṇaaṃ darasaïdavvaṃ. «tā tumaṃ kaṃ pi lāsiaṃ aṇṇesia saṅgīda|sālāe āgaccha tti.» tā jāva lāsiaṃ aṇṇesemi.⌟ *(parikramy' âvalokya ca)* ⌜kā puṇa esā gahida|varaṇā pacchā harisid'|ukkaṇṭhidā via ido ev' āgacchadi?⌟ *(nipuṇam avalokya)* ⌜kadhaṃ pisa|sahī Cūda|mañjarī? tā jāva edāe saha uvajjhāa|samīvaṃ gacchāmi.⌟ *(iti pratipālayati.)*

(tataḥ praviśati yathā|nirdiṣṭā lāsikā.)

CŪTAMAÑJARĪ: *(sa|vismayaṃ sa|harṣaṃ ca)* ⌜aho! mahā|ppahāvo rāesī Dussanto! *(s'|âsūyam)* aho, mahā|balo so hado Dujjao dāṇava|balo.⌟ *(vicārya)* ⌜adhavā Dussanto yyeva jeṇa sāradhi|dudīeṇa yyeva aṇea|paharaṇa|sāhasāiṃ vikiranto khaṇeṇa yyeva ṇihado so Dujjaya|dāṇāva|balo.⌟ *(nṛtyati.)*

7.5 PRATHAMĀ: ⌜sahi Cūda|mañjarie. ukkaṇṭhidā via lakkhīasi?⌟

DVITĪYĀ: *(vilokya)* ⌜kadhaṃ, Pārijāda|mañjarī? sahi, savvaṃ kadhaïssaṃ. tumaṃ dāva kahiṃ patthida tti pucchissaṃ?⌟

PRATHAMĀ: ⌜sahi, saṅkheveṇa kadhaïssaṃ. ahaṃ khu rāesiṇo Dussantassa dāṇava|vijaa|vavadeseṇa ajja maṅgala|ṇimittaṃ kiṃ pi pekkhaṇaaṃ daṃsīadi tti uvajjhāassa āṇāe ubhe yyeva saāsaṃ.⌟

(Enter a celestial dancer.)

CELESTIAL DANCER: My teacher Nárada has told me that, these days, the royal sage Dushyánta, ascending from the world of mortals, has gone to slay a demon at the bidding of blessed Indra. After I saluted him and sang his praises he charged me with staging a performance as a blessing for good fortune in front of an audience of experts. "Go find a dancer and come to the pavilion of dance!" So now I am looking for a dancer. *(strolls about gazing)* Who is this coming my way, seemingly yearning and satisfied at once, as if she had just received an ornament.* *(looks carefully)* Why, it's my dear friend Chuta·máñjari! Well, I will bring her along to the teacher.* *(She waits.)*

(Then enters, as described, a dancer.)

CHUTA·MÁÑJARI: *(astonished and delighted)* Oh! What great power the royal sage Dushyánta has. *(scornfully)* Oh! The mighty demon Dúrjaya is slain. *(reflecting)* To be precise, Dushyánta alone with his charioteer, scattering countless thousands of missiles, in a flash annihilated the powerful demon Dúrjaya. *(She dances.)*

FIRST: My friend Chuta·máñjari. You seem lovelorn? 7.5

SECOND: *(looking)* Is it you, Parijáta·máñjari? My friend, I will tell you everything. But first, let me ask, where are you going?

FIRST: My friend, I will tell you in brief. I have been instructed by the preceptor to stage something celebratory today on the occasion of the royal sage Dushyánta's triumph over the demon, so we are both going to see him.

DVITĪYĀ: *(s'|ôtkaṇṭham)* ⌜āsi avasaro edassa. idāṇīṃ puṇo macca|loaṃ patthide edassiṃ mahā|rāe kassa daṃsīadi?⌟

PRATHAMĀ: *(s'|āśaṅkam)* ⌜sahi, kiṃ Mahendassa maṇo|radhā sampādia gado uda aṇṇadha tti?⌟

7.10 DVITĪYĀ: ⌜sahi, suṇu! ajja yyeva go|sagga|samaeṇa varaṃ Dujjaa|dāṇava|jīvida|savvassa|sesam geṇhia jāva a tiasa|vilāsiṇī sa|rasa|hiaāiṃ avaṇim ahippaṭṭhido. ado a me haris'|ôkkhaṇṭhāṇaṃ kāraṇaṃ.⌟

PRATHAMĀ: ⌜sahi, tae piaṃ ṇivedidaṃ jaṃ yeva uvajjāeṇa Puru|vaṃsa|rāesiṇo purado kayyam kādum āṇattaṃ. taṃ yeva gīdaṃ kadua ettha yyeva karemha.⌟

DVITĪYĀ: ⌜jaṃ de roadi evaṃ taṃ. jaṃ yeva gīdaṃ mae lavidaṃ tae vā saha ṇaccamha.⌟

PRATHAMĀ: ⌜sahi, evaṃ karemha.⌟ *(ubhe gāyataḥ.)*

⌜*a|visaa|gamaṇaṃ* kaṃ caṇa
  aṇṇaṃ ca sa|rāaṃ ālī mahu|samao
aṇṇaṃ kuṇaï visaṇṇaṃ
  pāḍaliĕ imāĕ bhūmīe.⌟

7.15 *(ity ante nartitvā niṣkrānte.)*

praveśakaḥ.

SECOND: *(with longing)* There may be cause for this. But now that the king is leaving to the world of mortals, for whom do we stage it?

FIRST: *(concerned)* My friend, did he leave after fulfilling great Indra's wishes or otherwise?

SECOND: My friend, listen! This very day, early in the morn- 7.10
ing he departs to earth, taking with him as a boon what remained of the demon Dúrjaya's life—and the affectionate hearts of the heavenly women. That is why I am at once happy and filled with longing.

FIRST: My friend, you bring me glad tidings: we are commanded by the preceptor to perform before the royal sage of the Puru lineage. Let's compose a song and sing it here.

SECOND: However you like. We can dance together to my song or your recitation.

FIRST: My friend, that is what we will do. *(Both sing.)*

> Springtime
> turns one bee *away from objects of sense:*
> *towards illicit behaviour,*
>   fills another with passion,
>   and makes another despondent,
> with the redness of its grounds.

(They dance at the end and exit.) 7.15

End of the prologue.

(tataf praviśaty ākāśa|yānena rath'|âdhirūḍho rājā Mātaliś ca.)

RĀJĀ: Mātale! anuṣṭhita|nideśo 'pi Maghavataḥ satkriyā|viśeṣād anupayuktam iv' ātmānaṃ samarthaye.

MĀTALIḤ: āyuṣman, ubhayam apy aparitoṣam. kutaḥ?

7.20 upakṛtya Hares tathā bhavāl̄
laghu satkāram avekṣya manyate
gaṇayaty apadāna|sammitāṃ
bhavataḥ so 'pi na satkriyām imām.

RĀJĀ: mā m" âivam. sa khalu mano|rathānām apy atibhūmi|vartī visarjan'|âvasare satkāraḥ. mama hi divaukasāṃ samakṣam ardh'|āsan'|ôpaveśitasya—

antar|gata|prārthanam antara|sthaṃ
Jayantam udvīkṣya kṛta|smitena
pramṛjya vakṣo hari|candan'|âktaṃ
mandāra|mālā Hariṇā pinaddhā.

MĀTALIḤ: kim iva n' āyuṣmān amareśvarād ārhati. paśya

sukha|parasya Harer ubhayaiḥ kṛtaṃ
tri|divam uddhṛta|dānava|kaṇṭakam
tava śarair adhunā nata|parvabhif
Puruṣa|kesariṇaś ca purā nakhaiḥ.

(Enter the king and Mátali on a flying vehicle.)

KING: Mátali! Alhough I have obeyed Indra's command, I consider myself unworthy because of the high regard he showed me.

MÁTALI: Your majesty, both of you are unrequited. How so?

After rendering such help to Indra 7.20
you think it trifling
when you consider his high regard.
He, for his part,
does not reckon this honor equal
to your great deed.

KING: It is not so. The honor shown to me as I departed greatly exceeded even my wishes. As I sat on half of his throne before the gods—

Indra, smilingly gazing at Jayánta,
who stood beside him,
—secretly aspiring to this honor—garlanded
me with a wreath of heavenly coral-flowers,
rubbing them against his chest daubed with
yellow sandal.*

MÁTALI: How could you not deserve it from the King of the Gods? Behold,

Two things extricated the thorns,
—the demons—from heaven
for Indra, who wishes for happiness:
your smooth arrows
and long ago the Man-lion's claws.

7.25 RĀJĀ: atra Śatakrator eva mahimā. paśya—

sidhyanti karmasu mahatsv api yan niyojyāḥ
sambhāvanā|guṇam avehi tam īśvarāṇām
kiṃ prābhaviṣyad Aruṇas tamasāṃ vadhāya
taṃ cet Sahasra|kiraṇo dhuri n' âkariṣyat.

MĀTALIḤ: sadṛśaṃ tav' âitat. *(stokam antaram atītya)* āyuṣman! itaf paśya, nāka|pṛṣṭha|pratiṣṭhitasya saubhāgyam ātma|yaśasaḥ.

vicchitti|śeṣaiḥ sura|sundarīṇāṃ
varṇair amī kalpa|lat"|ântareṣu
saṃcintya gīta|kṣamam artha|tattvaṃ
divaukasas tvac|caritaṃ likhanti.

RĀJĀ: Mātale, asura|samprahārā|utsukena pūrvaṃ dūram adhirohatā na lakṣito mayā svarga|mārgaḥ. tat katamasmin pathi marutām vartāmahe?

7.30 MĀTALIḤ:

tri|srotasaṃ vahati yo gagana|pratiṣṭhām
jyotīṃṣi vartayati cakra|vibhakta|raśmiḥ
tasya vyapeta|rajasaf Pravahasya vāyor
mārgo dvitīya|hari|vikrama|pūta eṣaḥ.

RĀJĀ: tataḥ khalu me sa|bāhya|antaḥ|karaṇo 'ntar|ātmā prasīdati. *(rath'|âṅge vilokya)* śaṅke megha|patham avatīrṇau svaḥ.

KING: Therein lies Indra's greatness. Look— 7.25

Know that when their servants succeed,
even in a great endeavour,
it is due to the honor
the great show their servants.
Would Dawn have the power to slay darkness,
if the thousand-rayed Sun did not place him
in the forefront of his chariot.

MÁTALI: That is worthy of you. *(proceeds a bit further)* Your majesty! Look here, the splendor of your fame has reached the vault of heaven.

The gods reflecting upon the significance
of your deed
paint it on the exteriors of the wishgranting vines
with the leftover makeup of the heavenly nymphs.

KING: Mátali, as I ascended yesterday, eager to fight the demon, I took no note of the geography of heaven. In which heavenly region are we travelling?

MÁTALI: 7.30

This is the region of the vapor-free Praváha-wind,
purified by the second step of Vishnu
which bears the celestial cascade
of the triple-streamed Ganges
and, with rays refracted in circles
makes the luminaries revolve.

KING: So that is why my inner self and my inner and outer senses are tranquil. *(looking at the wheels)* I think we have descended to the region of clouds.

MĀTALIḤ: *(sa|smitam)* katham avagamyate?

RĀJĀ:

7.35 ayam ara|vivarebhyaś cātakair niṣpatadbhir
haribhir acira|bhāsāṃ tejasā c' ânuliptaiḥ
gatam upari ghanānāṃ vāri|garbh'|ôdarāṇām
piśunayati rathas te śīkara|klinna|nemiḥ.

MĀTALIḤ: kṣaṇam ūrdhvam āyuṣmān ātm'|âdhikāra|bhūmau vartiṣyate.

RĀJĀ: *(adho 'valokya)* Mātale, veg'|âvataraṇād āścarya|darśanaḥ khalu sampadyate manuṣya|lokaḥ. tathā—

śailānām avarohat' îva śikharād
unmajjatāṃ medinī
parṇeṣv antara|līnatāṃ vijahati
skandh'|ôdayāt pādapāḥ
sandhānaṃ tanu|bhāva|naṣṭa|salilā
vyaktā vrajanty āpagāḥ
ken' âpy utkṣipat" êva paśya bhuvanaṃ
mat|pārśvam ānīyate.

MĀTALIḤ: *(sa|bahumānam ālokya)* aho udagra|ramaṇīyā pṛthivī.

7.40 RĀJĀ: Mātale, katamo 'yaṃ pūrv'|âpara|samudr'|âvagāḍhaḥ kanaka|niṣyanda|śobhī sāṃdhya iva megha|parighaḥ sānumān ālokyate?

MÁTALI: *(smiling)* How did you guess?

KING:

Your chariot 7.35
with *chátaka* birds flying through
the gaps between its spokes,
with its horses tinged by lightning flashes,
its fellies damp,
betrays that it has passed above
clouds pregnant with rain.

MÁTALI: In a moment you will be in the world you rule.

KING: *(looking down)* Because of our swift descent the world of mortals appears strange. For—

The earth seems to recede
from the emerging mountains,
the trees give up their concealment
by leaves as their trunks rise up,
the rivers,
deprived of water by their thinness,
made whole, become visible.
Look! It is as if has thrown up the earth
and brought it near to me.

MÁTALI: *(looking respectfully)* Ah, the earth is beautiful beyond compare.

KING: Mátali, which mountain is this, plunging into the 7.40
eastern and western oceans, resplendent, dripping with gold like a wall of clouds at sunset?

MĀTALIḤ: āyuṣman, eṣa Hema|kūṭo nāma kimpuruṣa|parvataf, paraṃ tapasvināṃ siddhi|kṣetram. paśya—

Svāyambhuvo Marīcer yaf
prababhūva Prajāpatiḥ
sur'|âsura|guruḥ so 'smin
sa|patnīkas tapasyati.

RĀJĀ: *(s'|ādaraṃ)* tena hy an|atikramaṇīyāni śreyāṃsi, pradakṣiṇīkṛtya bhagavantaṃ gantum iyāva.

MĀTALIḤ: prathamaḥ kalpaḥ! *(avataraṇaṃ nāṭayitvā)* etāv avatīrṇau svaḥ.

7.45 RĀJĀ: *(sa|vismayam)* Mātale!

upoḍha|śabdā na rath'|âṅga|nemayaf pravartamānaṃ na ca dṛśyate rajaḥ a|bhūtala|sparśanatayā niruddhatis tav' âvatīrṇo 'pi ratho na lakṣyate.

MĀTALIḤ: etāvān eva Śatakrator āyuṣmataś ca viśeṣaḥ.

RĀJĀ: katamasmin pradeśe Māric'|āśramaḥ?

MĀTALIḤ: *(hastena darśayan)*

MÁTALI: Your majesty, this is Golden Peak, the mountain of the *kim·púrushas*, the greatest place for ascetics to attain of spiritual power.

Praja·pati, born
from the self-existent Maríchi
the parent of the gods and demons,
practices austerities here with his wife.

KING: *(respectfully)* Good fortune must not be overlooked. Let us circumambulate and go to the blessed one.

MÁTALI: Our primary duty! *(acting the descent)* We have descended.

KING: *(with amazement)* Mátali! 7.45

The fellies of the wheel make no sound,
no dust is seen to be set in motion.
Although your chariot has alighted it has gone unnoticed,
—it has not jolted because it has not touched the earth.

MÁTALI: That is the extent of the difference between you and Indra.

KING: Which way to Máricha's hermitage?

MÁTALI: *(indicates with his hand)*

7.50 valmīk'|ârdha|nimagna|mūrtir uraga-
tvag|brahma|sūtr'|ântaraḥ
kaṇṭhe jīrṇa|latā|pratāna|valaye-
n' âtyartha|sampīḍitaḥ
aṃsa|vyāpi śakunta|nīḍa|nicitaṃ
bibhraj jaṭā|maṇḍalam
yatra sthāṇur iv' âcalo munir asāv
abhyarka|bimbaṃ sthitaḥ.

RĀJĀ: namo 'smai kaṣṭa|tapase!

MĀTALIḤ: *(saṃyata/pragrahaṃ kṛtvā)* etāv Aditi|parivardhita|mandāra|vṛkṣakaṃ Prajāpates tapo|vanaṃ praviṣṭau svaḥ.

RĀJĀ: aho vismayaḥ! svargād adhika|nirvṛtti|sthānam amṛta|hradam iv' âvagāḍho 'smi.

MĀTALIḤ: *(rathaṃ sthāpayitvā)* avatīryatām!

7.55 RĀJĀ: *(s'|âbhinayam avatīrya)* bhavān, katham idānīm?

MĀTALIḤ: samyantrito 'yam āste rathaḥ. vayam apy avatarāmaḥ. *(tathā kṛtvā)* ita ita āyuṣman. *(ubhau parikramya)* āyuṣman, dṛśyantām atra|bhavatām siddharṣīṇāṃ tapo|vana|bhūmayaḥ.

RĀJĀ: nanu vismayād ubhayam apy avalokayāmi.

Where that sage stands facing the sun, 7.50
immobile like a post,
His body half buried in an anthill,
wearing a second sacred thread made of
snake-skin,
his throat crushed by the coil
of a withered vine's runner,
bearing a mass of matted hair covering his
shoulders, full of bird's nests.

KING: Homage to the great ascetic!

MÁTALI: *(secures the reins.)* Now we have entered the penance grove of Praja·pati, where the coral-trees are tended by Áditi.

KING: How amazing! I seem to be immersed into a pool of nectar, a place of greater repose than is heaven.

MÁTALI: *(stopping the chariot)* Descend!

KING: *(acts descending)* What now? 7.55

MÁTALI: *(both walk about)* The secured chariot remains here. I too will get down. *(does so)* This way, this way, Your majesty. *(both walk about)* Your majesty, behold the penance groves of the perfect sages.

KING: But I look upon both with wonder:

prāṇānām anilena vṛttir ucitā
sat|kalpa|vṛkṣe vane
toye haima|sahasra|pattra|subhage
naktaṃ|divaṃ sad|vratam
dhyānaṃ ratna|śilā|gṛheṣu vibudha|
strī|saṃnidhau saṃyamo
yat kāṅkṣanti tapobhir anya|munayas
tasmiṃs tapasyanty amī.

MĀTALIḤ: utkarṣiṇī khalu mahatāṃ prārthanā. *(parikramataḥ. ākāśe)* vṛddha|śākalya kiṃ|vyāpāro bhavān? *(karṇaṃ dattvā)* kiṃ bravīṣi? eṣa Dākṣāyaṇyā pati|vratā|puṇyam adhikṛtya pṛṣṭaḥ, tasyās tad vyākarot' îti pratipāly'|âvasaraḥ khalu prastāvaḥ. *(rājānaṃ dṛṣṭvā)* asminn aśoka|pādape tāvad āyuṣmān āstām yāvat tvām Prajā|pataya āvedayāmi.

7.60 RĀJĀ: yathā bhavān manyate *(sthitaḥ)*

(niṣkrānto) MĀTALIḤ:

RĀJĀ: *(nimittaṃ sūcayitvā)*

mano|rathāya n' āśaṃse
bāho sphurasi kiṃ vṛthā?
pūrv'|âvadhīritaṃ śreyo
duḥkhaṃ hi parivartate.

NEPATHYE: ⌜mā khu mā khu cabaladaṃ karehi! siṅgha, kadhaṃ kadhaṃ yeva attaṇo pakidiṃ daṃsesi.⌟

In a forest of wishgranting trees,
they are used to maintaining the vital energies
by means of air,
in water blessed with thousands of golden leaves
they perform their twilight ablutions,
in jewelled caves they meditate,
in the midst of heavenly nymphs they practise restraint,
—in the midst of that which other sages strive for
with their penances,
these sages perform their austerities.

MÁTALI: High-minded are the wishes of the great. *(They walk about; Mátali calls in the air)* Old Shakályа! How is his honor engaged? *(listening)* What do you say? He has been asked by Áditi about the virtues of a good wife and he is explaining them to her, therefore my petition must await an opportune moment. *(looking at the king)* Sit by this *ashóka* tree until I announce you to Praja·pati.

KING: As you wish. *(Waits.)* 7.60

MÁTALI: *(Exit.)*

KING: *(acting a portent)*

I have no hope for my desire,
O arm, why are you throbbing in vain?
Previously scorned good fortune,
turns into grief.

OFFSTAGE: Don't! Don't misbehave! Lion, how you show your character.

7.65 RĀJĀ: *(karṇaṃ dattvā)* abhūmir iyam avinayasya. ko nu khalv avinayaṃ niṣidhyate? *(śabd'|ânusāreṇ' âvalokya, vismay'|âbhinaya|pūrvakam)* aye! anurudhyamānas tāpasībhyām abāla|sattvo bālaḥ.

ardha|pīta|stanaṃ mātur
  āmarda|kliṣṭa|kesaram
vilambinaṃ siṃha|śiśuṃ
  kāreṇ' āhatya karṣati.

(tataf praviśati yathā|nirdiṣṭa|karmā tāpasībhyām anurudhyamāno bālaḥ.)

BĀLAḤ: ⌜jimbha! jimbha, le śiṅgha! dantāiṃ de gaṇaïssaṃ.⌟

PRATHAMĀ: ⌜aviṇīda! ki tti ṇo avacca|ṇivvisesāiṃ sattāiṃ vippakaresi? pavaṭṭadi de saṃrambho. thāṇe kkhu isi|jaṇeṇa «Savva|damaṇo» tti kida|ṇāma|heo si.⌟

7.70 RĀJĀ: kiṃ nu khalu bāle 'sminn aurasa iva putre snihyati me manaḥ? *(vicintya)* nūnam an|apatyatā māṃ vatsalayati.

DVITĪYĀ: ⌜esā kesariṇī tumaṃ laṅghedi jaï se puttaaṃ ṇa muñcesi.⌟

BĀLAḤ: *(sa|smitam)* ⌜ammahe! baliam khu bhīde mhi!⌟ *(ity adharaṃ daśayati.)*

RĀJĀ: *(sa|vismayam)*

mahatas tejaso bījaṃ
  bālo 'yaṃ pratibhāti me
sphuling'|âvasthayā vahnir
  edhopekṣa iva sthitaḥ.

KING: *(listening)* This is no place for misdemeanor. Who can it be that metes out justice? *(his gaze traces the sound, acts surprise)* Oh! It is a boy not young in strength of character, being restrained by two female ascetics. 7.65

Striking a baby lion with his hand,
he drags it along,
its mane dishevelled by rough handling,
resisting,
half finished drinking from its mother's breast.

(Enter a boy, engaged as described, being restrained by two female ascetics.)

BOY: Open your jaws! Hey, open your jaws, lion! I want to count your teeth.

FIRST ASCETIC: Bad boy! Why are you hurting the animals who are no different than children to us? Your vehemence is increasing. Rightly the sages call you Sarva·dámana.*

KING: *(pondering)* Why should my heart take to this boy as if he were my own? *(pondering)* It must be that my childlessness makes me fond of children. 7.70

SECOND ASCETIC: That lioness will pounce on you if you will not release her son.

BOY: *(smiling)* Oh, I'm terrified! *(Bites his lip.)*

KING: *(amazed)*

This child seems to me a seed
of great brilliance,
like fire in its spark-state,
waiting for fuel.

7.75 PRATHAMĀ: ⌜vacchaa! muñca edam bālaṃ maïndaṃ. aṇṇaṃ de kīḷaṇaaṃ dāissaṃ.⌟

BĀLAḤ: ⌜kahiṃ śe? dehi me eṇaṃ!⌟ *(iti dakṣiṇa|hastaṃ prasārayati.)*

RĀJĀ: kathaṃ? cakra|varti|lakṣaṇam anena dhāryate. tathā hy asya—

pralobha|vastu|praṇaya|prasārito
  vibhāti jāla|grathit'|âṅguliḥ karaḥ
a|lakṣya|pattr'|ântaram iddha|rāgayā
  nav'|ôṣasā bhinnam iv' âika|paṅka|jam.

PRATHAMĀ: ⌜suvvade, ṇa sakko eso āsāsa|metteṇā sañjāmidum. tā gaccha. mama kerae uḍae Maṅkaṇaassa isi|kumāraassa vaṇṇaa|cittido maṭṭia|maūrao ciṭṭhadi. taṃ se uvāhara.⌟

7.80 DVITĪYĀ: ⌜tadhā!⌟ *(iti niṣkrāntā.)*

BĀLAḤ: ⌜tāva imiṇā yeva kīḷiśaṃ.⌟

TĀPASĪ: *(vilokya hasati.)*

RĀJĀ: spṛhayāmi durlalitakāy' âsmai. *(niḥśvasya.)*

FIRST ASCETIC: Child! Let go of this baby lion! I will give you another toy. 7.75

BOY: Where is it? Give it to me! *(He stretches out his right hand.)*

KING: What? He bears the mark of an emperor. For—

His hand, extended to request
a thing he is enticed by,
  its fingers webbed,*
shines like a solitary lotus,
  the gaps between its petals not yet visible,
as it begins to open with the red glow
  of the early dawn.

FIRST: My dear, it is not possible to restrain him with promises. So go, in my hut there is a brightly painted clay peacock belonging to the infant seer Mánkanaka. Fetch it for him.

SECOND: As you say! *(Exit.)* 7.80

BOY: For now I will just play with this one.

ASCETIC: *(Looking, laughs.)*

KING: I am drawn to this stubborn child. *(Sighs.)*

ālakṣya|danta|mukulān a|nimitta|hāsair
  avyakta|varṇa|ramaṇīya|vacaḥ|pravṛttīn
aṅk'|āśraya|praṇayinas tanayān vahanto
  dhanyās tad|aṅga|rajasā paruṣī|ābhavanti.

7.85 TĀPASĪ: *(s'|âṅguli|tarjanam)* ⌜bhodu! ṇa maṃ gaṇayasi!⌟ *(pārśvam avalokya)* ⌜ko ettha isi|kumāraāṇaṃ?⌟ *(rājānaṃ dṛṣṭvā)* ⌜bhadda|muha! ehi, moāvehi dāva imiṇā dummoha|hatth|aggeṇa ḍimba|kariṇā bādhīamāṇaṃ bāla|maïndaaṃ.⌟

RĀJĀ: tathā! *(ity upagamya)* ayi maharṣi|putra!

evam āśrama|viruddha|vṛttinā
  saṃyamī kim iti janmadas tvayā
sattva|saṃśraya|sukho 'pi dūṣyate
  kṛṣṇa|sarpa|śiśun" êva candanaḥ.

TĀPASĪ: ⌜bhodu, ṇa kkhu aam isi|kumārao.⌟

RĀJĀ: ākāra|sadṛśaṃ ceṣṭitam ev' âsya kathayati. sthāna|pratyayāt tu vayam atarkiṇaḥ. *(siṃhaṃ mocayitvā yath"|âbhyarthitam anuṣṭhitam. bāla|sparśam anubhūy' ātmagatam)*

7.90 anena kasy' âpi kul'|âṅkureṇa
  spṛṣṭasya gātreṣu sukhaṃ mam' âivam!
kāṃ nirvṛtiṃ cetasi tasya kuryād
  yasy' âyam aṅgāt kṛtinaf prasūtaḥ.

Lucky are they, who
carrying their sons
  become grubby with the dust
    from their bodies,
whose teeth blossom forth in causeless laughter,
whose speech is delightfully indisinct,
who are fond of resting on their father's laps.

ASCETIC: *(threatening with her finger)* All right! You will not heed me! *(looking aside)* Are any of the hermit boys here? *(seeing the king)* Kind sir! Please come and free the tormented lion cub from this unruly boy whose grip is hard to loosen. 7.85

KING: Indeed! *(approaches)* Here now, son of a great seer!

Why are you thus dishonoring
  your self-possessed father
—as a young cobra does a sandal-tree—
with deeds out of keeping with a hermitage,
  even though it pleases him
  that beings take refuge in him?

ASCETIC: Actually, this is no young seer.

KING: His actions which befit his appearance betray him. I was misled by relying on his surroundings. *(He does as requested by releasing the lion. To himself after touching the boy.)*

Such is my joy 7.90
  as my limbs touch this child
  of someone elses family!
What delight must he bring to him
  from whose body he has sprung.

TĀPASĪ: *(ubhāv avalokya)* ⌜acchariaṃ, acchariaṃ!⌟

RĀJĀ: kim iva?

TĀPASĪ: ⌜assa bālassa a|sambaddhe vi bhadda|muhe saṃvādiṇī āidi tti vimhidamhi. avi a accanta|pariidassa via appaḍilomo eso de saṃvutto.⌟

RĀJĀ: *(bālam upalālayan)* na cen muni|kumāro 'yam atha ko 'sya vyapadeśaḥ?

7.95 TĀPASĪ: Puru|vaṃso.

RĀJĀ: *(sva/gatam)* katham ek'|ânvayo mama? ataḥ khalu mad|anukāriṇam atra|bhavatī manyate. *(prakāśam)* asty etat Pauravāṇām antyaṃ kula|vratam.

bhavaneṣu sudhā|siteṣu pūrvaṃ
  kṣiti|rakṣ'|ârtham uśanti ye nivāsam
niyat'|âika|yati|vratāni paścāt
  taru|mūlāni gṛhī|bhavanti teṣām.

na punar ātma|gatyā mānuṣāṇām eṣa viṣayaḥ.

TĀPASĪ: ⌜ṇaṃ jadhā bhadda|muho bhaṇādi. acchara|saṃbandheṇa uṇo imassa bālassa jaṇaṇī ettha yyeva guruṇo tavo|vaṇe pasūdā.⌟

7.100 RĀJĀ: *(ātma/gatam)* dattaṃ dvitīyam idam āśaṅkā|jananam. *(prakāśam)* tatra|bhavatī kim|ākhyasya rājarṣef patnī?

TĀPASĪ: ⌜ko tassa dhamma|dārā|pariccāiṇo ṇāma|heaṃ geṇhissadi?⌟

RĀJĀ: *(sva/gatam)* iyaṃ khalu kathā mām eva lakṣyī|karoti? kiṃ tāvad asya śiśor mātaraṃ nāmataf pṛcchāmi? athav" ânyāyaf para|dāra|vyavahāraḥ.

ASCETIC: *(looking at both)* Amazing! Amazing!

KING: What is?

ASCETIC: I am amazed at the resemblance between you and this boy, although you are not related. Moreover, he is easy-going with you as if you were someone very familiar.

KING: *(caressing the boy)* If he is not a young sage then what is his name?

ASCETIC: He is a descendent of Puru. 7.95

KING: *(to himself)* What, he shares my lineage? So that is why she thinks he resembles me. *(aloud)* The Páuravas follow an ultimate family tradition.

> At first they reside in stuccoed palaces
> to protect the earth,
> later they dwell among tree-roots,
> where only ascetic vows are observed.

But mortals may not come here of their own accord.

ASCETIC: It is as you say, sir. But because this boy's mother is related to a nymph she gave birth to him here in the penance grove of the Father of the Gods.

KING: *(to himself)* I have been given a second reason for 7.100
suspicion. *(aloud)* Her ladyship is the wife of what royal sage?

ASCETIC: Who would utter the name of him who rejected his lawful wife?

KING: *(to himself)* Does this tale refer specifically to me? Can I ask for the name of the boy's mother? But no, it is improper to concern oneself with another's wife.

(praviśya mṛn/maya/mayūra/hastā) DVITĪYĀ TĀPASĪ: ⌜Savva|damaṇa! saüntaļlavaṇṇaṃ pekkha.⌟

BĀLAḤ: *(sa/dṛṣṭi/kṣepam)* ⌜kahiṃ ajju?⌟ *(ubhe prahasite.)*

7.105 PRATHAMĀ: ⌜ṇāma|sādisseṇa chalido mādu|vacchalāo.⌟

DVITĪYĀ: ⌜vaccha, Saüntalā bhaṇadi: «imassa kittima|maūrassa ramaṇīadaṃ pekkha tti.»⌟

RĀJĀ: *(sva/gatam)* kiṃ Śakuntal" êti mātur ākhyā? santi punar nāma|dheya|sādṛśyāni. api nāma mṛga|tṛṣṇik" êva n' âyam antena prastāvo me viṣādāya kalpate.

BĀLAḤ: ⌜attike, loadi me bhaddālake eśe maūle.⌟ *(iti krīḍanakam ādatte.)*

DVITĪYĀ: *(ālokya, sa/saṃbhramam)* ⌜ammo! rakkhā|karaṇḍao se maṇi|bandhe ṇa dīsadi.⌟

7.110 RĀJĀ: alam āvegena. nanv ayam asya siṃha|śāvaka|mardāt paribhraṣṭaḥ. *(ādātum icchati.)*

UBHE: ⌜mā khu ṇaṃ ālambiṭṭhā! kadhaṃ, gahidaṃ yeva ṇena?⌟ *(sa/vismayam uro/nihita/haste paras/param avalokayataḥ.)*

RĀJĀ: kim|arthaṃ pratiṣiddho 'smi?

PRATHAMĀ: ⌜suṇādu ayyo! maha|ppahāvā esā khu «Avarāidā» ṇāma mah"|osahī imassa dāraassa jāda|kamma|samae bhaavadā Mārīeṇa diṇṇā. edaṃ kila mādā|pidaro attāṇaaṃ vā vajjia avaro bhūmi|paḍidaṃ ṇa geṇhadi.⌟

(enter with a clay peacock in her hand) SECOND NUN: Sarva·dámana! Look at the pretty bird.

BOY: *(casting a glance)* Where is Mama?* *(Both laugh.)*

FIRST: The similarity of the word has misled him since he 7.105
loves his mother.

SECOND: Child, Shakúntala says: "Look how lovely this toy peacock is."

KING: *(to himself)* His mother's name is Shakúntala? But then again, there are similarities of name. Like a mirage it may lead to my ultimate disappointment.

BOY: Auntie, I like this pretty peacock. *(He takes the toy.)*

SECOND: *(looking, agitated)* Oh no! I can't see the amulet on his wrist.

KING: Don't worry. It must have slipped off as he wrestled 7.110
the lion cub. *(He wishes to pick it up.)*

BOTH: Don't touch it! What, he has already touched it? *(Astonished, they look at one another, their hands placed on their chests.)*

KING: Why are you trying to stop me?

FIRST: Listen, sir! This is a potent herb called "Invincible" that Marícha gave to this boy at his birth ceremony. Nobody other than his mother, his father and himself can pick it up if it falls to the ground.

RĀJĀ: atha gṛhṇāti kiṃ bhavati?

7.115 PRATHAMĀ: ⌜tado sappo bhavia aṇṇaṃ daṃsedi.⌟

RĀJĀ: atha bhavatībhyāṃ kadā cid asyāf pratyakṣī|kṛtā vikriyā?

UBHE: ⌜aṇeaso.⌟

RĀJĀ: *(sa|harṣam)* tat kiṃ khalv idānīṃ pūrṇam api manorathaṃ n' âbhinandāmi? *(bālaṃ pariṣvajate.)*

DVITĪYĀ: ⌜Sañjade, ehi! imaṃ vuttantaṃ ṇiama|ṇivvudāe Saüntalāe ṇivedamha.⌟

7.120 PRATHAMĀ: ⌜evaṃ karemha.⌟ *(iti niṣkrānte tāpasyau.)*

BĀLAḤ: ⌜muñca maṃ! jāva ajjū|śakāśām gaścāmi.⌟

RĀJĀ: putraka, may" âiva saha mātaram nandayiṣyasi.

BĀLAḤ: ⌜mama khu tāde Duśśante, ṇa tumaṃ.⌟

RĀJĀ: *(sa|smitam)* eṣa vivāda eva māṃ pratyāyayati.

7.125 *(tataf praviśaty eka|veṇī|dharā Śakuntalā.)*

KING: What happens if someone does pick it up?

FIRST: Then it turns into a snake and bites the stranger. 7.115

KING: Have you seen this transformation yourselves?

BOTH: Many times.

KING: *(joyfully)* Then why should I not rejoice in the fulfiment of my hope? *(He embraces the boy.)*

SECOND: Samyáta, come! Let us tell this to Shakúntala who has completed her religious duties.

FIRST: Let's go. *(Exeunt ambo.)* 7.120

BOY: Let me go! I'm going to Mama.

KING: Son, we will go and delight your mother together.

BOY: My father is Dush-yán-ta, not you.

KING: *(smiling)* This rebuttal is my proof.

(Enter Shakúntala with her hair in a single braid.) 7.125

ŚAKUNTALĀ: ⌜viāra|kāle vi païdittham tam Savva|damaṇassa osahiṃ suṇia ṇa me āsāso attaṇo bhāa|dheesu. adhavā jadhā me Akkha|mālāe ācakkhidaṃ tadhā sambhāvīadi edaṃ.⌟

RĀJĀ: *(Śakuntalāṃ dṛṣṭvā)* aye! iyam atra|bhavatī Śakuntalā!

vasane paridhūsare vasānā
  niyama|kṣāma|mukhī kṛt'|âika|veṇiḥ
atiniṣkaruṇasya śuddha|śīlā
  mama dīrghaṃ viraha|vratam bibharti.

ŚAKUNTALĀ: *(rājānaṃ dṛṣṭvā)* ⌜ṇa kkhu ayya|utto via. tā ko ṇu kkhu eso kida|rakkhā|maṅgalaṃ dāraaṃ me hattha|saṃsaggeṇa dūsedi?⌟

7.130 BĀLAḤ: *(mātaram upetya)* ⌜ajjue! eśe ke vi palake maṃ māṇuśe puttake tti ālavadi.⌟

RĀJĀ: priye, krauryam api me tvayi prayuktam anukūla|pariṇāmaṃ saṃvṛttam. yato 'ham idānīṃ tvayā pratyabhijñātam ātmānam icchāmi.

ŚAKUNTALĀ: *(sva|gatam)* ⌜hiaa, samassasa samassasa! paharia ṇivutta|macchareṇa aṇukampidamhi devveṇa. *(sa|harṣam)* ayya|utto yyeva eso!⌟

SHAKÚNTALA: I have heard that Sarva·dámana's amulet remained in its natural state even when it should have changed, but I am not comforted about my fortune. But maybe it is possible, as Aksha·mala has told me.

KING: *(seeing Shakúntala)* Ah! It is the lady Shakúntala!

> Wearing gray clothes,
> her face drawn because of her religious restraints,
> her hair tied in a single braid,
> she, pure in character, is enduring
> the long penance of separation
> from merciless me.

SHAKÚNTALA: *(seeing the king)* He does not seem like my husband. Then who is this, who defiles my magically protected son with the touch of his hand?

BOY: *(going to his mother)* Mama! This is some human 7.130
stranger who calls me "son."

KING: My beloved, the cruelty that I showed you has resolved into a happy ending. For I now wish for you to recognize me.

SHAKÚNTALA: *(to herself)* My heart, take courage, take courage! After striking me down, fate, its anger vented, has taken pity on me. This is my husband!

RĀJĀ:

smṛti|bhinna|moha|tamaso
  diṣṭyā pramukhe sthit" âsi me sumukhi
uparāgānte śaśinaḥ
  samupanato rohiṇī|yogaḥ.

7.135 ŚAKUNTALĀ: ⌜jaadu jaadu ayya|utto. . .!⌟ *(ity ardh'|ôkte bāṣpa|kaṇṭhī bāṣpaṃ viharati.)*

RĀJĀ: priye—

bāṣpeṇa pratiṣiddhe 'pi
  jaya|śabde jitaṃ mayā
yat te dṛṣṭam asaṃskāra|
  pāṭal'|âuṣṭham idaṃ mukham.

BĀLAḤ: ⌜ajjue, ke va eśe?⌟

ŚAKUNTALĀ: ⌜vaccha, bhāa|dheāiṃ me puccha.⌟ *(roditi.)*

7.140 RĀJĀ: *(praṇipatya.)*

sutanu hṛdayāt pratyādeśa|vyalīkam upaitu te
  kim api manasaḥ saṃmoho me tadā balavān abhūt
srajam api śirasy andhaḥ kṣiptāṃ dhunoty ahi|śaṅkayā
  prabala|tamasām evaṃ|prāyāḥ śubheṣv api vṛttayaḥ.

KING:

> By good fortune, fair faced one,
> you stand before me,
>   the darkness of my delusion dispelled
>   by recollection.
> At the end of the eclipse
> the moon and the red star Róhini
>   are united.*

SHAKÚNTALA: Victory, victory, my husband...! *(She stops mid-sentence, her throat chocked with tears.)* 7.135

KING: My beloved–

> Though the word "victory" is choked by tears,
> I am victorious,
> because I have beheld your face,
>   with its pale, unadorned, lips.

BOY: Mama, who is this?

SHAKÚNTALA: Son, ask my fate. *(She weeps.)*

KING: *(falls to the ground.)* 7.140

> O slender lady,
> may the pain of rejection depart
>   from your heart;
> somehow I was greatly deluded then.
> A blind man shakes off even a garland
>   cast upon his head fearing it to be a serpent;
> those in deep darkness act like this
>   even towards auspicious things.

ŚAKUNTALĀ: ⌜utthedu ayya|utto. ṇaṃ mama suha|paḍibandhaaṃ purā|kadam tesu diasesu pariṇām'|âhimuhaṃ āsi, jeṇa s'|âṇukkoso vi ayya|utto maï tadhāviho saṃvutto.⌟ *(rāj" ôttiṣṭhati.)* ⌜adha kadham ayya|utteṇa sumārido aam jaṇo?⌟

RĀJĀ: uddhṛta|viṣāda|śalyaḥ kathayiṣyāmi.

mohān mayā sutanu pūrvam upekṣitas te
yo bāṣpa|bindur adharaṃ paridhāvamānaḥ
taṃ tāvad ākulita|pakṣma|vilagnam adya
kānte pramṛjya vigat'|ânuśayo bhavāmi.

7.145 *(iti yath"|ôktam anutiṣṭhati.)*

ŚAKUNTALĀ: *(pramṛṣṭa|bāṣpā nāma|mudrāṃ dṛṣṭvā)* ⌜ayya|utta! ṇaṃ taṃ aṅgulīaṃ!⌟

RĀJĀ: atha kim? asmād adbhut'|ôpalambhān mayā smṛtir upalabdhā.

ŚAKUNTALĀ: ⌜samīhidaṃ kāduṃ kkhaṇeṇa jaṃ tadā ayya|uttassa paccaa|karaṇe dullahaṃ me saṃvuttaṃ.⌟

RĀJĀ: tena hy ṛtu|samavāgam'|āśaṃsi pratipadyatāṃ latā kusumam.

7.150 ŚAKUNTALĀ: ⌜ṇa se vīsasāmi. ayya|utto yyeva ṇaṃ pāredu.⌟

(praviśya) MĀTALIḤ: diṣṭyā dharma|patnī|samāgamena putra|mukha|darśanena c' āyuṣmān vardhate.

SHAKÚNTALA: Stand up, my husband. In those days, surely, some former deed of mine, a hindrance to my happiness, was on the verge of bearing fruit, whereby you, though compassionate, became so changed. *(The king stands up.)* Then how did my husband come to remember me?

KING: I will draw out the dart of sorrow and tell you.

> O slender lady, once,
> the tear that troubled your lip
> was ignored because I was deluded,
> now, I will wipe it away
> as it clings to your tremulous eyelashes
> and free myself from regret.

(Does as stated.) 7.145

SHAKÚNTALA: *(sees the ring as her tear is wiped off)* My husband! Why, it's the ring!

KING: Of course! My memory returned when it was miraculously found again.

SHAKÚNTALA: It could have fulfilled my desire in a flash, but I could not find it when I needed to convince my husband.

KING: Then let the vine receive the flower to announce the arrival of spring.

SHAKÚNTALA: I do not trust it. Let my husband wear it. 7.150

MÁTALI: *(entering)* Congratulations, reunited with your lawful wife and looking upon the face of your son, your Majesty thrives again.

RĀJĀ: suhṛt|saṃpāditvād uttara|phalo hi me mano|rathaḥ. Mātale, na khalu vidito 'yam Ākhaṇḍalasy' ârthaḥ?

MĀTALIḤ: ehi, bhagavāṃs te Mārīco darśanaṃ vitarati.

RĀJĀ: Śakuntale, avalambyatāṃ putraḥ. tvāṃ puraskṛtya bhagavantaṃ draṣṭum icchāmi.

7.155 ŚAKUNTALĀ: ⌜arihāmy ayya|utteṇa saha samīvaṃ gantuṃ?⌟

RĀJĀ: ācaritam etad abhyudaya|kāleṣu, ehy ehi! *(sarve parikrāmanti.)*

(tataf praviśaty Adityā saha ārdh'|āsana|stho Mārīcaḥ)

MĀRĪCAḤ: *(rājānam avalokya)* Dākṣāyaṇi,

putrasya te raṇa|śirasy ayam agra|gāmī
  Duḥṣyanta ity abhihito bhuvanasya bhartā
cāpena yasya vinivartita|karma jātam
  tat koṭimat kuliśam ābharaṇaṃ Maghonaḥ.

7.160 ADITIḤ: ⌜sambhāvaṇīā se kkhu āidī.⌟

MĀTALIḤ: bhūtala|pate! etau putra|prīti|piśunena cakṣuṣā divaukasāṃ pitarāv avalokayataḥ. tad upasarpa.

KING: My desire bears most excellent fruit, since it has been achieved by a friend. Mátali, did not Indra know of this matter?

MÁTALI: Come, the reverend Marícha grants you an audience.

KING: Shakúntala, hold our son. I wish to see the reverend with you going before me.

SHAKÚNTALA: Am I worthy of going with my husband? 7.155

KING: It is customary on festive occasions, come come! *(All walk about.)*

(Enter Marícha sharing a seat with Áditi.)

MARÍCHA: *(looking at the king)* Dakshâyani,

> This is the lord of the earth, Dushyánta by name,
> frontmost in the battles of your son Indra.
> Because of his bow Indra's sharp thunderbolt
> has become an idle ornament.

ÁDITI: His appearance is indeed honorable. 7.160

MÁTALI: King of the earth! The parents of the gods are looking upon you with a glance that reveals a parental fondness. Approach.

RĀJĀ: Mātale,

prāhur dvādaśadhā sthitasya munayo
  yat tejasaḥ kāraṇam
bhartāraṃ bhuvana|trayasya suṣuve
  yad yajña|bhāg'|ēśvaram
yasminn ātma|bhavaf paro 'pi puruṣaś
  cakre bhavāy' āspadam
brahm'|ânantara|viśva|yoni|sahitaṃ
  dvandvaṃ tad etad|vaśi.

MĀTALIḤ: atha kim?

RĀJĀ: *(praṇipatya)* ubhābhyām api vāṃ Vāsava|niyojyo Duḥṣyantaf praṇamati.

MĀRĪCAḤ: vatsa, ciraṃ pṛthivīṃ pālaya!

ADITIḤ: ⌜vatsa, appaḍiraho hohi!⌟

ŚAKUNTALĀ: ⌜dāraeṇa sahitā pāda|vandaṇaṃ karemi.⌟

MĀRĪCAḤ: vatse, ciram a|vidhavā bhava!

Ākhaṇḍala|samo bhartā
  Jayanta|pratimaḥ sutaḥ
āśīr anyā na te yojyā
  «Paulomī|pratimā bhava!»

ADITIḤ: ⌜jāde, bhaṭṭiṇo bahu|madā hohi! aaṃ ca de dehao vacchao uhaa|pakkhaṃ alaṅkāredu. tā uvavisadha.⌟

MĀRĪCAḤ: *(ek'|âikaṃ nirdiśan)*

diṣṭyā Śakuntalā sādhvī
  sad|apatyam idaṃ bhavān
śraddhā vittaṃ vidhiś c' êti
  tritayaṃ tat samāgatam.

KING: Mátali,

> This is the couple, which the sages declare to be
> the source of the twelvefold brilliance,*
> which gave birth to Indra, the lord of the Gods
> who take a share in the sacrifice,
> in which the Soul that transcends even
> the self-born Brahma found a birthplace.*

MÁTALI: Assuredly.

KING: *(bowing)* Indra's servant Dushyánta bows to you both. 7.165

MARÍCHA: Child, long may you protect the earth!

ÁDITI: Child, be peerless in battle!

SHAKÚNTALA: I worship your feet with my son.

MARÍCHA: Child, long may you not be a widow!

> With a husband like Indra 7.170
> with a son like Jayánta,
> there can be no other blessing than this:
> "Be like Paulómi!"

ÁDITI: My daughter, may your husband honor you. May your son be an ornament to both of your families. Please sit. *(All sit with Praja·pati's permission.)*

MARÍCHA: *(pointing to one after another)*

> By good fortune,
> faithful Shakúntala, this perfect son, your Majesty,
> —faith, wealth, and law,
> this triad is united.

RĀJĀ: bhagavan, prāg abhipreta|siddhif paścād darśanam ity apūrvo bhagavato 'nugrahaḥ. paśyatu bhagavān—

7.175 udeti pūrvaṃ kusumaṃ tataf phalaṃ
ghan'|ôdayaf prāk tad|anantaraṃ payaḥ
nimitta|naimittikayor ayaṃ vidhis
tava prasādasya puras tu sampadaḥ.

MĀTALIḤ: evaṃ viśva|guravaf prasīdanti.

RĀJĀ: bhagavan, imām ājñā|karīṃ vo gāndharveṇa vivāha|vidhin" ôpayamya kasya cit kālasya bandhubhir ānītāṃ smṛti|śaithilyāt pratyādiśann aparāddho 'smi tatra|bhavataḥ Kaṇvasya. paścād enām angulīyaka|darśanād ārūḍha|smṛtir ūḍha|pūrvām anugato 'smi. tac citram eva me pratibhāti.

yathā gajo n' êti samakṣa|rūpe
tasminn apakrāmati saṃśayaḥ syāt
padāni dṛṣṭvā tu bhavet pratītis
tathā|vidho me manaso vikāraḥ.

MĀRĪCAḤ: vatsa, alam ātm'|âpacāra|śaṅkayā! sammoho 'pi tvayy upapannaḥ. yataḥ śrūyatām.

7.180 RĀJĀ: avahito 'smi.

MĀRĪCAḤ: yad" âiv' Âpsaras|tīrth'|âvataraṇāt pratyakṣa|vaiklavyāṃ Śakuntalām ādāya Menakā Dākṣāyaṇī|sakāśam āgatā tad" âiva dhyānād adhigato 'smi Durvāsasaḥ śāpād iyaṃ tapasvinī saha|dharma|cāriṇī pratyādiṣṭā n' ânyath" êti. sa c' âṅgulīyaka|darśan'|âvasāraḥ.

KING: Blessed one, your grace is unprecedented: first the fulfilment of our wishes, then the sight of you. See,

> The flower grows first, then the fruit, 7.175
> the clouds appear first, then the rain,
> —this is the order of cause and effect,
> but good fortune came before your grace.

MÁTALI: Such is the favor of the parents of the world.

KING: Blessed one, I married this servant of yours by the rite of mutual consent. After some time her kinsfolk brought her to me. I rejected her because of a loss of memory and offended against the reverend Kanva. Later, I remembered that I had married her after I saw the ring. This appears strange to me.

> It is as if one were to deny an elephant
> visibly before one,
> then doubt once it has gone,
> but seeing its footprints one perceives it,
> —such was the aberration of my mind.

MARÍCHA: Child, stop worrying that you have done wrong! You were deceived. Listen.

KING: I am attentive. 7.180

MARÍCHA: When Ménaka, descending from nymphs' bathing place, took the obviously frail Shakúntala, and came to Áditi, I realized through meditation that the poor girl had been rejected by her husband because of the curse of Durvásas, and that the opportunity to end it was the sight of the ring.

RĀJĀ: *(s'|ôcchvāsam)* eṣo 'haṃ vacanīyān mukto 'smi!

ŚAKUNTALĀ: *(ātma|gatam)* ⌜diṭṭhiā a|kāma|paccādesī ayya| utto. ṇa uṇa sattam attāṇaṃ sumarāmi. adhavā ṇa sudo dhuvam aṇṇa|hiaāe mae sāvo. jado sahīhiṃ accādareṇa sandiṭṭhamhi bhaṭṭiṇo aṅgulīaam daṃsehi tti.⌟

MĀRĪCAḤ: vatse, vidit'|ārth" âsi. tad idānīṃ saha|dharma| cāriṇaṃ prati na tvayā manyuḥ kāryaḥ. paśya—

7.185 śāpād asi pratihatā smṛti|lopa|rūkṣe
bhartary apeta|tamasi prabhutā tav' âiva
chāyā na mūrcchati mal'|ôpahata|prasāde
śuddhe tu darpaṇa|tale sulabh'|âvakāśā.

RĀJĀ: yathā bhagavān āha.

MĀRĪCAḤ: vatsa, kac|cid abhinanditas tvayā vidhivad asmābhir anuṣṭhita|jāta|karmā putra eṣa Śākuntaleyaḥ?

RĀJĀ: bhagavan, atra khalu me vaṃśa|pratiṣṭhā.

KING: *(draws in his breath)* I am freed from blame!

SHAKÚNTALA: *(to herself)* What a blessing, my husband rejected me without wanting to. But I cannot recall being cursed. Surely I must not have heard the curse because my heart was elsewhere—my friends were so insistent that I must show the ring to my husband.

MARÍCHA: Child, you have perceived the truth. Therefore, do not now show anger towards your husband. Look—

You were rejected by your husband, 7.185
  made cruel by his loss of memory.
Now that his darkness has lifted,
  sovereignty is yours.
An image does not take form in a mirror
  if its brightness is dirtied,
but it easily does if it is clear.

KING: As the blessed one says.

MARÍCHA: Child, I hope you have accepted the son of Shakúntala, for whom I have performed the birth rites?

KING: Blessed one, in him is supported my line.

MĀRĪCAḤ: tathā tat. bhāvinaṃ cakra|vartinam enam ava-gacchatu bhavān. paśya—

7.190 rathen' ânudghāta|stimita|gatir ā|tīrṇa|jaladhif
purā sapta|dvīpāṃ jayati vasudhām a|pratirathaḥ.
ih' âyaṃ sattvānāṃ prasabha|damanāt Sarva|damanaf
punar yāsyaty ākhyāṃ Bharata it lokasya bharaṇāt.

RĀJĀ: bhagavatā kṛta|saṃskāre sarvam asminn āśaṃsāmahe.

ADITIḤ: ⌜imāe ṇandaṇā|manoradha|sampattīe Kaṇṇo vi dāva suda|vitthāro karīadu. Meṇaā idha yyeva saṇṇihidā.⌟

ŚAKUNTALĀ: ⌜maṇo|gadaṃ me mantidam bhaavadīe.⌟

MĀRĪCAḤ: sarvam etat tapaḥ|prabhavāt pratyakṣaṃ tatra|bhavataḥ Kaṇvasya.

7.195 RĀJĀ: hanta! khalu na samabhikruddho guruḥ.

MĀRĪCAḤ: tath" âpy asau priyam asmābhiḥ śrāvayitavyaḥ. kaḥ ko 'tra bhoḥ.

(praviśya) ŚIṢYAḤ: bhagavan, ayam asmi.

MARÍCHA: That is a fact. Know him to be the future emperor. Behold—

> Crossing the ocean with his chariot
> his motion steady without jolts,
> an unrivalled warrior he will soon conquer the earth
> with its seven continents. Here he is known as Sarva·dámana,
> because he tames the animals by force,
> he will become known as Bhárata,
> because he supports the earth.

KING: Since the blessed one performed his rites I can hope for all of this for him.

ÁDITI: Kanva too should be told in detail about how her wishes have been fulfilled. Ménaka is nearby.

SHAKÚNTALA: You have said what is my heart.

MARÍCHA: All this is evident to his reverence Kanva through the power of his penance.

KING: Ah! The guru is not angry.

MARÍCHA: Nevertheless he ought to hear the good news from me. Who waits in attendance?

(entering) DISCIPLE: Your reverence, here I am.

MĀRĪCAḤ: vatsa Gālava, mad|vacanād idānīm eva vihāyasā gatvā tatra|bhavate śrī|Kaṇvāya priyam āvedaya, yathā Śakuntalā Durvāsasaḥ śāpa|vinivṛtti|samupāgata|smṛtinā Duḥṣyantena pratigṛhīt" êti.

ŚIṢYAḤ: yad ājñāpayati bhagavān. *(praṇamya niṣkrāntaḥ)*

7.200 MĀRĪCAḤ: *(rājānaṃ prati)* vatsa, tvam api s'|âpatya|dāraḥ saṃnihitaṃ sakhyur Ākhaṇḍalasya ratham āruhya sva|rāja|dhānīṃ pratiṣṭhasva.

RĀJĀ: yad ājñāpayati bhagavān.

MĀRĪCAḤ: vatsa,

kratubhir ucita|bhāgāṃs tvaṃ surān bhāvay" âlaṃ
  sura|patir api vṛṣṭyā tvat|praj"|ârthaṃ vidhattām
iti samam upakāra|vyañjita|śrī|mahimnor
  vrajati bahu|titho vāṃ sauhṛdayyena kālaḥ.

RĀJĀ: bhagavan yathā|śakti śreyase 'haṃ yatiṣye.

7.205 MĀRĪCAḤ: vatsa, tad ucyatām. kiṃ te bhūyaf priyam upaharāmi.

RĀJĀ: yad ataf paraṃ me bhagavān prasādaṃ kartum arhati, tataḥ—

MARÍCHA: My child Gálava, tell his reverence the illustrious Kanva the good news in my words, namely that Shakúntala has been received by Dush-yán-ta whose memory has returned at the end of the curse of Durvásas.

DISCIPLE: As your reverence commands. *(Bows and exits.)*

MARÍCHA: *(to the king)* Child, mount your friend Indra's 7.200
chariot which is right here with your son and wife and set out for your own capital city.

KING: As your reverence commands.

MARÍCHA: Child,

May you cherish richly the Gods,
  entitled to their share, with offerings;
may the King of the Gods in turn send rain
  for your subjects;
thus, in like manner,
the greatness of your magnanimity
  made visible by these favors,
may much time pass with your friendship.

KING: Blessed one, I will strive for good with all my power.

MÁRICHA: Child, say now, what further favor shall I grant 7.205
you?

KING: If beyond this the reverend wishes to show me a favor, then—

pravartatāṃ prakṛti|hitāya pārthivaḥ!
Sarasvatī śruti|mahatāṃ mahīyatām!
mam' âpi ca kṣapayatu nīla|lohitaf
punar|bhavaṃ parigata|śaktir ātma|bhūḥ!

(iti niṣkrāntāḥ sarve.)

saptamo 'ṅkaḥ.

7.210 *samāptaṃ c' êdam Abhijñāna/śakuntal'/ākhyaṃ mahā/nāṭakam.*

kṛtiḥ śrī/prasād'/āsādita/sarva/vidyasya mahā/kaveḥ Kālidāsasya.

May the king be devoted to the welfare
of his subjects!
May Sarásvati be honored by the learned!
May Self-born Shiva, whose power encompasses
all,
put an end to my rebirth!

(Exeunt omnes.)

End of the seventh act.

The end of the play called 7.210
"The Recognition of Shakúntala."

The work of the great poet Kali·dasa
who attained all knowledge by the grace of fortune.

CHĀYĀ

The following is a Sanskrit paraphrase *(chāyā)* of the Prakrit passages (marked with ⌜corner brackets⌟) in the play. References are to chapter and paragraph.

1.5 ārya! iyam asmi. ājñāpayatu āryaḥ ko niyogo 'nuṣṭhīyatām iti.

1.7 suvihita|prayogatay" āryasya na kiñ|cit parihāsyate.

1.10 evaṃ nv idam. anantara|karaṇīyam idānīm ārya ājñāpayatu.

1.14 tathā.

1.15 kṣaṇa|cumbitāni bhramaraiḥ subhaga|sukumāra|kesara|śikhāni, avataṃsayanti pramadā dayamānāḥ śirīṣa|kusumāni.

1.17 nūnaṃ prathamam ev' āryeṇ' ājñaptaṃ yathā <na> abhijñāna|śakuntalā nām' âpūrvaṃ nāṭakaṃ prayogen' âdhikriyatām iti.

1.66 ita itaf priya|sakhyau.

1.69 hale Śakuntale!

1.69 tvatto 'pi khalu tāta|kāśyapasy' āśrama|vṛkṣakāf priyā iti tarkayāmo yena navamālikā|pelav" âpi tvam etasy' ālavāla|pūraṇe niyuktā.

1.70 na kevalaṃ tāta|niyoga iti. bahu|māno yāvan mamāpi. sahodarī|sneha eteṣv asty eva.

1.71 hale Śakuntale! udakaṃ lambhitā grīṣma|kāla|kusuma|dāyino gulmakā. idānīm atikrānta|samaye 'pi vṛkṣān siñcāmaḥ. tasmād anabhisandhita|pūrvo dharmo bhaviṣyati.

1.72 abhinandanīyaṃ mantrayathaḥ.

1.76 eṣa vāt'|ērita|pallav'|âṅgulībhis tvarayat' îva māṃ bakula|vṛkṣakaḥ. yāvad enaṃ sambhāvayāmi.

1.79 hale Anasūye! atipinaddhena Priyaṃvadayā valkalena niyantrit" âsmi. tac chithilaya tāvad enam.

1.80 atra payodhara|vistārayitṛkam ātmanaḥ yauvanam upālabhasva.

1.83 hale Śakuntale! eṣā tāta|Kāśyapena tvam iva saṃvardhit" âlindake mādhavī|latā. prekṣasv' âinām. kiṃ vismṛtā te?

1.84 ātm" âpi vismariṣyate.

1.85 hale Śakuntale! tiṣṭh' êh' âiva muhūrtakaṃ tāvad bakula|vṛkṣa|samīpe.

1.86 kim iti?

1.87 tvayā samīpa|sthitayā latā|sanātha iva me bakula|vṛkṣakaf pratibhāti.

1.88 ataḥ khalu Priyaṃvad" âsi.

1.91 hale Śakuntale! iyaṃ svayam|vara|vadhūḥ sahakārasya tvayā kṛta|nāmadheyasya vana|toṣiṇo nava|mālikā.

1.92 hale! ramaṇīye kāle 'sya pādapa|mithunasya vyatikaraḥ saṃvṛttaḥ. iyaṃ nava|kusuma|yauvanā. ayam api baddha|phalatay" ôpabhoga|kṣamaḥ sahakāraḥ.

1.93 hale Anasūye! jānāsi kiṃ|nimittaṃ Śakuntalā Vana|toṣiṇam atimātraṃ paśyat' îti.

1.94 na khalu vibhāvayāmi.

1.95 yathā Vana|toṣiṇ" ânusadṛśena pādapena saṅgatā nava|mālikā, api nām' âivam aham apy ātmano 'nurūpaṃ varaṃ labha iti.

1.96 eṣa nūnaṃ ātmanas te citta|gato manorathaḥ.

1.100 aho. salila|seka|saṃbhrānto navamālikām ujjhitvā vadanaṃ me madhu|karo 'nuvartate.

1.103 hale! paritrāyadhvaṃ mām anena kusuma|pāṭaccareṇ' âbhibhūyamānām!

1.104 ke āvāṃ paritrāṇe? Duṣṣyamtam ākranda. rāja|rakṣitāni khalu tapo|vanāni bhavanti.

1.106 n' âiṣa me purato 'tidhṛṣṭo viramati. tad anyato gamiṣyāmi.

1.106 hā dhik! katham ito 'pi mām anusarati.

1.110 na khalu kiṃ cid atyāhitam. iyaṃ punar naf priya|sakhī madhu|kareṇ' ākulīkriyamāṇā kātarī|bhūtā.

1.113 idānīm atithi|viśeṣa|lābhena.

1.114 svāgatam āryasya!

1.115 halā Śakuntale! gaccha tvam uṭajataḥ phala|miśram upāhara, iha pād'|ôdakam asty eva.

1.117 ten' âsmiṃs tāvat pādapa|chāyā|śītalāyām sapta|parṇa|vedikāyām ārya upaviśya muhūrtaṃ pariśramam apanayatu.

1.119 hale Śakuntale! ucitaṃ no 'tithi|paryupāsanam. tad ih' ôpaviśāmaḥ.

1.120 kiṃ nu khalv imaṃ prekṣya tapo|vana|virodhino vikārasya gamanīy" âsmi saṃvṛttā?

1.122 Anasūye! ko nu khalv eṣa catura|gambhīr'|ākṛtir madhuraṃ priyam ālapan prabhavantaṃ dākṣiṇyam iva karoti.

1.123 sakhi! mam' âpi kautūhalam asty eva. tat prakṣyāmi tāvad enam.

1.123 āryasya no madhur'|ālāpa|janito visrambho mantrayati. katamaṃ punar āryo varṇam alaṅkaroti? kiṃ|nimittaṃ vā sukumāreṇ' āryeṇa tapo|van'|āgamana|pariśramasy' ātmā pātrī|kṛtaḥ?

1.124 hṛdaya, mā uttāmya! yat tvayā cintitaṃ tad anasūyā mantrayati.

1.126 sa|nāthā dharma|cāriṇaḥ.

1.128 hale Śakuntale! yady adya tāta iha saṃnihito bhavet. . .

1.129 tataḥ kiṃ bhavet?

1.130 tata imam atithiṃ jīvita|sarvasven' âpi kṛt'|ârthaṃ kuryāt.

1.131 ayi! apetam. kim api hṛdaye kṛtvā mantrayathaḥ. na khalu śroṣyāmi.

1.133 ārya! anugrahe 'py abhyarthanā.

1.135 śṛṇotv āryaḥ! asti Kauśika iti gotra|nāmadheyo mahā|prabhāvaḥ rāja'|ṛṣiḥ.

1.137 taṃ sakhī|jane prabhavam avagaccha. ujjhita|śarīra|saṃrakṣaṇ'|ādibhis tāta|Kāśyapo 'syāf pitā.

1.139 purā kila tasya rāja'|ṛṣer ugre tapasi vartamānasya kim api jāta|śaṅkair devair Menakā nām' âpsarā niyama|vighna|kāriṇī prahitā.

1.141 tato vasant'|ôdaya|samaye tasyā unmādayitṛ rūpaṃ prekṣya. . .

1.143 atha kim?

1.148 punar iva vaktu|kāma āryaḥ.

1.151 tena hi vicāriteṇ' âlaṃ. niyantraṇ'|ânuyogyas tapasvi|janaḥ.

1.154 ārya! dharma|caraṇe 'py eṣa par'|ādhīno janaḥ. gurof punar asyā anurūpa|vara|pratipādane saṅkalpaḥ.

1.157 Anasūye! gamiṣyāmy aham.

1.158 kiṃ|nimittam?

1.159 imām asambaddh'|ālāpinīṃ priyaṃvadām āryāyai Gautamyai nivedayiṣyāmi.

1.160 sakhi na yuktam āśrama|vāsino janasy' âkṛta|satkāram atithi|viśeṣaṃ visṛjya svacchandato gamanam.

1.164 hale caṇḍi! na te yuktaṃ gantum.

1.165 kim iti?

1.166 vṛkṣa|secanake dve me dhārayasi. tābhyāṃ tāvad ātmānaṃ mocaya, tato gamiṣyasi.

1.172 tena hi n' ârhat' îdaṃ ca rājño 'ṅgulīyakaṃ viyoga|kāritaṃ. āryasya tava vacanena nām' âiṣ" ânṛṇ" âiva mama. halā Śakuntale mocit" âsy anukampin" āryeṇa. atha vā mah"|ânubhāvena. kṛtajñ" êdānīṃ bhaviṣyasi.

1.173 n' êdaṃ vismariṣyate yady ātmanaf prabhavāmi.

1.174 hale! kim idānīṃ sāṃprataṃ na gacchasi?

1.183 ārya anen' ākranditena paryākulāḥ smaḥ. tad anujānīhi na uṭaja|gamanāya.

1.185 asambhāvita|satkāraṃ bhūyo 'pi tāvat pratyavekṣaṇā|nimittaṃ prekṣaṇa|nimittaṃ lajjāmahe āryaṃ vijñāpayitum. vidita|bhūyiṣṭho 'si naḥ saṃprataṃ yad idānīm upacāra|madhyasthatay" âparāddhāḥ smas tan marṣayasi.

1.187 hale Śakuntale! ehi śīghrataram! ākul" āryā Gautamī bhaviṣyati.

1.188 hā dhik! ūru|sthambhena vikal" âsmi saṃvṛttā.

2.2 bhoḥ! dṛḍho 'smi! etasya mṛgayā|śīlasya rājño vayasya|bhāvena nirviṇṇaḥ. ayaṃ mṛgo 'yaṃ vāraha iti. madhyaṃ|dine 'pi grīṣma|virala|pādapa|chāyāsu vaṇa|rājīṣu bhramyate. mayā patra|saṃkara|kaṣāyāṇi pīyante kaṭukāny uṣṇāni giri|nadī|jalāni.

aniyata|velāṃ śūla|māṃsa|śakuna|māṃsa|bhūyiṣṭham adyate. turaga|yāna|khaṇḍīkṛta|sandhi|bandhanānām aṅgānāṃ rātrim api n' âsti prakāmaṃ śayitavyam. tato mama mahaty eva pratyūṣe dāsyāf putraiḥ śakuna|lubdhakaiḥ karṇa|ghātinā vana|grahaṇa|kolāhalena pratibodhye. etāvat" âpi me prāṇā na niṣkrāntāḥ. tato gaṇḍ'|ôpari piṭikā saṃvṛttā. hyo 'smāsv avahīneṣu tatra|bhavato mṛg'|ânusāreṇ' āśrama|padaṃ praviṣṭasya kila tāpasa|kanyakā Śakuntalā nāma mam' âdhanyatayā darśitā. sāmprataṃ nagara|gamanasya saṃkathām api na karoti. adya tām eva sañcintayato vibhātam akṣṇoḥ. tat kā gatiḥ. yāvad enaṃ kṛt'|ācāra|parikramaṃ kutra prekṣye. eṣa rājā bāṇāsana|hastābhir yavanībhif parivṛto vana|puṣpa|mālā|dhārita iv' āgacchati. tad yāvad enam upasarpāmi. bhavatu. aṅga|sammarda|vihvala idānīṃ bhūtv" êh' âiva sthāsyāmi. yata evam api tāvad viśrāmaṃ labhe.

2.9 bho rājan! na me hastaf prasarati vāṅ|mātrakena jāpyase.

2.11 kutaḥ kila svayam akṣyākulīkṛty' âśru|kāraṇam pṛcchasi.

2.13 bhoḥ! tvayā nāma rāja|kāryāṇy ujjhitvā tādṛśān krīḍā|prasādān vana|car'|âika|vṛttinā bhavitavyam. yat satyaṃ pratyahaṃ śvāpada|śakun'|ânugamanaiḥ saṃkṣobhita|saṃdhi|bandhānām aṅgānām anīśo 'smi saṃvṛttaḥ. tat prasīda! māṃ varjaya! ek'|âham api tāvad viśramyatām.

2.16 atra|bhavān kim api hṛdaye kṛtvā mantrayate. araṇye mayā ruditam.

2.20 ājñāpayatu bhavān.

2.22 api modaka|khādikāyām?

2.24 gṛhītaḥ kṣaṇaḥ.

2.26 ājñāpayatu bhartā.

2.28 yad bhart" ājñāpayati.

2.32 eṣa khalv anuvacana|datta|karṇa ito datta|dṛṣṭir eva bhartā tvāṃ pratipālayati. tasmād upasarpatv āryaḥ.

2.37 atra|bhavān prakṛtim āpannaḥ. tvaṃ tāvad aṭavīto 'ṭavīm bhrama yāvan sīsa|śṛgāla iva jīrṇa'|rkṣasya mukhe patiṣyasi.

2.44 gaccha sāṃprataṃ dāsyāf putra!

2.47 yad bhart" ājñāpayati.

2.48 kṛtaṃ bhavatā nirdhūmako daṃśa|pratīkāraḥ. tat sāmpratam etasmin āvāsa|pādapa|chāyā|parivṛte vitāna|sanāthe āsane yathāsukhaṃ upaviśatu bhavān yāvad aham api sukhāsana|stho bhavāmi.

2.52 nanu bhavān agrato me tiṣṭhati.

2.54 bhavatu. n' âsya prasaraṃ vardhayiṣyāmi. yadā tāvat sā tāpasa|kanyak" âbhyarthanīyā tat kiṃ tayā dṛṣṭayā.

2.56 tat katham etat?

2.59 yady api na Kāśyapasya maha"|rṣer aurasā duhitā tath" âpi kiṃ tayā dṛṣṭayā?

2.62 yathā kasy' âpi piṇḍa|kharjūrair udvejitasya tintilikānām abhilāṣo bhavati tathā strī|ratna|paribhāvino bhavata iyaṃ prārthanā.

2.64 tat khalu ramaṇīyaṃ nāma yad bhavato 'pi vismayaṃ janayati.

2.67 pratyādeśa idānīṃ rūpavatīnām!

2.70 tena hi laghu pariṇayatu bhavān mā kasy' âpi tapasvina iṅgudī|taila|cikkaṇa|śīrṣasy' āraṇyakasya haste patiṣyati.

2.72 atha bhavantam antareṇa kīdṛśas tasyāś citt'|ânurāgaḥ?

2.75 kiṃ khalu sā bhavato dṛṣṭa|mātrasy' âiv' âṅkam ārohatu?

2.78 gṛhīta|pātheyo bhavasi. katham punaf punas tapo|vana|gamanam iti prekṣe.

2.80 eṣa cintayāmi... mā khalu mam' âlīka|paridevitaiḥ samādhiṃ bhāṅkṣīḥ. bhoḥ! ko 'nya upāyaḥ? nanu bhavān rājā?

2.82 nīvāra|ṣaṣṭha|bhāgaṃ tāvat svāmy upaiti.

2.87 jayatu jayatu bhartā. etau dvau ṛṣi|kumārau pratīhāra|bhūmim upasthitau.

2.89 ayaṃ praveśayāmi.

2.91 ita ito bhavantaḥ.

2.104 ayam idānīm anukūlā|gala|hastaḥ.

2.106 yad bhart" ājñāpayati.

2.112 prathamam aparibādham āsīt. rākṣasa|vṛtt'|ântena punaḥ sāṃpratam viṣāda|darśinā viśeṣitam.

2.114 eṣa cakrākī bhūto 'smi.

2.115 bhartaḥ! sajjo ratho bhartur vijaya|prasthānam udīkṣate. eṣa punar nagarato devīnāṃ sakāśataḥ Karabhaka upasthitaḥ.

2.117 atha kim?

2.119 yad bhartā ājñāpayati.

2.121 jayatu jayatu bhartā. devya ājñāpayanti āgamini caturthe divase putra|piṇḍako dānako nāma upavāso bhaviṣyati. tatra dīrgh'|āyuṣ" âvaśyaṃ saṃnihitena bhavitavyam.

2.123 Triśankur iv' ântare tiṣṭha.

2.127 sādhu! rākṣasa|bhīrukaṃ māṃ gaṇayiṣyati.

2.129 tena hi yathā rāj'|ânurāgeṇa gantavyaṃ tathā gamiṣyāmi.

2.131 tena hi yuva|rājo 'smi saṃvṛttaḥ.

2.134 evam etat!

3.19 sakhi Śakuntale! api sukhayati te nalinī|patra|vātaḥ?

3.20 kiṃ vā vījayato māṃ sakhyau?

3.25 halā Śakuntale! anantarajñā vayaṃ madana|vṛttānteṣu. tath" âpi kiṃ tu yādṛś"|ītihāsa|gateṣu madana|vṛttānteṣu kāmayamānasy' âvasthā śrūyate tādṛśaṃ ca lakṣāvahe. tat kathaya kiṃ|nimittaṃ te 'yam āyāsaḥ. vikāraṃ khalu param'|ârthato 'jñātv" ânārambhaf pratīkārasya.

3.27 balavān ca me 'bhiniveśo na ca śaknomi sahasā nivartitum.

3.28 sakhi suṣṭhu eṣā bhaṇati. kim nv etam ātmana upadravaṃ nigūhasi? anudivasaṃ ca parihīyase 'ṅgakaiḥ. kevalaṃ lāvaṇyamayī chāyā tvāṃ na muñcati.

3.31 kasya v" ânyasya kathayiṣyāmi. kiṃ tv āyāsayitr" îdānīṃ vo bhaviṣyāmi.

3.32 ata eva no nirbandhaḥ. saṃvibhaktaṃ khalu duhkhaṃ sahya|vedanaṃ bhavati.

3.35 yataf prabhṛti sa tapo|vana|rakṣitā rāja'|rṣir mama darśana|pathaṃ gataḥ, tata ārabhy' ôdgaten' âbhilāṣeṇ' âitad|avasth" âsmi saṃvṛttā.

3.38 evaṃ yadi vo 'bhimataṃ tat tathā mantrayethāṃ māṃ yathā tasya rāja'|rṣer anukampanīyā bhavāmi. anyathā māṃ siñcatam idānīm śānty|udakena.

3.40 Anasūye! dūre|gata|manmath" êyam akṣamā kāla|haraṇasya. yasmin baddha|bhāvā, sa api lalāma|bhūtaf pauravāṇām. tat tvaritavyam ev' âsy' âbhilāṣam anuvartitum.

3.41 yathā bhaṇasi. sakhi diṣṭy" ânurūpas te 'bhilāṣaḥ. sāgaraṃ varjayitvā kutra vā mahā|nadyā gantavyam?

3.42 ka idānīṃ sahakāram atimukta|latayā pallavituṃ n' êcchati?

3.44 kaf punar upāyo bhaved yena sakhyā avilambitaṃ nigūḍhaṃ mano|rathaṃ sampādayāvaḥ?

3.45 nipuṇaṃ prayatitavyam iti cintanīyaṃ bhavet. śīghram iti na duṣkaram.

3.46 katham iva?

3.47 sa rāja'|rṣir asyāṃ snigdha|dṛṣṭi|sūcit'|âbhilāṣa imāni divasāni prajāgara|kṛśa iva lakṣyate.

3.50 Anasūye! madana|lekha idānīṃ kriyatām. taṃ sumano|gopitaṃ kṛtvā deva|śeṣ'|âpadeśena tasya rājño haste pātayiṣyāmi.

3.51 rocate me sukumāraf prayogaḥ. kiṃ vā Śakuntalā bhaṇati?

3.52 niyogo 'pi vikalpyate.

3.53 tena hy upanyāsa|pūrvam ātmanaś cintaya kim api sulalitaṃ pada|bandhanam.

3.54 cintayiṣyāmi. avadhīraṇā|bhīrukaṃ punar vepate me hṛdayam.

3.57 ātma|guṇ'|âvamānini! ka idānīm śāradīyaṃ jyotsnāṃ ātapa|treṇa vārayiṣyati?

3.58 niyojitā 'smi!

3.61 halā cintitaṃ mayā gītikā. asaṃnihitāni punar lekha|sādhanāni.

3.62 nanv asmin śuk'|ôdara|sukumāre nalinī|patre pattra|cheda|bhaktyā nakhair nikṣipta|varṇaṃ karoṣi. tataḥ śṛṇumo 'sy' âkṣarāṇi.

3.63 śṛṇuta tāvad enāṃ saṅgat'|ârthā na vā.

3.64 avahite svaḥ!

3.66 tava na jāne hṛdayaṃ mama punaḥ kāmo divā ca rātrau ca, niṣkṛpa tapati balīyas tav' âbhimukha|mano|rathāny aṅgāni.

3.69 svāgataṃ yathā|cintita|phalasy' âvalambino mano|rathasya.

3.70 hṛdaya! tath" ôttamy' êdānīṃ na kiṃ cit pratipadyase.

3.73 itaḥ śilā|tal'|âikadeśam anugṛhṇātu vayasyaḥ.

3.75 labdh'|âuṣadhaḥ sāmpratam upaśamaṃ gamiṣyati kālena.

3.76 kālen' êti kim? paśya, megha|nād'|āhatām iva mayūrīṃ nimeṣ'|ântareṇa pratyāgataṃ priya|sakhīṃ.

3.78 mahā|bhāga! dvayor api yuvayor anyony'|ânurāgaf pratyakṣaḥ. sakhī|snehaf punar māṃ punarukta|vādinīṃ karoti.

3.80 tena hi śṛṇotu mahārājā.

3.82 iyam naḥ sakhī tvām ev' ôddiśya bhagavatā madanen' êdam īdṛśam avasth"|ântaraṃ nītā. tad arhasy abhyupapatty" âsyā jīvitam avalambitum.

3.84 halā! alam antaḥ|pura|vihāra|paryutsukasya rāja'|rṣer uparuddhena.

3.87 vayasya bahu|vallabhāḥ rājānaḥ śrūyante. yathā naḥ sakhī bandhu|jane 'śocanīyā bhavati tathā nirvāhaya.

3.90 anugṛhīte svaḥ.

3.91 hale marṣayataṃ lokapālaṃ yat kiṃ c' âsmābhir upacār'|âtikrameṇa visrambha|pralāpiṇībhir bhaṇitam.

3.92 yena tan mantritaṃ sa marṣayatu. anyasya janasya ko 'tyayaḥ. parokṣaṃ ko vā kiṃ na mantrayati?

3.95 etāvatā punas te tuṣṭir bhavet?

3.96 virama durlalite! etāvad|avasthay" âpi me krīḍasi.

3.97 priyaṃvade, eṣa mṛgapotaka itas tato datta|dṛṣṭir utsuko nūnaṃ mātaram paribhraṣṭām anveṣati. tat saṃyojayiṣyāmi tāvad enam.

3.98 nanu capalakaḥ khalv eṣas. ekākinī niyojayituṃ na pārayasi. tad aham api te anuvartituṃ kārayiṣyāmi.

3.99 hale! anyatarā vo gacchatu. anyath" âśaraṇ" âsmi.

3.100 yaf pṛthivyāḥ śaraṇaṃ sa tava samīpe.

3.101 kathaṃ gataṃ eva?

3.104 na mānanīye jane ātmānam aparādhayiṣye.

3.107 sakhī|mātra|śaraṇā kaṃ vā śaraṇayiṣyāmi?

3.109 na khalv āryaṃ, daivam upālabhe!

3.111 katham idānīm upālapsye ya ātmano 'nīśāṃ para|guṇair mām upahāsayati?

3.116 Paurava! muñca māṃ!

3.118 kadā?

3.120 madan'|âvaṣṭabdho 'pi n' ātmanaḥ kanyakā|janaf prabhavati. bhūyo 'pi tāvat sakhī|janam anumānayiṣyāmi.

3.122 Paurava rakṣa vinayam. ita ita ṛṣayaḥ sañcaranti.

3.124 Paurava! anicchā|pūrako 'pi darśana|mātra|sukha|do na te 'yaṃ jano vismartavyaḥ.

3.127 hā dhik! na me caraṇau puromukhau prabhavataḥ. ebhir ārya|putrasya kuravakair vyavahitā paścād latā|maṇḍapakasya prekṣiṣye tāvad asya bhāv'|ânubandham.

3.130 imaṃ śrutvā na me 'sti vibhavo gantuṃ.

3.133 aho! durbala|śithilatayā prabhraṣṭam api etan mṛṇāla|valayaṃ mayā na vijñātam.

3.136 ato 'param asamarth" âsmi vilambitum. bhavatu. eten' âiva vyapadeśen' âsy' ātmānaṃ darśayiṣyāmi

3.139 aṅga. ardha|pathe smṛtv" âitasya hasta|bhraṃśino mṛṇāla|valayasya kṛte sannivṛtt" âsmi. ākhyātam iva me hṛdayena tvayā gṛhītam iti. tat kṣip' êdaṃ mā muni|jana ātmānam māṃ ca sūcayiṣyasi.

3.141 kena?

3.143 kā gatiḥ!

3.147 tvarayatv ārya|putraḥ!

3.149 kāla|kṣepaḥ kuśalah. yat te rocate.

3.152 na tāvad enaṃ paśyāmi. pavana|kampinā karṇ'|ôtpala|reṇunā kaluṣīkṛtā me dṛṣṭiḥ.

3.154 anukampitā bhaveyam. kiṃ punar na te viśvasimi!

3.156 eṣa eva ta atyupakāro 'viśrambha|janakaḥ.

3.163 pratijñātaṃ manthara iv' ārya|putraḥ saṃvṛttaḥ.

3.165 bhavatu! prakṛti|sth" âsmi saṃvṛttā. lajje punar anupakāriṇī priya|kāriṇa ārya|putrasya.

3.168 asaṃtoṣeṇa kiṃ kariṣyasi?

3.170 āryā Gautamī!

3.171 Paurava! eṣā mama śarīra|vṛttānt'|ôpalambhāya tātasya dharma|kaṇīyasy upasthitā. tad viṭap'|ântarito bhava.

3.174 atyāhitam. iha devatā|sahāyā tiṣṭhasi.

3.175 idānīm eva Mālinīm avatīrṇāf Priyaṃvadā|miśrāḥ.

3.176 api laghuka|santāpāni te 'ṅgāni?

3.177 asti viśeṣaḥ.

3.178 vatse, pariṇato divasaḥ. tad ehi, uṭajam eva gacchāmaḥ.

3.179 hṛdaya, mano|ratha|durlabhaṃ janaṃ prāpya kāla|haraṇaṃ karoṣi, anuśaya|vighaṭṭitasya kathaṃ te sāmpratam. latā|gṛhaka! āmantraye tvāṃ punar api paribhogāya.

4.2 Priyamvade! yady api gāndharveṇa vidhinā nirvṛtta|kalyāṇā Śakuntal" ânurūpa|bhartṛ|gāminī saṃvṛttā tath" âpi na nirvṛtaṃ me hṛdayam.

4.3 katham iva?

4.4 adya sa rāj" êṣṭi|parisamāptāv ṛṣibhir visarjita ātmano nagaraṃ praviśy' ântaḥ|pura ito|gataṃ smarati vā na v" êti.

4.5 atra viśvastā bhava. na tādṛśā ākṛti|viśeṣāḥ guṇa|virodhino bhavanti. etāvat punaś cintanīyam. tāta idānīm imaṃ vṛttāntaṃ śrutvā na jāne kiṃ pratipatsyata iti. . .

4.6 sakhi! yathā māṃ paśyasi tathā tātasy' ânumataṃ priyaṃ ca.

4.7 katham iv' ânumataṃ priyaṃ ca?

4.8 kim anyat. guṇavate kanyakā pratipādayitavy" êty ayaṃ tāvat prathamo 'sya saṅkalpaḥ. taṃ yadi daivam eva sampādayati nanv aprayāsena kṛt'|ârtho guru|janaḥ.

4.9 evam nv etat.

4.9 sakhi avacitāni khalu bali|karma|paryāptāni kusumāni.

4.10 sakhi! Śakuntalāyā api saubhāgya|devat" ârcanīyā.

4.11 yujyate.

4.13 sakhi! atithin" êva niveditam.

4.14 sakhi! nan'|ūṭaja|samnihitā Śakuntalā.

4.15 āṃ adya punar hṛdayeṇa na saṃnihitā.

4.16 tena hi bhavatu etāvadbhiḥ kusumaiḥ.

4.19 hā dhik! eva saṃvṛttam. kasminn api pūj"|ârhe 'parāddhā śūnya|hṛdayā priya|sakhī.

4.20 na khalu yasmiṃs tasmin sulabha|kopa eṣa Durvāsā maha"|ṛṣir, hutāśa iva tvarita|pād'|ôddhārayā gatyā gantuṃ pravṛttaḥ.

4.21 ko 'nyo huta|vahād dagdhuṃ prabhaviṣyati. Anasūye! gaccha pādeṣu patitvā prasāday' âinaṃ yāvad aham argh'|ôdakam upakalpayāmi.

4.23 aho! āvega|skhalitayā prabhraṣṭam agra|hastāt puṣpa|bhājanam me. tat punar api avaceṣyāmi.

4.24 sakhi śarīra|baddhaḥ kopa iva kasya so 'nunayaṃ gṛhṇāti. kiṃ ca punaḥ s' ânukrośaḥ kṛtaḥ.

4.25 tasmin bahv etad api. tataḥ kathaya katham iva.

4.26 yadā nivartituṃ n' êcchati tadā vijñāpito mayā: bhagavan! prathama|bhaktim avekṣy' âdy' ātma|prabhāva|vijñāta|sāmarthyasya duhitṛ|janasya bhagavat" âparādho marṣitavya iti.

4.27 tatas tataḥ?

4.28 tataḥ: «na me vacanam anyathā|bhavitum arhati. ābharaṇ'|âbhijñāna|darśanena mama śāpo nivartiṣyate» iti mantrayann ev' ântarhitaḥ.

4.29 śakyam idānīm āśvasitum. asti tena rāja'|ṛṣiṇā saṃprasthitena sva|nāma|dhey'|âṅkitam aṅgulīyaṃ smaraṇīyam iti Śakuntalāyāḥ svayam eva haste pinaddham. tasmiṃś ca sv'|ādhīne 'yam upāyo bhaviṣyati.

4.30 hale Priyaṃvade! prekṣasva prekṣasva! vāma|hast'|ôpanihita|
vadan" ālikhit" êva sakhī bhartṛ|gatayā cintay" ātmānam apy
eṣā na vibhāvayati kiṃ punar āgantukam?

4.31 halā Anasūye! dvayor ev' āvayor eṣa śāpa|vṛttāntas tiṣṭhatu.
rakṣaṇīyā khalu prakṛti|pelavā sakhī.

4.32 ka idānīṃ tāp'|ôdakena nava|mālikāṃ siñcati.

4.45 evam api nāma viṣaya|parāṅ|mukhasy' âpy etan na viditam
yathā tena rājñā Śakuntalāyā an|āryat" ācaritavy" êti.

4.47 pratibuddh" âpi kiṃ karayiṣyāmi. na ma utthitāyāś cintite-
ṣu prabhāta|vyāpāra|karaṇīyeṣu hastāf pādā vā prabhavanti.
sa|kāma idānīṃ kāmo bhavatu, yena snigdha|hṛdayā sakhy
asatya|sandhe jane padaṃ kāritā. atha vā na tasya rāja'|ṛṣer
aparādho Durvāsaḥ|kopo 'tra viprakaroti. anyathā kathaṃ tā-
dṛśo rāja'|ṛṣis tādṛśāni vacanāni mantrayitv" âitāvataḥ kālasya
lekha|mātram api na visarjayati. ito 'ṅgulīyam asy' âbhijñā-
naṃ visarjayāmaḥ. atha vā duḥkha|śīle tapasvi|jane ko 'bhyar-
thyatām. na ca sakhi|gamanena doṣa iti vyavasitam idānīṃ
pārayāmaḥ Prabhāsa|nirvṛttasya tāta|Kāśyapasya Duṣyanta|
pariṇītām āpanna|sattvāṃ ko 'pi Śakuntalāṃ nivedayiṣyati.
itthaṃ|gate kiṃ nu khalv asmābhiḥ kartavyam?

4.49 Śakuntalāyāf prasthāna|kautukāni kriyantām.

4.50 sakhi kathaṃ nv etat?

4.51 Anasūye. śṛṇu. idānīṃ sukha|śayita|vibuddhāyāḥ Śakuntalāyās
samīpaṃ gat" âsmi yāvat tāṃ lajj"|âvanataṃ pariṣvajya tāta|
Kāśyapaḥ svayam abhinandati. diṣṭyā dhūm'|ôparuddha|dṛṣṭer
api janasya pāvaka eva āhutiṣ patitā. suśiṣya|pratipādit" êva vi-
dy" âśocanīy" âsi me saṃvṛttā. tad ady' âiva' ṛṣi|parigṛhītaṃ
tvāṃ bhartuḥ sakāśaṃ visarjayām' îti.

4.52 atha kena ākhyātas tātasy' âyaṃ Śakuntalā|vṛttāntaḥ?

4.53 tātasya śaraṇaṃ praviṣṭasya śarīraṃ vinā chandovatyā vācā.

4.54 katham iva.

4.57 sakhi priyaṃ me, kiṃ tv Śakuntalā nīyata ity utkaṇṭhā|sādhāraṇaṃ paritoṣam samudvahāmi.

4.58 utkaṇṭhāṃ vinodayiṣyāvaḥ. s" êdānīṃ nirvṛtā bhavatu.

4.59 tena hy etasmiṃś cūta|śākh"|âvalambite nārikela|samudgake tan|nimittam eva kāl'|ântara|kṣamā kṣiptā mayā sa|kesara|guṇā. tāṃs tvaṃ hasta|sannihitān kuru yāvad aham asyā mṛga|gorocanāṃ tīrtha|mṛttikāṃ dūrvā|kisalayāni maṅgala|samālabhan'|ârthaṃ viracayāmi.

4.62 Anasūye, tvaraya tvaraya! ete khalu Hastināpura|gāmina ṛṣayaḥ sajjībhavant' îti.

4.63 sakhi, ehi gacchāmaḥ.

4.64 eṣā sūry'|ôdaya eva visarjitā pratīṣṭa|nīvāra|bhājanakābhis tāpasībhir abhinandyamānā Śakuntalā tiṣṭhati. tad upasarpāva enām.

4.66 jāte! bhartur bahu|māna|yuktakaṃ mahā|devī|śabdaṃ adhigaccha.

4.67 vatse vīra|prasavinī bhava.

4.69 sakhi! sumaj|janaṃ te bhavatu!

4.70 svāgataṃ priya|sakhyoḥ. ito niṣīdatam.

4.71 halā Śakuntale! ṛjugatā bhava yāvat te maṅgala|samālabdhaṃ aṅgaṃ kriyatām.

4.72 ucitam idam api bahumantavyam. durlabham idānīṃ me sakhī|maṇḍanaṃ bhaviṣyati.

4.73 sakhi na ta eṣṭavye maṅgala|kāle roditavyam.

4.74 ābharaṇ'|ârhaṃ rūpam āśrama|sulabhaif prasādhanair viprakriyate.

4.78 vatsa Hārīta. kuta etat?

4.83 hale! adbhuta|saṃpattiḥ sūcitā, bhartur gehe 'nubhavitavyā te rāja|lakṣmīḥ.

4.85 sakhi! kalyāṇin" îdanīm asi. koṭara|saṃbhav" êva madhukarī puṣkara|madhum abhilaṣasi.

4.86 anupabhukta|bhūṣaṇo 'yaṃ janaḥ. citra|karma|paricayen' êdānīṃ te 'ṅgeṣv ābharaṇa|niyogaṃ karoti.

4.87 jane vo nipuṇatvam.

4.94 halā Śakuntale avasita|maṇḍan" âsi. paridhehi sāṃpratam imaṃ pavitraṃ kṣauma|nirmokaṃ.

4.97 eṣa te ānanda|parivāhiṇā cakṣuṣā pariṣvajamāna iva gurur upasthitaḥ. tad ācāram asya pratipadyasva.

4.98 tāta vande.

4.101 bhagavān! varaḥ khalv eṣo, n' āśīḥ.

4.117 jāte. jñāti|jana|snigdham abhyanujñāta|gaman" âsi tapo|vana|devatābhiḥ. tat praṇama bhagavatīḥ.

4.118 halā Priyaṃvade ārya|putra|darśan'|ôtsukay" âpy āśramaṃ parityajantyā duḥkha|duḥkhena me caraṇau puromukhaf prabhavanti.

4.119 na kevalaṃ tava viraha|paryutsukās sakhya eva. yāvat tvay" ôpasthita|viyogasya tapo|vanasy' âpy apekṣyam avasth"|ântaram. tathā ca.

4.120 ullalati darbha|kabalā mṛgī pariśrānta|nartanā mayūrī. apasṛta|pāṇḍu|pattrā dhunvanty aṅgān' îva latāḥ.

4.121 tāta, latā|bhaginīṃ tāvan mādhavīm āmantrayiṣye.

4.123 eādhavi. pratyāliṅga māṃ śākhā|mayair bāhūbhir adya|prabhṛti dūra|vartinī te bhaviṣyāmi.

4.126 eṣā dvayor api vo haste nikṣepaḥ.

4.127 ayaṃ janaḥ kasya sandiṣṭaḥ.

4.129 tāta! eṣ" ôṭaja|paryanta|cāriṇī garbha|mantharā mṛga|vadhūḥ. yad" āsanna|prasavinī bhavet tadā me kam api priyaṃ nivedayitāraṃ visarjayiṣyatha.

4.132 ko nu khalv eṣa mātrākrānta iva punar vasanasy' ântaṃ gṛhṇāti?

4.135 vatsa kiṃ sahavāsa|parityāginīṃ kaitava|snehām anveṣasi? acira|prasūt'|ôparatayā jananyā vinā vardhito 'si/ idānīm api mayā virahitaṃ tvāṃ tātaś cintayiṣyati. tat pratinivartasya.

4.142 sakhi! na sa āśrame cintanīyo 'sti yas tvayā virahayantyā n' ôtsukīkṛto 'dya prekṣasva tāvat.

4.143 padminī|pattr'|ântaritāṃ vyāhṛtāṃ n' ânuvyāharati jāyām, mukh'|ôdvyūḍha|mṛṇālas tvayi dṛṣṭiṃ dadāti cakravākaḥ.

4.144 sakhi! satyam eva nalinī|patr'|ântaritam priyaṃ saha|caram aprekṣamāṇ" āturaṃ cakravāky ārasati duṣkaraṃ khalv ahaṃ karomi.

4.146 ady' âpi vinā priyeṇa gamayati rātriṃ visūraṇā|dīrghāṃ, hanta gurukam api duḥkham āśā|bandhas sahayati.

4.157 etāvat khalv ev' âitad vadhū|jana upadeśaḥ.

4.157 jāte, evaṃ khalv avadhāraya.

4.159 tāta kim ita eva priya|sakhyo nivartante?

4.161 katham idānīṃ tātena virahitā kari|sārtha|paribhraṣṭā kareṇuk" êva prāṇān dhārayiṣye.

4.168 hale! etaṃ dve eva māṃ samaṃ pariṣvajethām!

4.169 sakhi sa rājā yadi pratyabhijñāna|mantharo bhavet tad" âsy' êdaṃ tadīya|nāmadhey'|âṅkitam aṅgulīyakaṃ darśaya.

4.170 ā sandeśen' ânukampit" âsmi.

4.171 mā bhaiṣīḥ. sneho vāmam āśaṅkate.

4.174 tāta, kadā nu khalu bhūyas tapo|vanaṃ prekṣiṣye?

4.177 jāte, parihīyate gamana|velā. tan nivartaya pitaram. atha vā cireṇ' âiṣā pitaraṃ na nivartayiṣyati. tan nivartayatu bhavān.

4.179 tāto nirutkaṇṭho bhaviṣyati, aham idānīm utkaṇṭhā|bhāginī saṃvṛttā.

4.184 hā dhik! antarhitā Śakuntalā vana|rājībhiḥ.

4.186 tāta Śakuntalā|virahitaṃ śūnyam iva tapo|vanam praviśāvaḥ.

5.12 bhoḥ! saṃgīta|śālikā. ten' âvadhānaṃ dehi tāla|gater viśuddhāyāḥ khalu vīṇāyāḥ svara|saṃyogāḥ śrūyante.

5.16 abhinava|madhu|lobha|bhāvitas tathā paricumbya cūta|mañjarīm, kamala|vasati|mātra|nirvṛto madhu|kara vismṛto 'sy enāṃ katham?

5.18 kiṃ tāvad asyā gītikāyā api gṛhīto bhagavat" âkṣar'|ârthaḥ?

5.20 gṛhītas tvayā parakīyair hastaiḥ śikhaṇḍake bhallūkaḥ. a|vīta|rāgasy' êva n' âsti me mokṣaḥ.

5.22 kā gatiḥ!

5.31 ita ito devaḥ.

5.39 eṣo 'bhinava|saṃmārjana|ramanīyaḥ saṃnihita|kapila|dhenur agni|śaraṇ'|ālindaḥ.

5.42 devasya bhuvana|pariṣvaṅga|nirvṛte catur|āśrame kuta etat? kiṃ tu sucarit'|âbhinandina ṛṣayo devaṃ sabhājayitum āgatā iti tarkayāmi.

5.50 aho! kim api vām'|êtaraṃ me nayanaṃ visphurati?

5.51 pratihatam amaṅgalam! sukhāni te bhartṛ|kula|devatā vitarantu.

5.55 deva! prasann' ôkha|rāgā dṛśyante svastha|karyā ṛṣayaḥ.

5.58 deva! kutūhalatayā bṛṃhit" âsmi. na me tarkaf prasīdati.

5.59 bhartaḥ, darśanīyā khalu asyā ākṛtir lakṣyate.

5.61 hṛdaya! kim evaṃ vepasi? ārya|putrasya bhāva|sthitiṃ smṛtvā dhīraṃ tāvad bhava.

5.76 bhadra|mukha! vaktukāmā tiṣṭhāmi, na ca me vadan'|âvakāśo 'sti. katham iti?

5.77 n' âpekṣito guru|jano 'nayā na c' âtra pṛṣṭā bandhavaḥ, ek'|âikena varite kiṃ bhaṇyatāṃ ekam|ekasmin?

5.78 kiṃ nu khalv ārya|putra bhaṇiṣyati?

5.80 huṃ! pāvako 'sya vacan'|ôpakṣepaḥ.

5.84 hṛdaya, saṃvardhitā khalu tav' āśaṅkā.

5.89 jāte! mā muhūrtakaṃ lajjasva. apaneṣyāmi tāvat tav' âvaguṇṭhanam. tato bhartā tvām abhijñāsyat' îti.

5.93 aho dharmāpekṣitā bhartuḥ! īdṛśaṃ nāma sukh'|ôpanatam strī|ratnaṃ dṛṣṭvā, ko 'nyo vicārayati?

5.96 hā dhik! katham pariṇaya eva sandehaḥ? bhagn" êdānīṃ me dūr'|ārohiṇī āśā!

5.100 idam avasth"|ântaraṃ gate tādṛśe muhūrta|rāge kiṃ vā smāritena sāmprataṃ tena? athav" ātm" êdāniṃ me śodhanīyo 'sti vivadiṣyāmy etat. ārya|putra! athavā saṃśayita idānīṃ me samudācāraḥ. Paurava! yuktaṃ nāma pur" āśrama|pade sad|bhāv'|ôttāna|hṛdayam imaṃ janaṃ samaya|pūrvaṃ pratāry' ēdṛśair akṣaraif pratyākhyātum.

5.103 yadi param'|ârthataf para|parigrahaṇa|śaṅkinā tvay" âivam uktaṃ, tad abhijñānena guruṇā tava sandeham apaneṣyāmi.

5.105 hā dhik! aṅgulīya|śūnyā me 'ṅgulī.

5.106 na khalu te Śakr'|âvatāre Śacī|tīrth'|ôdakam avagāhamānāyāf prabhraṣṭo 'ṅgulīyakaḥ?

5.108 atra tāvad vidhinā darśitaṃ prabhutvam. aparaṃ te kathayiṣyāmi.

5.110 na khalu tatr' âika|divase nava|mālikā|maṇḍape nalinī|pattra|bhājana|gatam udakaṃ tava hasta|saṃnihitam āsīt?

5.112 tat|kṣaṇaṃ ca mama kṛtaka|putro Hariṇaka upasthitaḥ. tatas tvay" âyaṃ tāvat prathamaṃ pivatv iti anukampiṇ" ôpacchanditaḥ. na punas te 'paricitasya hast'|âbhyāsa upagataḥ. paścāt tasminn ev' ôdake mayā gṛhīte praṇaya|prakāśa|pūrvaṃ prahasito 'si. bhaṇitaṃ ca tvayā: «sarvaḥ sa|gandhe viśvasiti dvāv apy atr' āraṇyakāv iti.»

5.114 mahā|bhāga! n' ârhasy etāvan mantrayitum. tapo|vana|saṃvardhitaḥ khalv ayaṃ jano 'nabhijñaḥ kaitavaysa.

5.117 ātmano hṛday'|ânumānena sarvaṃ prekṣase! ko 'nyo dharma|kañcuka|praveśinas tṛṇa|channa|kūp'|ôpamasya tav' ânukārī bhaviṣyati?

5.122 yūyam eva pramāṇaṃ jānītha dharma|sthitiṃ ca lokasya, lajjā|vinirjitā jānanti khalu kiṃ nu mahilāḥ?

5.123 suṣṭhu tāvat svacchanda|cāriṇī kṛt" âsmi y' âham asya Puru|vaṃśa|pratyayena hṛdaya|śastra|dhārasya mukha|madhuno hast'|âbhyāsam upagatā.

5.135 huṃ! anena tāvat kaitavena vipralabdh" âsmi. yūyam api māṃ parityaktum icchatha. tat kā gatiḥ?

5.136 vatsa Śārṅgarava! anugacchty eṣā karuṇā|parideviṇī Śakuntalā. pratyādeśa|kaluṣe bhartari kiṃ vā putrikā me karotu?

5.151 bhagavati Vasu|dhe! dehi me vivaram!

6.2 are kumbhīraka kathaya kutra tvay" âiṣa mahā|maṇi|bandhan'|ôtkīrṇa|nām'|âkṣaro rājakīy'|âṅgulīyakaḥ samāsāditaḥ?

6.3 prasīdantu prasīdantu bhrātṛka|miśrāḥ! ahaṃ khalv īdṛśasya karmaṇo na kalyaḥ!

6.4 kiṃ nu khalu śobhano brāhmaṇa iti kṛtvā rājñā pratigraho dattaḥ?

6.5 jānīth' êdānīm! ahaṃ Śakrāvatāra|vāsiko dhīvaraḥ. . .

6.6 pāṭac|cara! kiṃ khalu te 'smābhir jātif pṛṣṭā?

6.7 Sūcaka kathayatu sarvam anukrameṇa. m" âinam antarā pratibandhīṣṭha.

6.8 yad ābutta ājñāpayati! bhaṇa bhaṇa!

6.9 so 'haṃ jāla|baḍiś'|ādibhir matsya|bandhan'|ôpāyaiḥ kuṭumba|bharaṇaṃ karomi.

6.10 viśuddha idānīṃ ta ājīvaḥ!

6.11 bhartaḥ!

6.12 sahajaṃ kila yad api ninditaṃ na khalu tat karma vivarjanīyam. paśu|māraṇa|karma|dāruṇo 'nukampā|mṛdur eva śrotriyaḥ.

6.13 tatas tataḥ!

6.14 ath' âika|divase khaṇḍaśo rohita|matsyo mayā kalpitaḥ. yāvat tasy' ôdar'|âbhyantare etad ratna|bhāsuram aṅgulīyakaṃ prekṣe. paścād ih' âitad vikrayāya darśayan gṛhīto bhāva|miśraiḥ. etāvāṃs tāvad etasy' āgamaḥ adhunā mārayata kuṭṭayata vā!

6.15 Jānaka! matsy'|ôdara|saṃsthitam iti n' âsti saṃdehaḥ. tath" âyam asya visra|gandhaḥ. āgama idānīm etasya vimarśayitavyam. tad etaṃ rāja|kulam eva gacchāmaḥ.

6.16 gaccha nātha granthi|bhedaka!

6.17 Sūcaka! iha māṃ gopura|dvāre 'pramattau pratipālayataṃ yāvad idam yath"|āgamam aṅgulīyakaṃ bhartur upanīya tadīya|śāsanaṃ pratīṣya niṣkrāmāmi.

6.18 praviśatv āvuttaḥ svāmi|prasādāya!

6.19 Jānaka, cirāyate khalv āvuttaḥ.

6.20 nanv avasar'|ôpasarpaṇīyā rājānaḥ.

6.21 vayasya sphurato mama hastāv asya pinaddhum.

6.22 n' ârhati bhrātṛ|bhrātṛko 'kāla|mārako bhavitum.

6.23 . . . eṣo 'smākam īśvaraf prāpto gṛhītvā rāja|śāsanam. sakulānāṃ mukhaṃ prekṣase 'thavā gṛdhra|śṛgālānāṃ balir bhaviṣyasi.

6.24 śīghraṃ śīghram etam. . .

6.25 hā hato 'smi!

6.26 muñcatam re muñcatam jāl'|ôpajīvinam. upapanno 'sya kil' âṅgulīyakasy' āgamaḥ. asmat|svāmin" âiva me kathitam.

6.27 yad ājñāpayati ābuttaḥ! Yama|vasatiṃ gatvā khaṇḍaṃ c' êva pratinivṛttaḥ.

6.28 bhartaḥ! tava me jīvitaḥ!

6.29 uttiṣṭha! eṣa bhartṛ" âṅgulīyaka|mūlya|sammitaf pāritoṣiko 'pi te dāpitaḥ.

6.30 anugṛhīto 'smi.

6.31 tathā nām' ânugraho yac chūlād avatārya hasti|skandhe pratiṣṭhāpitaḥ.

6.32 āvutta! pāritoṣikaḥ kathayati mah"|ârha|ratnena ten' āṅgulīyakena bhartuf prathama|bahu|matena bhavitavyam.

6.33 na ca tasmin mah"|ârha|ratnam iti bahu|mānaṃ bhartus tarkayāmi.

6.34 kiṃ khalu?

6.35 tarkayāmi tasya darśanena ko 'pi abhilaṣito jano bhartrā smṛta iti, yatas tat prekṣya muhūrtam prakṛti|gambhīraḥ paryutsuka|manāḥ saṃvṛttaḥ.

6.36 sādhu mantritaṃ nām' āvuttena.

6.37 nanu bhaṇāmy asya kṛte mātsyalikā|śatror iti.

6.38 bhartaḥ! ito 'rdhaṃ yuṣmākaṃ sumano|mūlyam bhavatu.

6.39 etāvad yujyate.

6.40 dhīvara, mahattarako hi sāmprataṃ priya|vayasyako 'si me saṃvṛttaḥ. kādambarī|sākṣikaṃ c' âsmākaṃ prathama|sauhṛdam iṣyate. tac chauṇḍika|śālaṃ gacchāmaḥ.

6.44 nirvartitaṃ mayā paryāya|nirvartanīyam apsaras|tīrtha|sāmnidhyaṃ. tad yāvad asya rājarṣer udantaṃ pratyakṣī|karomi. Menakā|sambandhena śarīra|bhūtā me Śakuntalā. tayā c' âitan|nimittam eva sandiṣṭa|pūrv" âsmi. kiṃ nu khal' ûtsavaṃ|dine 'pi nirutsav'|ārambham iva rāja|kulaṃ dṛśyate. athav" âsti me vibhavaf praṇidhānena sarvaṃ jñātum. kiṃ tu sakhyā ādara ānītavyaḥ. bhavatu. eṣāṃ tāvad udyāna|pālinīnāṃ tiraskariṇī|pracchannā pārśva|parivartinī bhūtv" ôpālabhiṣye.

6.47 ātāmra|harita|vṛntaka ya ucchvasito 'si surabhi|māsasya, dṛṣṭaś ca cūta|kṣāraka kṣaṇa|maṅgalakam iva prekṣe.

6.48 hale Parabhṛtike kiṃ nv idam ekākinī mantrayase.

6.49 sakhi, cūta|latikāṃ dṛṣṭv" ônmattā parabhṛtikā bhavati.

6.50 katham upasthito madhu|māsaḥ?

6.51 madhu|karike, tav' êdānīṃ kāla eṣa mada|vibhram'|ôdgītānām.

6.52 sakhi, avalambasva yāvad agra|pāda|pratiṣṭhāpitā bhūtvā Kāmadevasy' ârcanaṃ karomi.

6.53 yadi mam' âpi ardham arcanaka|phalasya.

6.54 hale! abhaṇite 'py etad bhavati, yata ekam eva no dvidhā|sthitaṃ śarīram. aho! apratibuddho 'pi cūta|prasava eṣa bandhana|bhaṅga|surabhir vāti. namo bhagavate Makara|dhvajāya!

6.55 arhasi me cūt'|âṅkura dattaḥ Kāmasya gṛhīta|dhanoḥ. saṃsthāpita|yuvati|lakṣaf paścāt|skhalitaḥ śaro bhavitum.

6.59 prasīdatv āryaḥ! agṛhīt'|ârthe āvām.

6.62 n' âtra saṃdehaḥ. mahā|prabhāvo rājarṣiḥ.

6.63 ārya, kati divasā asmākaṃ Mitrā|vasunā rāṣṭriyeṇa bhartuf pāda|mūlāt preṣitānāṃ, ih' ā krīḍā|gṛhe pratikarm' ârpitam. ato na kad" âpi śruta|pūrva eṣa asmābhir vṛttāntaḥ.

6.65 ārya, kautūhalyaṃ yad anena janena śrotavyaṃ tat kathayatv āryaḥ kiṃ nimittaṃ bhartrā vasanta|kaumudī pratiṣiddh" êti?

6.66 utsava|priyā rājānaḥ. atra guruṇā kāraṇena bhavitavyam.

6.68 ārya! śrutaṃ rāṣṭriya|mukhād yāvad aṅgulīyaka|darśanam.

6.71 priyaṃ me!

6.73 yujyate.

6.74 etu etu bhavān.

6.79 sthāne khalu pratyādeśa|vimānit" âpi Śakuntalā yad asya kṛte tāmyati.

6.82 īdṛśāny asyās tapasvinyā bhāga|dheyāni.

6.83 laṅghita eṣa bhūyaḥ Śakuntalā|vātena. na jāne kathaṃ cikitsitavyo bhaviṣyati.

6.86 yad deva ājñāpayati.

6.89 kṛtaṃ bhavatā nirmakṣikam. sāmprataṃ śiśira|vicchede ramaṇīye 'smin pramada|vane sukhaṃ vihariṣyāmaḥ.

6.92 tiṣṭha tāvat. imaṃ daṇḍakaṃ cūta|manmathake pātaye.

6.94 nanu khalu bhavatā medhāvinī lipi|karī saṃdiṣṭā. mādhavī|maṇḍapa imāṃ kṣaṇaṃ pratipālayiṣyāmi. tatra me citra|phalake sva|hasta|likhitāṃ tatra|bhavatyāḥ Śakuntalāyāḥ pratikṛtim ānay' êti.

6.96 etu bhavān.

6.97 eṣa maṇi|śilā|paṭṭaka|sa|nātho mādhavī|maṇḍapako viviktatayā niḥśabdaṃ svāgaten' êva pratīcchati priya|vayasyam. upaviśāmaḥ. niṣīdatu bhavān.

6.100 na vismarāmi. kiṃ tu sarvaṃ kathitaṃ tvay" âiva vṛttam. parihāsa|vikalpa eṣa na bhūt'|ârtha iti. rahasya|bheda|bhīruṇā may" âpi mṛt|piṇḍa|manda|buddhinā tath" âiva gṛhītam. api ca bhavitavyatā balavatī.

6.101 evaṃ nv idam.

6.103 kiṃ nv idam. īdṛśam upanataṃ. kadā punaḥ sat|puruṣāḥ śoka|baddha|dhairyā bhavanti? nanu pravāten' âpi girayo niṣprakampāḥ.

6.106 aho. īdṛśī kaṣṭ'|âvasthā. asya saṃtāpen' âhaṃ rame.

6.107 asti deva tarkaḥ. ken' âpi tatra|bhavaty ākāśa|gāmin" âvahit" êti.

6.109 aho! mohaḥ khalu vismayanīyo na punaf pratibodhaḥ.

6.110 yady evaṃ tad asti khalu samāgamo 'pi kālena tatra|bhavatyā.

6.112 na khalu mātā|pitarau bhartṛ|virahitām duhitaraṃ ciraṃ draṣṭuṃ pārayataḥ.

6.115 mā evam bhaṇa! nanu khalv aṅgulīyakam eva nidarśanam. evam ev' âvaśyaṃ|bhāvino 'cintanīyāḥ samāgamā bhavat' îti.

6.118 sakhi, dūre vartase. ekākinī tāvat karṇa|sukham anubhavāmi.

6.119 bho vayasya! idam aṅgulīyakaṃ ken' ôdghātena tatra|bhavatyā hasta|saṃsargaṃ prāpitam?

6.121 tatas tataḥ?

6.125 ramaṇīyas te vidhinā darśito mārgaḥ.

6.126 atha kathaṃ dāsyāf putrasya rohita|matsyasya baḍiśam iv' âitad aṅgulīyakaṃ mukhe praviṣṭaṃ?

6.129 pūrv'|âpara|virodhī eṣa vṛttānto vartate.

6.132 eṣa khalu bhartā. yāvad enam upasarpāmi. jayatu, jayatu bhartā! iyaṃ citra|gatā bhartrī.

6.133 he he bhoḥ! svabhāva|madhur" ākṛtiḥ khalu. sādhu vayasya sādhu. kim bahunā? svānt'|ânupraveśa|śaṅkay" ālapana|kutūhalaṃ māṃ janayati.

6.134 aho, vayasyasya vartikā|rekhāyā nipuṇatā! jāne sakhy agrato me tiṣṭhati.

6.136 ayam eva sarvaṃ pratipanno yad asmi vaktukāmā.

6.137 bhoḥ, tisras tatra|bhavatyo dṛśyante. sarvā darśanīyāḥ. katam" âtra tatra|bhavatī Śakuntalā?

6.138 moha|dakṣas tapasvī. avaśyaṃ na me pratyakṣā sakhī.

6.140 tarkayāmi y" âiṣ" âvaseka|snigdha|pallavām aśoka|latikāṃ saṃśritā śithila|keśa|bandh'|ôdvamat|kusumena baddha|sveda|bindunā vadanakena viśeṣa|namita|śākhābhyāṃ bāhu|latābhyām ucchvasita|nīvinā vasanen' ēṣat|pariśrānt" êv' ālikhit" âiṣ" âtrabhavatī Śakuntalā. itarāḥ sakhyaḥ.

6.144 ārya Mādhavya! avalambasva citra|phalakaṃ yāvad gacchāmi.

6.145 kim aparaṃ atra abhilikhitavyam?

6.146 asaṃśayaṃ yo yaḥ sakhyā me 'bhirucitaf pradeśas taṃ tam ālikhitukāmo bhaviṣyat' îti tarkayāmi.

6.149 tathā tarkayāmi pūritam anena citra|phalakaṃ kūrc'|âlakānāṃ tāpasānām.

6.151 kim iva?

6.152 vana|vāsasya tasyāś ca saukumāryasya yad anusadṛśaṃ bhaviṣyat' îti.

6.154 kiṃ nv atrabhavatī rakta|kuvalaya|śobhin" âgra|hastena mukham apavārya cakita|cakit" êva sthitā. he he bhoḥ! eṣa dāsyāf putraḥ kusuma|pāṭac|caro madhu|karo 'tra|bhavatyā vadana|kamalam abhilaṣati.

6.156 bhavān ev' âvinīt'|ânuśāsi vāraṇe prabhavati.

6.159 abhijātaṃ khalu vāritaḥ.

6.160 pratiṣiddha|vām" âiṣā jātiḥ.

6.163 evaṃ tīkṣṇa|daṇḍasya kathaṃ te na bheṣyati? eṣa unmattakaḥ khalu! aham apy īdṛśasya saṃsargeṇa īdṛśa|varṇa iva saṃvṛttaḥ.

6.164 mam' âpy ātmano 'nantaraṃ gaṇaya y" âham idānīṃ pratibuddhā.

6.166 aho! dhīre 'pi jane rasaf padaṃ karoti.

6.167 bhoḥ, citraṃ khalv etat.

6.170 smṛtaṃ tvayā pratyādeśa|vimānanaṃ Śakuntalāyāḥ sakhyā dṛṣṭaṃ khalu pratyakṣam asmābhiḥ.

6.171 bhartā, devyāḥ Kula|prabhāyāf parijaṇen' ântar"| âvacchinnas te vartikā|karaṇḍakaḥ.

6.173 bahu|māny" âsya Kula|prabhā. atha vā n' âitat kiṃ cit. vipañcyāḥ khalv asannidhāna eka|tantur apy arghati.

6.176 bhartaḥ, idam ap' îdānīṃ citra|pratikṛtaṃ Piṅgalikā|miśrā apahastitaṃ yatante.

6.177 bhinn" êdānīm asy' āśā.

6.179 jayatu jayatu bhartrī!

6.180 apeta bhoḥ! Medhāvinīṃ mṛgīm iv' ânusaranty upasthit" ântaḥ|pura|vyāghrī Piṅgalikā.

6.182 ātmānam iti bhaṇa!

6.183 sakhi, eṣā pratikṛtir api te pratipakṣasy' âlaṅghanīyā kriyate.

6.184 eṣa enaṃ gopayāmi yatra pārāvatīṃ varjayitv' âparo na prekṣate.

6.185 jayatu jayatu devaḥ!

6.187 bhartaḥ, patra|hastāṃ māṃ prekṣya pratinivṛttā.

6.189 deva, amātyo vijñāpayati. artha|jātasya gaṇanā|bahulatay" âikam eva paura|kāryam avekṣitaṃ tad devaḥ soḍhum arhati.

6.191 yad bhart" ājñāpayati.

6.193 deva idānīm eva Keśava|śreṣṭhino duhitā nirvṛtta|pumsavanā jāyā śrūyate.

6.195 yad deva ājñāpayati.

6.197 iyam asmi.

6.200 idaṃ nāma atra ghoṣayitavyam. deva, kāle ghuṣṭam iv' âbhinanditaṃ deva|śāsanaṃ mahā|janena.

6.202 pratihatam āśaṅkitam!

6.204 asamśayaṃ sakhīm eva hṛdaye kṛtvā nindito 'nen' ātmā.

6.207 imaṃ pattrakaṃ preṣayatā kiṃ smāritam amātyena yat prekṣya tāvad bhartur jal'|âvasekaḥ saṃvṛttaḥ? athavā na so 'buddhi| pūrvakaṃ pravartate.

6.210 sadṛśaṃ khalu te vyavadhānam. vayaḥ|sthaf prabhur aparāsu devīṣu anurūpa|putra|janmanā pūrva|puruṣāṇām an|ṛṇo bhaviṣyat' îti. na me vacanaṃ pratigṛhṇāti! athav" ânurūpam ev' âuṣadham ātaṅkaṃ nivārayati.

6.213 samāśvasitu samāśvasitu bhartā!

6.214 idānīm ev' âinaṃ nirvṛtaṃ karomi. athavā mahatībhif punar devatābhir etad darśitam. na śakyo may" ân|anujñātayā hasta|saṃsargaṃ netum. bhavatu. yajña|bhāg'|ôtsukā devā eva tathā kariṣyanti yath" âiṣa rājarṣis tayā saha|dharma|cāriṇyā samāgamiṣyati. kariṣyanti katham eva tatra prekṣe. yāvad anena vṛtt'|ântena priya|sakhīṃ samāśvāsayāmi.

6.215 abrāhmaṇyaṃ abrāhmaṇyaṃ bhoḥ! abrāhmaṇyaṃ!

6.217 tapasvī Piṅkalikā|miśrānāṃ mukhe patito bhaviṣyati.

6.238 dhāva bhoḥ!

6.240 kathaṃ idānīṃ na bheṣyāmi? eṣa māṃ ko 'pi paścān|moṭita|śiro|dharam ikṣum iva sthira|bhaṅgam eva kartum icchati!

6.242 jayatu jayatu bhartā! etac char'|āsanaṃ hast'|āvāpa|sahitam.

6.249 abhidhāva bhoḥ! aham bhavantaṃ prekṣe. eṣa bhavān māṃ na prekṣate. marjāra|gṛhīta iv' ônduro nirāśo 'smi jīvite saṃvṛttaḥ.

6.257 bhoḥ! aham anena paśu|māreṇa mārito manāg asmi!

6.270 yad bhavān ājñāpayati.

7.2 ājñaptaṃ hi guruṇā Nāradena yath" âiteṣv eva divaseṣu martya|lokād uttīrṇena rājarṣiṇā Duśyantena bhagavataḥ Puran|darasya priya|kāriṇā dānava|vadha|nimittaṃ gantavyam. yāvad abhyarcy' êmaṃ hy āpṛcchyamāno nikṣipati tāvad eva mayā vibudha|pratyakṣaṃ maṅgala|nimittaṃ kim api prekṣaṇakaṃ darśayitavyam. «tat tvaṃ kām api lāsikām anveṣya saṅgīta|śālāyām āgacch' êti.» tad yāval lāsikām anveṣayāmi. kā punar eṣā gṛhīta|varaṇā paścādd harṣit'|ôtkaṇṭhit" êv' êta ev' āgacchati? kathaṃ priya|sakhī Cūtamañjarī? tad yāvad etayā sah'|ôpādhyāya|samīpaṃ gacchāmi.

7.4 aho! mahā|prabhāvo rājarṣir Duṣyantaḥ. aho, maha|balaḥ sa hato Durjayo dānava|balaḥ. athavā Dusṣyanta eva yena sārathi|dvitīyen' âiva aneka|praharaṇa|sāhasāni vikiran kṣaṇen' âiva nihataḥ sa Durjaya|dānava|balaḥ

7.5 sakhi, Cūta|mañjarī. utkaṇṭhit" êva lakṣyase?

7.6 katham, Pārijāta|mañjarī? sakhi, sarvaṃ kathayiṣyāmi. tvaṃ tāvat kutra prasthit" êti prakṣyāmi?

7.7 sakhi, saṅkṣepena kathayiṣyāmi. ahaṃ khalu rājarṣer Duśyantasya dānava|vijaya|vyapadeśen' âdya maṅgala|nimittaṃ kim api prekṣaṇakaṃ darśyata ity upādhyāyasy' ājñay" ôbhe eva sakāśam.

7.8 āsīd avasara etasya. idānīṃ punar martya|lokaṃ prasthita etasmin mahā|rāje kasya darśyate?

7.9 sakhi, kiṃ Mahendrasya mano|rathān sampādya gata ut' ânyath" êti?

7.10 sakhi, śṛṇu! ady' âiva go|sarga|samayena varaṃ Durjaya|dānava| jīvita|sarvasva|śeṣam gṛhītvā yāvac ca tridaśa|vilāsinī sa|rasa|hṛdayāny avanim abhiprasthitaḥ. ataś ca me harṣ'|ôtkaṇṭhānāṃ kāraṇam.

7.11 sakhi, tvayā priyaṃ niveditaṃ yad ev' ôpādhyāyena Puru|vaṃśa|rājarṣef purataḥ kāryaṃ kartum ājñaptam. tad eva gītaṃ kṛtv" âtr' âiva kurvaḥ.

7.12 yat te rocata evaṃ tat. yad eva gītaṃ mayā lapitaṃ tvayā vā saha nṛtyāvaḥ.

7.14 a|viṣaya|gamanaṃ kaṃ can' ânyaṃ ca sa|rāgam āliṃ madhu| samayaḥ/ anyaṃ karoti viṣaṇṇaṃ pāṭaly" âsyā bhūmyāḥ.

7.64 mā khalu mā khalu capalatāṃ kuru! siṃha, kathaṃ katham ev' ātmanaf prakṛtim darśayasi.

7.68 jṛmbha! jṛmbha, re siṃha! dantāni te gaṇayiṣyāmi.

7.69 avinīta! kim iti no 'patya|nirviśeṣāṇi sattvāni viprakaroṣi. pravartate te saṃrambhaḥ. sthāne khalv ṛṣi|janena «Sarva|damana» iti kṛta|nāma|dheyo 'si.

7.71 eṣā kesariṇī tvāṃ langhayati yady asyāf putrakaṃ na muñcasi.

7.72 aho balīyaḥ khalu bhīto 'smi!

7.75 vatsaka! muñca etaṃ bālaṃ mṛg|êndraṃ! anyaṃ te krīḍanakaṃ dāsyāmi.

7.76 kutra saḥ? dehi ma enam!

7.79 suvrate, na śakya eṣa āśvāsa|mātreṇa saṃyamitum. tad gaccha. māmaka uṭaje Maṅkanakasya ṛṣi|kumārakasya varṇaka|citrito mṛttikā|mayūrakas tiṣṭhati. tam asy' ôpāhara.

7.80 tathā!

7.81 tāvad anen' âiva krīḍiṣyāmi.

7.85 bhavatu. na māṃ gaṇayasi. ko 'tra ṛṣi|kumārakāṇām? bhadra|mukha! ehi, mocaya tāvad anena durmoca|hast'|âgreṇa ḍimba|kariṇā bādhyamānaṃ bāla|mṛgendram.

7.88 bhavatu, na khalv ayam ṛṣi|kumāraḥ.

7.91 āścaryam, āścaryam!

7.93 asya bālasy' âsaṃbaddhe 'pi bhadra|mukhe samvādiny ākṛtir iti vismit" âsmi. api c' âtyanta|paricitasy' êv' â|pratiloma eṣa te samvṛttaḥ.

7.95 Puru|vaṃśaḥ.

7.99 nanu yathā bhadra|mukho bhaṇati. apsaraḥ|saṃbandhena punar asya bālasya janany atr' âiva guros tapo|vane prasūtā.

7.101 kas tasya dharma|dāra|parityāgino nāma|dheyaṃ grahīṣyati.

7.103 Sarvadamana! śakunta|lāvaṇyaṃ paśya.

7.104 kutra mātā.

7.105 nāma|sādṛśyena vañcito mātṛ|vatsalakaḥ.

7.106 vatsa, Śakuntalā bhaṇati: «asya kṛtrima|mayūrasya ramaṇīyatvaṃ paśy' êti.»

7.108 attike, rocate me bhadrālaka eṣa mayūraḥ.

7.109 aho rakṣā|karaṇḍakam asya maṇi|bandhe na dṛśyate.

7.111 mā khalv enam ālambiṣṭhāḥ! katham, gṛhītam ev' ânena?

7.113 śṛṇotv āryaḥ. mahā|prabhāv" âiṣā khalv Aparājitā nāma mah"|âuṣadhir asya dārakasya jāta|karma|samaye bhagavatā Mārīcena dattā. etāṃ kila mātā|pitarāv ātmānaṃ vā varjayitv" âparo bhūmi|patitāṃ na gṛhṇāti.

7.115 tataḥ sarpo bhūtv" ânyaṃ daśati.

7.117 anekaśaḥ.

7.119 saṃyate, ehi. imaṃ vṛttāntaṃ niyama|nirvṛtāyāḥ śakuntalāyāḥ nivedayāvaḥ.

7.120 evaṃ kurvaḥ

7.121 muñca mām! yāvan mātṛ|sakāśaṃ gamiṣyāmi.

7.123 mama khalu tāto Duṣyantaḥ, na tvam.

7.126 vikāra|kāle 'pi prakṛti|sthāṃ tāṃ Sarva|damanasy' âuṣadhiṃ śrutvā na me āśvāsa ātmano bhāga|dheyeṣu. athavā yathā me 'kṣa|mālay" ākhyātaṃ tathā sambhāvyata etat.

7.129 na khalv ārya|putra iva. tataḥ ko nu khalv eṣa kṛta|rakṣā|maṅgalam dārakaṃ me hasta|saṃsargeṇa dūṣayati.

7.130 mātaḥ! eṣa ko 'pi parako māṃ mānuṣaf putraka ity ālapati.

7.132 hṛdaya, samāśvasihi samāśvasihi! prahṛtya nirvṛtta|matsareṇ' ânukampit" âsmi daivena. ārya|putra ev' âiṣaḥ!

7.135 jayatu jayatv ārya|putraḥ. . . !

7.138 mātaḥ ka ev' âiṣaḥ?

7.139 vatsa, bhāga|dheyāni me pṛccha.

7.142 uttiṣṭhatv ārya|putraḥ. nanu mama sukha|pratibandhakaṃ purā|kṛtaṃ teṣu divaseṣu pariṇām'|âbhimukham āsīd, yena s'|ânukrośo 'py ārya|putro mayi tathā|vidhaḥ saṃvṛttaḥ.

7.142 atha katham ārya|putreṇa smṛto 'yaṃ janaḥ?

7.146 ārya|putra! nanu tad angulīyakam.

7.148 samīhitaṃ kartuṃ kṣaṇena yat tad" ārya|putrasya pratyaya|karaṇe durlabhaṃ me saṃvṛttam.

7.150 n' âsya viśvasimi. ārya|putra ev' âitat pārayatu.

7.155 arhāmy ārya|putreṇa saha samīpaṃ gantum?

7.160 sambhāvanīy" âsya khalv ākṛtiḥ.

7.167 apratiratho bhava!

7.168 dārakeṇa sahitā pāda|vadanaṃ karomi.

7.171 jāte, bhartur bahu|matā bhava. ayaṃ ca te deha|jo vatsaka ubhaya|pakṣam alaṅkarotu. tad upaviśata.

7.171 sarve Prajā|paty|abhimatam āsanam upaviśanti.

7.183 diṣṭy" â|kāma|pratyādeśy ārya|putraḥ. na punaḥ saptam ātmā-naṃ smarāmi. athavā na śruto dhruvam anya|hṛdayayā mayā śāpah. yataḥ sakhībhyām atyādareṇa saṃdiṣṭ" âsmi bhartur aṅgulīyakaṃ darśay' êti.

7.192 anayā nandanā|mano|ratha|sampattyā Kaṇvo 'pi tāvac chruta|vistāraḥ kriyatām. Menak" êh' âiva saṇṇihitā.

7.193 mano|gataṃ me mantritaṃ bhagavatyā.

NOTES

Bold *references are to the English text;* ***bold italic*** *references are to the Sanskrit text. An asterisk (*) in the body of the text marks the word or passage being annotated.*

1.1 The eight forms of Śiva *(aṣṭa/mūrti)* are: 1. fire, 2. the offering (*havis* n.), 3. the sacrificer (*hotrī* f.), 4. sun, 5. moon, 6. space, 7. earth, 8 air.

1.10 Here I print the particle ***ṇu***, preceded by a nasal, and followed by *edaṃ*, reduced to a bare *ṇ* enclosed by two center-dots, although one could argue that it really is in *sandhi* with the preceding nasal and/or the following *edaṃ*. The alternative of hyphenating *ṇ'* seemed potentially too confusing in view of the negative particle *ṇa*, even though the Kashmirian text usually would write *ṇa edaṃ*. I also opted against compounding as in *adhavā*.

1.15 The most natural interpretation of this verse is that the ladies are kind because they make themselves even more beautiful by such graceful adornment.

1.26 An allusion to Śiva's mythological feat of chasing the sacrifice *(yajña)* fleeing in the guise of a deer.

1.30 **Uneven /** ***udghātinī:*** This is commonly translated as "churned up," but it is also possible to interpret as "rising." This might even be contextually more suited: the king is rising to a higher plane of being by entering the environs of the sacred hermitage. His actions there have consequences that are more far-reaching.

1.67 **To the right /** ***dakṣiṇena:*** see *Pāṇini* 2.3.31 *enapā dvitīyā* for the use of the accusative in conjunction with an adverb in *-ena*.

1.83 **Verandah**: Cf. *Gāthāsaptaśatī* 48d, *āliṃdae vasio*: "he spent the night *(vasio)* on the verandah [by the gate]," *āliṃdo bahirdvāraprakoṣṭhaḥ*.

1.97 The king is here worried she may be a brahmin, and thus beyond his marital aspirations. In the "Maha·bhárata"'s version of the tale Shakúntala explicitly boasts to him that she is superior, for she has inherited her mother's power to fly. In Kali·dasa's tale she lacks this power, she is more human than divine Ápsaras.

1.106 *Paṭ'|ântareṇa:* MONIER-WILLIAMS dictionary alleges that this is probably a mistake for *paṭāntam*, thus "standing on the edge of her garment," which seems very improbable.

1.125 The king is not of course lying. The expression "office of dharma" *(dharmādhikāra)* is a transparent metaphor for the duties of the king, and the Páurava he means is of course his own father who bestowed the crown upon him. Similarly "Vedavit" might have been his name.

1.135 The sage in question is the warrior sage Viśvāmitra.

2.24 Lit. "the moment is taken [by me]," which might either intend: "I await," or, "It's now or never!" The king does however delay his revelation.

2.35 **Probe the commander's frame of mind:** lit. "I will follow the commander's thoughts."

2.62 Or ***strī/ratna*** might here stand for Lakshmi, the Goddess of beauty and fortune. Thus: "you who care not even for the Goddess of beauty and fortune."

2.114 *Cakkākī:* I take the term as intending both the epic "wheel-guard" *(cakra/goptṛ)*, a warrior who protected the chariot's wheels and a "goose" *(cakr'|âṅkī)*.

2.116 *Ajjū:* This form is not given in most dictionaries. The commonly encountered *Ajjukā* normally denotes a "courtesan."

2.121 It is also possible that what is meant is "the fourth day after today."

2.123 **Tri·shanku:** The mythical king stuck midway between heaven and earth. See *Rāmāyaṇa* 1.57–60.

3.6 *Kāmayāna-:* On the originality of this unusual present participle see GOODALL & ISAACSON (2003:370).

3.34 *Hāva* is one of the ten types of coquetry.

3.94 ***Aṅga/recit'/ârdhe:*** This reading appears to suggest that Shakúntala has shyly shrunk away from Dushyánta.

3.109 **King:** the word *āryaputra* denotes both "king" and also "husband."

3.129 I take the *khalu* as an interrogative particle. The Bengali recension makes the question clearer by reading *katham* in place of *tathā (pāda b)*.

4.23 Considerations of ritual purity forbid her to just pick up the flowers that have fallen to the ground.

4.59 Or emend: *guṇḍā,* cf. the Bengal recension.

4.64 ***Pratīṣṭa:*** *=aṅgīkṛta.*

4.129 Or: "someone dear."

5.115 *Pāṇini* 2.2.38: *tāpasa/vṛddhā = vṛddha/tāpasā.*

6.8 **Brother-in-law:** The police captain is the king's brother-in-law.

6.23 The Prakrit form ⌜***śakula***⌟ can in Sanskrit be either *sakula,* "family," or it can remain *śakula* meaning "fish;" hence: "you will see fish-faces again." If this pun is intended, the guard is insulting the fisherman's family.

6.47 **Seasonal blessing**: or "an instant blessing." The red and white colors are auspicious signs of the fertility of spring.

6.49 The first gardener's name, **Para·bhrítika**, means "female cuckoo."

6.95 Or, if the word *saṃsthāna* is interpreted in consonance with the other recensions the sense would be rather "such (i.e. the painting) is the abode of my heart."

6.99 The Bengal recension's reading is here smoother: *sarvam idaṃ smarāmi Śakuntalāyāḥ prathama/darśana/vṛttāntaṃ.*

6.114 The Kashmirian recension presents the syntactically most difficult version of this verse, the predicate *(vidheya)* being predominant. It is possible that the Mithilā recension's *sudatī* ("fine-toothed" for *tad atītam*) is original, for there exists ample motivation for redactors to remove it. The rhetorician Vámana had taught that the grammatical form *sudatī* is unacceptable (*Kāvy'|âlaṅkāra|sūtra|vṛtti* 5.2.67: *sudaty|ādayaḥ pratividheyāḥ.)* In *pāda* c an original reading of *s" âsannivṛttyai sudatī mam' âiṣa* can account for all of the variants. Note how appropriate is the use of "fine-toothed" for the juxtaposition with the cliff precipice.

6.141 The king means that the buffoon might just have noted that he has smeared the sketch of Shakúntala by repeatedly touching it out of affection. Kali·dasa's phrasing makes it sound as if he is talking about the signs of love-making.

6.153 Note that the colors of these two ornaments are red and white, the colors of an Indian wedding.

6.191 **Dhana·vriddha** means "abounding in wealth."

6.200 This at least is the sense the redactor presumably intended. The dictionaries do not seem to give this sense for ***ghuṭṭhaṃ***, however.

6.207 KANJILAL reads as *soa|buddhi|puravaṃ*.

7.2 ***gahida|varaṇā pacchā***: an emendation by Burkhard. I am uncertain of the precise significance of *varaṇa* here; perhaps it is a "gift," or a "favor."

7.2 The sage **Nárada** is celebrated as a great authority on music and dance.

7.22 The courtly circumlocution implies that Indra removed the garland from his own neck.

7.69 **Sarva·dámana** means "All-tamer."

7.78 Webbed fingers were considered the mark of a universal emperor.

7.104 The Prakrit phrase used by the second nun in the previous speech was ***saünta/lavaṇṇaṃ*** which the boy is interpreting as ***Saüntala***. . . .

7.134 **Róhini** is the star Aldebaran.

7.163 **Twelvefold brilliance:** The twelve months.

7.163 **Soul:** The Vámana incarnation of Vishnu.

INDEX

Sanskrit words are given in the English alphabetical order, according to the accented CSL pronunciation aid. They are followed by the conventional diacritics in brackets.

k	ṭ	t	p	ṅ	n	ṃ	ḥ	āḥ	aḥ	k/kh
g	ḍ	d	b	ṅ	n	ṃ	r	ā	o	g/gh
k	ṭ	c	p	ṅ	ṃś	ṃ	ś	āś	aś	c/ch
g	ḍ	j	b	ṅ	ñ	ṃ	r	ā	o	j/jh
k	ṭ	ṭ	p	ṅ	ṃṣ	ṃ	ṣ	āṣ	aṣ	ṭ/ṭh
g	ḍ	ḍ	b	ṅ	ṇ	ṃ	r	ā	o	ḍ/ḍh
k	ṭ	t	p	ṅ	ṃs	ṃ	s	ās	as	t/th
g	ḍ	d	b	ṅ	n	ṃ	r	ā	o	d/dh
k	ṭ	t	p	ṅ	n	ṃ	ḥ	ā	aḥ	p/ph
g	ḍ	d	b	ṅ	n	ṃ	r	ā	o	b/bh
ṅ	ṇ	n	m	ṅ	n	ṃ	r	ā	o	*nasals* (n/m)
g	ḍ	d	b	ṅ	n	ṃ	r	ā	o	y/v
g	ḍ	d	b	ṅ	n	ṃ	*zero*[1]	ā	o	r
g	ḍ	l	b	ṅ	l̃[2]	ṃ	r	ā	o	l
k	ṭ	c ch	p	ṅ	ñ ś/ch	ṃ	ḥ	āḥ	aḥ	ś
k	ṭ	t	p	ṅ	n	ṃ	ḥ	āḥ	aḥ	ṣ/s
gg h	ḍḍ h	dd h	bb h	ṅ	n	ṃ	r	ā	o	h
g	ḍ	d	b	ṅ/ṅṅ[3]	n/nn[3]	m	r	ā	a[4]	*vowels*
k	ṭ	t	p	ṅ	n	m	ḥ	āḥ	āḥ	*zero*

[1]ḥ or r disappears, and if a/i/u precedes, this lengthens to ā/ī/ū. [2]e.g. tān+lokān=tāl̃ lokān.
[3]The doubling occurs if the preceding vowel is short. [4]Except: aḥ+a=o '.

Permitted finals: (*Except* āḥ/aḥ)

Initial

k	t	ṭ	p	ṅ	n	m	ḥ/r	āḥ	aḥ